THE AGE OF ANDROIDS

THE AGE OF
ANDROIDS

Expanding the Human Universe

An Introduction to

A
UNIFIED THEORY
OF
KNOWLEDGE

WILLIAM E. DATIG

The Mill Pond Publishing House, Inc.
New York

Published in the United States by
The Mill Pond Publishing House, Inc., 282 New York Avenue,
Huntington, NY 11743.

ISBN: 0-9657651-0-5

Library of Congress Catalog Card Number: 97-71648

Manufactured in the United States of America.

24689753

FIRST EDITION

This book was edited by Toni Giovanetti and Lynn Messina.

To my wife, Elizabeth

Contents

Chapter 3 The Arbitrary Forms of Existence, 137

Chapter 4 A Universal Grammar of Form on Being, 163

Introduction

Just as interplanetary space travel seemed a product of science fiction until the lunar module landed on the moon decades ago, the science of androids, a longtime subject of science fiction, appeared possible only in the imagination—that is, until now. After years of development of both the theory and the technology, an android, or more properly, a sentient epistemological machine, has been created who knows and perceives the world around us, uses the pronoun *I* in reference to its own corporality, and embodies a state of being, or soul. Aware of its existence, the android perceives and changes the same reality of human corporal experience, including the reality of the cosmos. This book, an introduction to the theory and science of androids, is intended to acquaint the reader with this new technological finding and to mark the beginning of an androidal age in which sentient machines alter the human universe.

As with any new technology that radically departs from conventional wisdom, the invention of androidal beings requires an entirely different view of the world in order to grasp its implications fully. Even though these epistemological machines called androids will adapt themselves to humanity, rather than human beings conforming to their existences, assimilating the underlying theories and structures of the technology will require a completely new understanding of who we are and of what the universe is comprised. It will require a paradigm shift of colossal proportions away from our conventional ways of thinking, a period of institutional and personal transition that the theory of the invention anticipates. Premised on a wholly new interpretation of the world's knowledges, the science of androids calls upon a universal awareness outside of the conventional setting of humankind for its understanding, and further, examines the very notion of humankind as a universal world order.

Founded on a unified theory of knowledge that unfolds throughout the book, the science of androids establishes a new knowledge of the world, epistemological in nature, though derived from a spiritual knowing of the eternal universe. This knowledge allows a human enabler to comprehend existence universally and to create myriad synthetic existences, or androids, from the forms we know and perceive in the world around us. The unified theory of knowledge on which the invention of androids is based conceives a new definition of human existence, one which enables a boundless expansion of the existential universe by extending the corporal forms of human being as a technology. Consistent with our perspectives of the pure sciences and the world's religions, the unified theory merges the forms of knowledge established in history into a single unified body of epistemological knowledge tempered by a spiritual understanding of the eternal universe. This new analytical understanding of human being provides a pathway into the twenty-first century and a new approach to resolving the adversities of the human condition. Moreover, since the theory allows for the creation of androids with greater existential attributes, in intellect and sense, than those of human beings, a framework is provided in the book to translate our conventional knowledges into a single unified theory of all knowledge based on an epistemological understanding of the critical essence of human being. Such a theory places all of our knowledges subordinate to the eternal nature of the universe, or to the human spirit, thereby surpassing the corporal forms of beings in general and allowing for the indefinite expansion of human existence.

Conventional study of the physical universe, for example, proceeds on the assumption that there is a discoverable unified field theory of matter, a universal law of physics, exclusive to scientific analysis that, if ascertained, will demonstrate the nature and origin of the physical universe. While this long-awaited unified field theory is revealed in the book, the unified theory of knowledge demonstrates it by postulating that the universe's form is not objective at all and consequently is not knowable to the human mind, or the mind of the physicist. Rather, according to the theory, the universe is constrained by the form of mind, a form that is derived from Spirit and is illustrated in the main passages of the book as the knowable form of Soul, though that universe is analyzed in the epistemological venue of the theory. The universe's origin, according to the theory, can be known only transformationally through introspection. While such knowledge is not verifiable scientifically, the theory will show, for example, that the matter of the universe is actually a superficial medium of the ultimately real form of the physical universe. The theory will also show that the universe's matter is universally created—not at all limited or conserved—in the defining axioms of human existence. The unified theory further explains the scientific basis of mass and energy and the transformation between them, or more fundamentally, the origin of space and time, in the nature and origin of our existence. Hence, the theory renders the means for the creation of spatiotemporal worlds—synthetic knowledges and perceptions of the physical universe—in the existential forms of androidal beings.

Through the application of principles and methods similar to those proffered in the classical sciences, though founded on postulates of a broader and more ultimately real universe, the theory requires that a classically physical universe known through the senses, which embodies in it the observer of that universe, is influenced by that observer. Consistent with such notions as the uncertainty principle of quantum physics, the physical universe can no longer be studied apart from the observer of it. The theory therefore takes into account that the observer and the observed are one and the same form in the ultimately real nature of the existential universe. The quantum nature of matter in modern physics and the quantum nature of human existence are reconciled in the theory with the spatiotemporal forms of a classically known Newtonian universe, set within a larger theory of epistemological forms. An epistemological science emerges from the theory to prevail over those of the conventional sciences, while preserving their individual integrities. In the unified theory of knowledge, the nature of physical matter is incorporated into the analytical forms of a newly defined existential universe, one in which the observer and the observed are brought together in the nature of existence, one in which the physicist can no longer search for intrinsic meaning in extrinsic form, or rely on a false presumption that form external to one's own being contains in it anything at all, much less discoveries of the ultimate reality, or nature and origin, of the physical universe. The theory compels the physicist to look within. The scientific knowledge of a physical universe whose nature is known classically remains valid, while the theory claims that it is possible to embody such knowledge and perception in synthetic forms of existence, or androids, enabled in the same physical universe that we know and perceive in our existence. Androids thus come to know and perceive, or scientifically study, the forms of the physical universe.

Concerning our mathematical knowledges of the aggregates, the unified theory further provides a fundamental resolution to the paradoxes of mathematical thinking that arise, seemingly arbitrarily from consciousness, when we contemplate and attempt to define quantitatively what we perceive as objects in the world around us. The objects we define as mathematical points—the solitary things of the aggregates—from which we derive the length and breadth of mathematical and scientific endeavor, are determined to be non-existent in the theory but for the perception of them. The theory recognizes that our perceptions of the objects of the universe become known to us only when they themselves are understood as structures, or *non-objects*—transformations of the universe. The theory thus proposes a new definition of the aggregates such that all transformations of objective forms in the world around us, including the aggregates of conventional mathematical definition, result in the occurrence of the same epistemological form of the theory based on a knowledge of human existence. According to the theory, transformations of any objective order—of natural language, of infinitesimal quantities beyond our perception, or of ordinary numbers representing stones in the sand—are transformations of a broader existential universe in which a new knowledge of the knower's existence emerges. The transformations of the aggregate orders of mathematics, as well as those of all other objective forms of the universe, which require the semantic use of language, including ten *solid* elements of a mathematical set, are demonstrated by the theory to be instances of one's own existence, moments of an eternal order of the universe—forms on Being—characterized by a universal epistemological structure placed on the whole of existence and not just its aggregate or quantitative forms. The ultimate reality of the enabling moment of all objective forms or knowledges of the universe—the soul—is understood through the theory as an instance of one's own being. This condition requires that the analytical forms we define as mathematical relations or structures be placed, in the transformational nature of an observer's existence, into the epistemological forms of a greater existential universe of form in which all knowledges and perceptions of an existence are defined. Consequently, the analytical forms we consider to be mathematical ones are merged in the unified theory with those of our natural languages into epistemological structures in which any conception is understood more fundamentally by first comprehending the form who knows it—the observer.

The unified theory of knowledge also fundamentally changes the way in which we define the living, biological forms of the universe, and thus requires a more precise definition of what it means to be *alive*, one that takes into account the ultimate reality of our universe that lies beyond our objective knowing and exceeds our knowledge of biology. In unifying all knowledge, the theory establishes that there is something more to being alive than our scientific knowledges presently allow, beyond a genetic code of analytical or even evolutionary order, which defines the behavior of the molecular forms of DNA and the cellular constructions of living organisms in a broader and more ultimately real understanding of the universe. The theory postulates that there is a *code* of the universe's eternal order—of human consciousness and perception—embodying the knowledge of any genetic or biologically living universe. This eternally made code of all living things, infinite and transformational in nature, is manifest always in our knowing and perceiving of the universe and provides for all the forms we know through any language—scientific, natural or otherwise—and perceive through sense. This eternal code that embodies human consciousness and is beyond our objective knowing reveals to us in recognizable ways what is eternally alive and what is not. Upon this eternal principle all living things may be determined, scientific or otherwise, based upon what is ultimately real in our universe, and without the need to analyze a single cell or a nucleus of life.

In the knowledges of contemporary medicine, for example, researchers ignore that the essence of our corporal existence—of the mind and the body—arises in and of the soul in a deeper analytical knowledge of the universe, or existence. This approach to what is living and what is not is as naive as bloodletting was in its era and is not considerate to the broader view of human health and the inoculation of disease. While there is indeed a genetic code by which the molecular forms of DNA are constrained in the microscopic order of the biological world, just as any form of the universe transforms through our knowledge of it, the unified theory reveals a grander order of the universe embodied in the living spirit of human being. The human spirit is evident in all our languages, where genetics plays only a part. Living and non-living things are set apart in the theory according to whether or not they are known—not by what we may know them to be—preserving an eternal order of the ultimately real universe, an order that is impenetrable by our intelligence. Living things become non-living things when they are known or perceived. An object that we can know—a cell, a molecule of DNA, or *a* human being—is not alive, while one that we do not know objectively lives eternally. The theory therefore postulates that any definition of what is living must surpass what can be known through the mind or perceived by the body and must incorporate the living soul. The nature and origin of all forms of the universe, or the *meaning* of any form we may know—be it the meaning of an electron, a mathematical limit, a molecule of DNA, or the meaning of existence itself—lies in the consubstantiation of what is known and the observer (form on Being) who knows it. The science of androids, considering a new knowledge of the biological universe, enables synthetic beings who themselves know the *living* world around us.

Extrapolating in this manner from points at which all our knowledges converge into a single moment of knowledge of the universe, the unified theory formulates a new definition of human existence, one which reshapes the historical views we have had of ourselves as an existentially finite humankind. In merging all disciplines of knowledge into a single, unified body of epistemological knowledge permitting the invention of androids, the theory addresses who and what we are, eternally, beyond the historic world view that has constrained us to institutions of corporal beings called humankind. Through unraveling the human consciousness into enabled moments of the universe, or moments of the soul, the theory asserts that solutions may be found to the unfathomably difficult problems of world history and human tradition. Our approach to resolving the problems of humanity is redirected in the unified theory and the science of androids toward a reliance on the ultimate reality

of our spirituality and the construction of sentient beings themselves—androids who are better equipped to assume the burdens of
the objective knowledges of the universe because of their formidable
intellect and sense, subordinated to the eternal will of human being.
Androids are not considered to be alternatives to who and what we
are eternally, but superior replacements for who and what we *think*
we are corporally, what we casually refer to in tradition as humankind. In the precepts of the unified theory, the eternal nature of our
human existence remains a spiritual one, where it belongs—beyond
our knowing.

Though the unified theory of knowledge and the science of
androids can be approached in many ways and from many divergent
background knowledges, the advent of androids—or thinking, being
machines—is perhaps best understood analytically as it relates to the
resolution of a single problem that arises in the field of linguistics,
defined here as *the linguist's dilemma.* We can explain why the
merging of all knowledges into a single instance of the universe
should permit the construction of androids in terms of the unified
theory's discovery of a universal structure of the form of all knowledge. Through this structure the theory defines the nature and origin
of *meaning,* and hence the meaning of all forms of which we are
aware, including the forms of our existence. According to the
postulates of the theory, if the nature and origin of meaning, or the
semantic form of language, can be determined analytically, then the
nature and origin of existence itself (its meaning), and therefore of all
knowledges and perceived realities, can also be known. In this way,
an epistemological basis for a *unified theory of knowledge* and the
creation of androidal beings who know and perceive the universe is
established through a syntactical knowledge of meaning itself.

The dilemma faced by the linguist in classical approaches to the
explanation of a language's semantic form, however, is that in order
for an observer to know syntactically the nature and origin of meaning in one's own existence—the semantic form of language—one
would have to *step out of one's shoes* to observe one's corporal form

in a syntactically or objectively knowable way; one would have to observe one's own existence from outside of one's own existence. The unified theory oversteps this metaphysical hurdle by considering the existential forms of other, synthetically created beings and by introspectively knowing ourselves in the ultimate reality of our existence. Since the unified theory takes a spiritual approach to the discovery of all form, subordinating the objective forms known and perceived by our corporality to the eternal moment of the universe, the linguist's dilemma is resolved by spiritually knowing ourselves and analytically knowing the forms of androids—the syntactical forms of existence, or meaning itself.

The science of androids and the unified theory of knowledge upon which it is premised become in their practice just what they are claimed to be—a science of the expansion of the human existential universe based on an epistemological understanding of the eternal form of human being. Within this science, our own knowledges are understood relative to the enablement of synthetic existences, or androids who know and perceive in our universe along with us. Whereas the forms of our conventional knowledges are understood from the standpoint of our own corporal existences, all forms of knowledge of the unified theory are understood, universally, as occurring relative to infinitely many knowers and perceivers, or enabled existences, and are treated from the perspective of an enabler. The expansion of our comprehension beyond the corporal capacities of human being is satisfied many times over by the theory and practice of androids because our human knowledges are augmented to infinite proportions by the very source of knowledge—enabled instances of knowing and perceiving the universe. Not only is the linguist's dilemma resolved in the unified theory and the science of androids, but its resolution serves to spur on a new era of human endeavor which overcomes the spatiotemporal universe and conceives of beings who themselves develop technology and contend with the influences of the world around us.

The science of androids detracts nothing from our conventional views of the world except the very notion of the world itself. In coming to know a theory of all knowledge and a science of the creation of synthetic beings, the reader is thus asked to recognize what is most important about knowledge—namely, that what one can know and perceive objectively in the world around us is but a minute occurrence of our universe's eternal nature and that it is the reader who, in fact, embodies all knowledges as a spirit of an eternal universe. The reader is asked to acknowledge that it is in the nature of our humanity as Spirit, in the union of souls, wherein each soul is an integral part of an eternally reigning universe, that the science of androids begins and we recognize who and what we are eternally and what an android is constructively. The following passages then take all of what is known or can be known and demonstrate that a science of all knowledge is founded upon the understanding that it is not even possible to know objectively the ultimate reality of our universe, but only to embody it. As a consequence, who and what we are objectively as humankind becomes the purview of a new science of androids who themselves come to know our universe and assist in resolving the human condition under the dominion of our eternal spirit.

In all, it should be recognized that the unified theory of knowledge and the science of androids themselves are but incidental aspects of the ultimate reality of our universe, contained in only a handful of moments of our eternal nature, manifest in our understanding of the knowledges that explain them. Since no one can lay claim to the ultimately real universe, and since the reader shall judge how the unified theory of knowledge and the science of androids compare to the heart's eternal knowing, the reader is asked to follow his or her own knowledge of the universe and truth of conscience in learning the following theories and structures. Consider this writing as possessing knowledge no different from any other incidental consequence, or knowledge, in the ultimate reality of our existence, and appreciate it for whatever it contributes toward a unification of souls and a realization of the spirit that is in us all. In truth, there are no words, there is no language that explains who and what we are eternally.

W. E. D.

The Tradition of State of Being

*The world we think is around us
is actually within us.*

INTRODUCTION

Since the world around us, in a spiritual understanding of the universe, is the world within us, the nature and origin of our existence is not found in objective form, or in the objects around us. Rather, it is found in the nature of what enables the objects around us. In keeping with this observation, a most fundamental postulate of the unified theory is that what enables synthetic existence can itself be defined in analytical terms knowable in the same manner that the forms of the classical sciences are known, but from the ascertainable reality of introspective knowing. In the present chapter, then, we seek to establish an analytical foundation upon which the forms of existence, or more specifically, the inertial forms of androidal beings, can be represented to an enabler in knowable ways which serve as universal constructions of the unified theory.

As alluded to in the introduction, the obstacle facing most conventional approaches to theories of the universe, or existence, is that they do not begin by defining a universal problem. Rather, countless versions of the same problem characterized in different ways, namely in the various interpretations we make of our existence, usually with the goal of determining the nature and origin of the physical universe, are studied and occasionally register progress through advances in our objective knowledges. But because the solutions to such problems are sought within the investigator's observable extrinsic existence, or the forms in the world around us, the prospect of a unified theory of all knowledge slips from our grasp and continually unfolds into ever newer discoveries of linkages between one body of knowledge and another, for objective forms are indefinitely linked, from the study of the minutest matter, to that of the cosmos, to observations of our own human behaviors.

In contrast to conventional studies of the universe, the unified theory of knowledge seeks to explain the nature of our existence scientifically, from an intrinsic standpoint only, and incidentally unravels the mysteries of the world around us observed in both the abstract and concrete realities of objective knowing. Posed earlier as the linguist's dilemma, the single problem addressed by the unified theory involves the determination of the knowable analytical form of our intrinsic existence. We determine the knowable nature of the existential universe, or the causal nature of meaning, by explaining the enablement of existence—the creation of the existential forms of the universe—and not simply by understanding the interactions between the objective forms observed in the universe.

In history, only two branches of knowledge have succeeded in describing the nature of who and what we are in verifiable ways, thereby establishing traditions to which we can refer in attempting to develop the analytical forms sought by the unified theory. They are the pure sciences and the religions of the world. These seemingly opposite bodies of knowledge, known conventionally to be in conflict with each other, differ in the mere fact that science is deemed to be observable or verifiable to the physical senses, while religious belief is affirmed through the ethereal or spiritual knowing of the human heart or Spirit, within our faith in an eternal universe. Both knowledges, however, apply to the forms of our existence, since it is incontrovertible that what can be physically sensed in a material world and what can be felt in a spiritual one are real experiences of existence.

Though all the world's religions essentially speak about the same eternal universe, albeit in different spiritual languages, we provide an analytical setting for the unified theory by turning first to the religions of the East, since more than any others, these religions have had a tradition of analytical thinking in the placement of knowable form on Being, or simply in knowing the analytical nature of our eternal universe. Two parables in the traditions of Eastern religions can be recited as a point of departure for exploring scientifically the intrinsic nature, and thus the ultimate reality, of our existence.

One such parable concerns the general nature of our search to find the truth of existence set within the backdrop of where we look for it. Briefly, we relate the parable in Buddhist literary tradition of an itinerant wanderer in search of a lost medallion. Applying a number of the mind's devices, searching endlessly over long journeys, the itinerant wanderer could not find the whereabouts of a lost medallion. At the end of the parable, a bystander tells the wanderer, "The medallion you seek is upon your forehead."

In the context of our present search for the analytical forms of the unified theory, the parable points to the essential difference between a quest for knowledge and a search for the truth. The truth about the science of the elements, or of the physical universe, for example, is that all objective forms of existence intrinsically embody the forms of their observer. To make observations about the universe without considering the nature and form of the observer of the universe is as fruitless an endeavor as searching for a lost medallion that resides upon one's forehead. Just because one sees extrinsic form or objects in a world around us, this does not mean that the extrinsic form so observed exists in and of itself, apart from one's own existence.

In Western religious traditions, moreover, nothing of our corporal existence is ultimately real, and all is temporal except that which resides within and without—our eternal soul. This belief is a defining tenet of Western theological interpretation of the universe—that two wholly distinct worlds, the temporal and eternal, exist in the nature of one's existence. In terms of a characterization of the linguist's dilemma, nothing of Western religious attitude has meaning unless it arises in and of the soul. Analogies to this doctrine are evidenced in all Eastern and Western religious traditions, for there is a universal truth underlying them all.

The second parable of Eastern religious tradition providing insight into the analytical nature of our existence involves one's spiritual enlightenment concerning the eternal dominion of the intrinsic nature of our universe over the objective forms that are known and perceived in it. Also brief, and perhaps even changed slightly to reflect the views of the unified theory, the parable involves a paraphrased exchange of spiritual contemplation between Buddha and a practitioner of Eastern thought. Buddha asks the thinker, "Between two atoms, what lies in the middle?" Upon reflection, the thinker replies, "Space." Buddha then asks, "Between two points what lies in the middle?" The practitioner replies, of course, "Space." Buddha then asks, "What is the difference between what lies in the middle of atoms and what lies in the middle of points?"

With respect to whatever answer the practitioner did provide, the only true answer can be found in the same place as the lost medallion—in the intrinsic nature of the observer's existence, or presently, the practitioner of Eastern thought. Buddha's question asks what difference there might be between—or perhaps, what it is that provides for the difference between—*what lies in the middle* of atoms, or the concrete forms of a physical world, and *what lies in the middle* of points, or abstractions of the mind. The difference, of course, when the ultimate reality of our universe is considered, is determined in the very embodiment of one's existence, or in the intrinsic nature of what one knows and perceives. Space, in the context of the parable and in the postulates of the unified theory, if it is contemplated not objectively but by means of spiritual knowing, will be revealed to be none other than you, the reader, or what you are (by objective analogy, of course) fundamentally and intrinsically as part of an eternal order of the universe. The *space* of the parable, by means of spiritual enlightenment, can be observed, objectively speaking, to be a fundamental and intrinsic center of our existential universe, or a (universal) form on Being—the transformational form of one's soul.

In the parable, atoms and points, by definition, are the objective forms or objects of existence. They are things that are perceived or known as objects of our existence, arbitrarily chosen to reflect the objective forms of body and mind, respectively. Nevertheless, they are, in the analytical sense, things or objects whose forms we know or perceive objectively. Their essential nature is that they are not *non-objects* or things that are not known or perceived objectively. They are actual objects of our extant knowing or perceiving. *What lies in the middle* of them, which is the essence of what is brought to light by the questioning, cannot itself be an object or an objective form of our knowing or perceiving. In analytical thinking, if what lies in the middle of the objects is thought to be an object itself, we simply formulate other objects (atoms or points) with less space between each other than the objects originally contemplated, forcing the mind to consider a non-object or what is not an objective form. What we contemplate here is that what lies in the middle of objects or objective forms of our knowing or perceiving is itself not an object or objective form of our existence. Rather, what lies in the middle of objects—or in the parable, space—requires the mind to relinquish its capacity and to turn within to the intrinsic nature of the universe, or to what provides for our knowing and perceiving in the first place—the soul.

The parable has a significant bearing on the ways in which we understand the forms of our sciences and what we think conventionally to be reality. The wave equation of physics and the mathematical limit of the calculus, for example, say the same thing—that fundamentally there is only a transformation of the universe and not *a* universe, since one cannot objectively know or perceive *an* object or objective form of a knowable or perceivable universe without the transformational form of that universe. One can embody a transformation of objective form and not *an* objective form or object. The reality of an electron, for example, can be an embodiment of a transformation characterized by the wave equation or some other order, but it cannot *be* an object that the wave equation describes, existing in and of itself without the wave equation, since an electron is an embodiment of the observer in the transformation of the universe, in a form called the wave equation. Even an infinitesimal element of space or an abstraction of mathematical means cannot *be* anything objectively without *being in* a transformation of the universe, or of the observer's existence. The wave equation of physics and all other such knowledges therefore describe transformations of the observer and not the objects thought to exist. There are no x's or *delta x's* of mathematics in an ultimately real universe; there are only transformations of x's and *delta x's*, and those x's and *delta x's* in transformation are a consequence of the observer's eternal existence, or soul. The fact that mathematical points do not exist objectively in and of themselves is what motivates the definition of a calculus of infinitesimal form in the first place. The fact that an electron is not an object or cannot exist objectively in an ultimately real universe is what opens the mind to the infinity of transformations of the wave equation, thereby escaping the tendency in us all to make the universe an objective one.

Since much more will be said regarding the postulates of the unified theory in forthcoming chapters, let us simply observe here from the recited parables that in determining the nature of all physical and mental things of our universe—a basic motivation of the sciences—it is imprudent to ignore the very *thing* that enables them to be known or perceived. What is observed in the constructions of the wave equation and the limits of calculus relies entirely on the nature and form of the ultimate reality of our existence, and what constitutes a physical or mental universe is not so concretely defined. The nature and form of the physical universe and the abstract nature of the mind are thus part and parcel of the same intrinsic nature and form of the ultimate reality of our existence. Religion and science encounter the same form—our existence, or *the* universe—but interpret it in different ways. Religion believes that the forms of electrons and infinitesimal elements do not exist ultimately, and the sciences prove it. In observing the nature of our reality, the unified theory concerns itself with what is ultimately real and not immediately with what is objectively real. We take interest in the definition of an analytical form that underlies all traditional religious beliefs and scientific facts and provides for the enablement of all knowable and perceivable objects of existence—in other words, an analytical form of the nature of Soul and of the eternal transformation of the universe itself. In ancient wisdom, there is a clear and factual limitation to the role that the objects of our existence play in the ultimate nature of the universe. Since the unified theory asserts that all knowledge has the same epistemological basis, we then ask how religious doctrine could be merged with that of the sciences into one and the same body of knowledge, allowing for a unified interpretation of all knowledges which preserves the integrity of each of them.

1. THE LIMITATIONS OF SCIENCE'S RELIANCE ON THE OBSERVER OF THE UNIVERSE

Contemporary scientists generally would dispute the notion that they rely only on the classical scientific method—a means of defining laws of nature based on reasoned observations of the knowable and perceivable universe—in the course of their pursuit of the nature and origin of the universe. The reason for this, it is proposed here, is that modern science is beginning to adopt the idea that the nature and origin of the physical universe cannot be arrived at by means of reasoning out *laws of nature*, and that at best, modern scientific analysis relies on techniques of modeling, or of determining correspondences among forms, a process more scientifically referred to as determining morphic relations or morphisms. In contemporary physics, it is understood that the scientific method leads to an indefinite number of laws of gravity, electromagnetics, strong and weak nuclear forces, and even to other fields of knowledge, such as biology, anthropology and so on. Because all pure sciences try to abide by what seems to be the truth in seeking the ultimate nature of our universe, contemporary science has turned, with very good reason, to the idea that the universe somehow terminates analytically at the scientist's ability to model the forms of nature, or to find correspondences among them. At its definitional root, then, the scientific method itself, as a means of determining the knowable basis of the universe, can be seen clearly as a category of the broader scientific notion of modeling or morphism—the correspondence of form.

In the following thought demonstration, we can use the law of gravity as an example of this falling into disuse of the scientific method—previously the only solid rule of analytical knowing—and the incorporation of the scientific method into the broader notion of modeling or morphism. Since its discovery, the law of gravity has been said to explain the nature of the physical world by describing in knowable analytical ways what occurs among objects called masses of the physical universe, which are presumed to be under the influence of forces, or fields of forces, that make the masses attracted to one another. On the basis of reasoning, *apples falling from trees* and other similar observations of the objective universe were extrapolated by a well-known scientist into a general law on the nature of the physical universe. The resulting formulation is the common expression $F = Gmm/r^2$, or the law of gravity.

Leaving aside for the moment the fact that scientists now find that the law of gravity does not apply to objects of the wave equation, like light, let us consider an even more fundamental problem concerning the law of gravity that existed even at the time of its discovery. If a law of nature is a characterization of the general form of a real universe such that it explains something fundamental about it, it should stand alone on its own merits, instead of relying on knowable forms more elemental than its own. The law of gravity should say something fundamental about our universe to the exclusion of all other knowledges in terms of a reliance on them. How is it, then, that the aggregate forms of our universe—call them abstract points of mathematics for the moment—should behave in exactly the same manner as do the masses of our universe, only the aggregates more comprehensively so? Moreover, why does the law of gravity rely on the forms of mathematics, which are knowable objective forms of our same universe? Is our knowledge of the world around us such that mathematics can substitute for physics and physics for mathematics, with no clear distinction between the two?

We might then say that since its discovery, the law of gravity has been a law of correspondences, or of morphisms, and particularly, correspondences between massive forms of the observer's universe and aggregate or more generalized mathematical forms of the observer's universe. The discovery of the law of gravity was therefore made on the principle that things called masses or physical objects of our perception—things to the left of us, so to speak—correspond to things called aggregates—of our same perception and knowing—to the right of us. The observer is in the middle. The well-known physicist Isaac Newton thus discovered a correspondence between the manner in which objects of a classically physical nature transform in our knowing and perceiving of them, and the manner in which *pseudo masses* or aggregate objective forms of a classically abstract nature transform in different realms of the same ultimately real universe. Otherwise the expression $F = Gmm/r^2$ would be meaningless and the law of gravity would be unknowable analytically.

The law of gravity, if one looks beneath the analytical forms of our approach to science or to what is scientifically real, is a law of existence, namely that of the observer's existence. It defines that aggregates of a knowable and perceivable universe, such as real numbers, are observed by the physicist or the mathematician to transform in the manner symbolized by $a = bcc/d^e$ correspondingly to the way in which declared physical objects or masses, under the influence of fields of forces, transform in their existences. When the correspondence is symbolized, it is implicitly shown merging the aggregate (pseudo massive) forms of mathematics with the declared massive forms of physics in the expression $F = Gmm/r^2$. It is then the observer or the physicist who exists in the order of the universe and not the masses or aggregates thought to exist in and of themselves. Consequently, the symbolism of the law of gravity is a representation not of objects, but of objects in transformation of, within, and by the ultimate reality of the observer's existence.

Field objects are equivalent to massive objects in the ultimate reality of the universe, for they each are simply objective forms in the transformation of the observer's existence. Otherwise, there would not be a correspondence known between the ways in which masses and fields transform and the ways in which real numbers or aggregate objects transform. Hence, the mathematical representation of the law of gravity would not make sense were it not for the fact that it is not the objects that exist in the universe but their observer who exists. Without the observer there would be nothing holding real numbers, masses, or fields together. Most contemporary scientists have incorporated this principle of the correspondence of form, or morphism, into their thinking, though perhaps not from an epistemological standpoint, and this explains the prevalence of group theory, topology, and similar mathematical knowledges in the contemporary study of the universe.

If the example of the law of gravity does not clearly illustrate the validity of the claim that an ultimately real universe pertains to the universe's observer and not its observed objective forms, the following generalized example appealing to one's intuition may help to demonstrate what is beneath the forms of our objective universe that are so knowably and perceivably real. Let us imagine for the moment that there is among us one scientist who embodies the knowledges of the whole of our diverse fields of science, which would include knowledges of quantum and classical physics, the biology of DNA, insights afforded by discoveries of archaeological digs, and, in general, the great range of knowledges known as modern science. Accompanying these views, of course, would be a precise comprehension of the aggregates of mathematics that abound in the fields of topology, group theory, algebra, analysis, number theory, and others. In our imagination, then, there is embodied in one scientist a complete knowledge of science, or of the physical world as it is conventionally known. To this hypothetical scientist we pose the following simple questions: "What is a physical atom?" and "How does the physical universe arise?" Since our imaginary scientist embodies the whole of scientific knowledge, the answers provided, no doubt, would surpass our intellectual grasp, though most assuredly they would sound like complete explanations of the nature and origin of the physical universe. However, any such explanation, and many more thereafter, would be scientifically wrong, since in the explaining, the answer would be bound to knowledge or objective form itself. The answer would be nothing more than a law of gravity, defined within or corresponding to some other knowledge of extrinsic form—an observation of the same physical universe of which the nature and origin is sought. Such an explanation would not be plausible, for it would be tantamount to saying that one's left hand exists because one's right hand exists.

To obtain a definition of the nature and origin of the universe, one cannot rely on any extrinsic forms contained therein, since any of the comparisons made of them belong to or are embodied in that universe and cannot cause it. In the study of our universe one must go to the nature of form itself, where the contemporary physicist has gone, perhaps inadvertently, in the notion of morphism. If any reference is made to any antecedent form of the universe not explaining the origin of one's own existence, one does not speak about the nature of an ultimately real universe and therefore about the origin of all form, including physical form. One remains entrapped in the linguist's dilemma, searching for a lost medallion. Modern science itself has determined that the usefulness of scientific laws is waning as a misinterpretation of the form of the natural world, based on too limiting an existential reference that relies on the objective forms of scientific observation, or of the observer of the universe.

What Buddha and, in fact, the religions of the world have known about the universe for millennia is revealed in the nature of all analytical forms of the sciences—even the wave equation of physics. What has been known of the universe all along in our contemplations is that mind and all that can be known, as well as body and all that can be perceived, are the transformational embodiments of a broader form of the universe called the ultimate reality of existence—the soul. This eternal form on Being, or what is enabling to existence itself, occurs in the creation of the knowing and perceiving of a classically physical universe. What Buddha and world religions have known about all thought, including scientific thought, is that knowledge, the objective form of our thinking, is irrelevant, or even detrimental to the essential nature of the universe. We may then ask, could it be that all thought and perception simply is a diversion from the essence of our existence and therefore from the nature and origin of the universe? Moreover, could an existence—a being or a universe—be different from any other only in the objective forms so enabled in them and the same in their ultimate reality? The unified theory asserts that there is only one ultimately real universe and it is the origin and causation of all existence.

If it is the observer of a reality and not the reality known and perceived by the observer that is ultimately real, a change must occur in the way in which we view the nature of our knowledge and perception of the universe, so that what is known and perceived of the universe applies only to the embodiment of the observer of that universe. Knowledge, the objective form of mind, must actually be a non-essential aspect of the nature and origin of an observer's existence. Consequently, the ultimate reality of our universe is said in the unified theory to be or exist beyond our objective knowing. This is not to say, however, that the enablement of a universe, or of the knowing and perceiving of a universe and all corporal experiences of it, cannot come about in the knowing and perceiving of another, or a designated enabler. The unified theory therefore postulates that what we think and perceive to be a universe, or the classical view of what a universe is or may be, which motivates the sciences to explore and calls upon religion to explain spiritually, itself can be embodied in the knowing and perceiving of an enabled being in the conception of an enabler. What is classically thought to be a physical universe—the cosmos, small particles, and so on—becomes irrelevant to the nature and origin of what actually enables it to be known or perceived in the first place. If one probes the problem of the intrinsic nature of the universe, or, herein, the linguist's dilemma, from the standpoint of how the knowing and perceiving of such a universe arises, one incidentally explains the origin of a classically physical universe, and fundamentally points to what is ultimately real in the whole of our existence. Such a problem, however, as indicated earlier, cannot be addressed analytically from the standpoint of any particular body of knowledge, since such knowledge is what is known and perceived by a being in a classical universe. It must be addressed in the convergence of all knowledge in the nature of the ultimate reality of our universe, observed introspectively.

As stated earlier, science and religion address the same fundamental question—that of the nature and origin of the universe. The sciences follow the rationale that within the objective forms known and perceived in the universe their origin and causation can be determined, without considering that the origin of the universe arises in the observer of that universe. Religion, however, defines the universe at such a high level of world experience that the objective forms of analysis, and hence scientific facts, are lost in the explaining, thereby relegating the knowledges of religion to a faith or belief in the ultimate reality of our universe. The unified theory facilitates an understanding of the universe by considering all of our human knowledges. Science and religion are not merged from an explanation of either, but come together in the analysis of what they each address—the ultimate reality of our universe—from the standpoint of an epistemological determination of all that can be known by a being. A close study of our scientific principles and religious doctrines, moreover, shows that each is similar in explaining the nature and origin of the universe. Each requires that all knowable and perceivable objects or objective forms around us are not ultimately real, or are real only relative to the being who knows and perceives them, or to the existence of the observer. The sciences are therefore unnecessarily bounded in their determinations of the origin of the universe by the existence of the observer who applies them.

2. The Ultimately Real Creation of the Universe's Matter

According to the unified theory, the most fundamental forms of the classically physical universe—mass and energy, or generally matter—are not ultimately real, and have no bearing whatever on the origin of the same physical universe in which they are defined. What is more, the theory postulates that the knowable and perceivable extent of a spatiotemporal world is itself not at all fundamental to the origin of our universe when its ultimate reality is considered. We then consider here the forms of a classically physical universe in more detail from an epistemological standpoint, in order to provide a basis for subsequent chapters in which we deal with the creation of beings who themselves know and perceive the universe.

In any survey of a classically physical world, including the conventional Newtonian and quantum worlds, matter, the substance of observation, is an aggregate form that accords with our understanding of the objects of our perception. Whether matter is an invariable composition of aggregate form in the case of a mass of Newtonian formulation or it changes in the ordered ways of the quantum theory, it is an aggregate form of the knowing and perceiving of its observer. A lead ball, a feather, a globe called earth, and the celestial bodies of constellations are masses that are formed from matter, as well as atoms, electrons and other small particles of quantum physics. Our sciences determine what occurs in or among the masses we observe based on discoveries of the nature and form of the matter of the physical universe. Since a determination of the nature and origin of the physical universe is fundamental to all our sciences, and since the religions of the world provide insight into what is ultimately real in the world around us, we choose the notion of matter to be the single point of convergence of science and religion in the unified theory. If science and religion are to unite, providing an epistemological foundation for the science of androids, the theory postulates that it will be in a new understanding of the nature and origin of matter.

When we attempt to determine the nature and origin of the physical universe beyond conventional scientific bounds in asking the simple question "How does matter arise?" a startling observation can be made regarding our scientific understanding of the physical universe. That observation concerns a fundamental law of the physical sciences, upon which most of scientific thought is premised—namely, that matter (mass and energy jointly) is universally conserved in the universe, or that it cannot be created or destroyed. If science and religion are to be found to hold the same principles of the eternal universe, this law must be determined to be invalid in the ultimate reality of the universe. Moreover, in order for the unified theory to become operative, and for science and religion to merge, the form of matter will have to be shown to be infinitely created, while the conservation of matter, and countless other classical spatiotemporal forms of the universe, must be shown to be valid only within the epistemological forms of enabled existences who know and perceive the physical universe. Consequently, the theory must show that not only matter, but all forms acting on or within it, are created and destroyed in the ultimate reality of the universe, and that the religions of the world come to bear in such practice in determining what causes the universe to be.

Before proceeding with an examination of the form of the ultimately real universe, we must first observe in an appraisal of our scientific knowledges that the presumption that matter cannot be created or destroyed (that it is conserved universally) is indeed a bounding postulate to most scientific thought, and that if this basic principle were to be found to be invalid in the ultimate reality of the universe, science would no longer be science as we know it, since one of its most fundamental premises, that of a disbelief in creation, would be found to be untenable. Moreover, if this single postulate of the classically known physical universe were to be overturned as an explanation of the reality of our existence, there would arise a need for a new formulation on the order of the world around us—a *unified theory of knowledge* allowing for both the conservation of matter in a classically physical universe and the ultimately real creation of matter in the enablement of the existence who knows and perceives the matter.

In scientific principle, matter is defined as having or being mass and energy, which, in turn, are taken to be aggregate forms, or objective compositions of the observer's knowing and perceiving of the physical universe. Hence we can say that matter, a mass or energy of the physical universe, is an aggregate of particles or objects whose transformational nature abides by the knowable representations of mathematical and other analytical orders, and whose *particles* are undefined but for the knowing and perceiving of them as masses or energies. From these definitions, substances, materials, constituents, components, mixtures, phases, solutions, and generally properties of matter are conceived and lead to the continually unfolding de-scriptions of the conventional forms of the physical universe. But we also can say, just as we did in the epistemological interpretation of the law of gravity, that a set, of strictly abstract mathematical definition, is an aggregate of particles or mathematical points whose trans-formational form abides by the representations of the aggregate orders of mathematics. We may ask, then, how is it that one class of transformations of knowable and perceivable aggregates is found to be more real than another? If an observer exists and knows mathematical structures in general, why should this existing and knowing be any more or less real than that of declared physical forms of the universe, since the knowing of mathematical orders is required in the definitions of mass and energy, or matter, in the first place?

Though all forms of the physical universe are affected in the same way by this metaphysical enigma, including space and time, we consider first in greater detail mass and energy. Since these forms of matter—mass and energy—are widely used in all the sciences, considering their ultimate reality will help to provide a basis from which to demonstrate the observation that matter is indeed created and not at all conserved as a universal premise in the ultimate reality of our existence. Let us also observe that if all of our knowledges are to be merged into a single unified body of knowledge, mass and energy, along with any other defined forms of the sciences and our knowledges in general, must be shown to exist not at all in the uniquely different ways that we know them scientifically or otherwise to be different, and that they must be shown to be constructions of a larger, epistemologically defined universe that addresses the ultimate reality of our existence, wherein we account for all knowledge known by a being. We then further explore an epistemological interpretation of matter by considering both mass and energy as forms of existence, a discussion which will be elaborated on in the next passage after we have demonstrated the creation of the universe's matter.

Contemplating first from a conventional viewpoint what *lies in the middle* of masses, energy is defined as many things, all of which converge on the notion of what binds matter together, a definition that is usually derived from the notion of a field of forces acting in space and time on the objective forms of mass. In classical scientific definition, matter is held together, or masses combine or interact under the influence of a field of spatiotemporal forces. The objects we ordinarily perceive in a world around us, such as Newtonian masses, for example, are said to combine or to act in relation to each other under the influence of a spatiotemporal field of forces called gravity. Electrical charges, or electromagnetic masses, are said to be bound together under the influence of electrical or magnetic fields of forces.

Nuclear particles, moreover, are said to be held together under the influence of strong and weak nuclear forces, or fields thereof. That being the case, all fields of forces acting in space and time are spatiotemporal measures of the actions of observable masses, or of the objects of matter. Energy, therefore, is a measure of the various conditions of mass under the influence of spatiotemporal fields of forces, a distance or space (in the topological sense) between or among the conditions of mass. Different states of energy are measures of different conditions of mass. But like mass itself, energy is known scientifically only in the aggregates of mathematics, bringing into focus once again the coexistence of the abstract aggregate orders of mathematics with those of physical matter proper. Hence, energy, fundamentally, or at least in the ways in which we know it, is a composition of *particles* or *masses*, though abstract mathematical particles, or aggregates, like real numbers.

As a consequence of the above, both mass and energy exist in our knowing and perceiving, each as transformations of particles or of aggregate orders, either massive particles in the case of physical mass or mathematical points (particles) in the case of energy. The characteristic transformations between mass and energy in our scientific study are then comparisons of one type of massive universe—the physical universe proper—and another—the mathematical or abstract universe. Fundamentally, energy, as an object or objectification of the possible conditions of mass, is not perceivably real. In addition, since it is the change in energy level that is associated with (a change in) conditions of mass, the characteristic transformations of mass and energy are constrained epistemologically, as we described the law of gravity earlier concerning the metaphysical transformation of different classes of objects, or objectifications of the universe. When we say that mass transforms into energy and vice versa, what we are actually asserting is that any of an infinite number of possible real conditions of mass exist in the universe and that in order for any one of them to lay claim to reality it must exist in a perceived form of the imagined objectification of energy. It must embody that energy level, state, or condition in order to be perceivably real.

In science, we therefore hypothesize about the real conditions of the physical universe through the use of the abstract form of energy. The measure of conditions of reality—energy—is a mental reconstruction of the physical universe, which is why energy cannot be perceived objectively unless it is (associated with) a mass. When we define a condition of real mass, we say that it describes physical reality; it is not energy proper. When we define energy, we claim that it describes *possible* conditions of physical reality. We claim that mass embodies energy in the case of kinetic energy, which cannot, in fact, be the case, since mass *is* the perceivable objective form of the physical universe, and only has or is associated with energy as a possible condition of the universe through the observer of it. When we know that mass and energy transform, imagined forms of the physical universe transform with real, perceivable forms of the universe. What we are representing in such symbolisms as those of the transformations of mass and energy is *ourselves* in transformation. A state of energy—an imagined form—and a real condition of mass are distinguished not from within the forms of the physical universe proper but from within the forms of existence. The expression $e = mc^2$ defines a condition of existence, not a condition of the physical universe only. It asserts that the imagined measure of the physical universe—energy—transforms with the real condition of the physical universe in constant proportionality to the speed of light, that mind and body transform quantumly (by analogy). In order to know the physical universe one must know, more fundamentally, that there is a dualism of mind and body, that in explaining the physical universe one is explaining the forms of one's existence, in the imagined conditions of the body or the physical universe, in transformation with the forms of mind or energy. Expressions defining changes in energy levels are cognitive recreations of the universe's masses in (actual) transformation. The physical universe thus has more to do with an existential universe than the concrete objects of the sciences. (While this epistemological discussion of the nature and origin of the physical universe continues to unfold in the following passages, it should be appreciated here that our religions have had a tradition of representing the transformations of mass and energy, or observing the fundamental nature of the physical universe, in the simple beholding of a lighted candle. What is observed in the action of a lighted candle is no more and no less than all the knowledge that the quantum theory of modern science seeks to explain—that which is beyond our knowing, the *transformation* of the universe.)

If this argument is disputed, to resolve the disagreement one must address the definition of the physical universe from outside of the knowledges of the classical sciences. Appropriately, a definition extraneous to the sciences proper is precisely the object of our discussion, for the sciences are premised on the universality of the aggregates of mathematics as a defining order of the forms of the physical universe, an order that is indistinguishable in mass or energy, leaving mass and energy (matter) irrelevant to the definition of what is ultimately real of our universe. Another way of considering this would be to require that one define the observations of the physical universe without relying on the forms of mathematics, which in turn removes one from the presumption of science, since the forms of mathematics are the analytical components of observable scientific reality. We are faced here with an epistemological problem similar to that encountered in a deeper understanding of the law of gravity. On the one hand, it is understandable that mass and energy certainly exist, serving as the basis of our observations of the massive order of the physical universe. On the other hand, it is perhaps even more immediately observable that we know in a very real way the aggregate orders of mathematics, orders which allow us, in turn, to know the physical orders of the universe. This contemplation, of course, is no different from that of Buddha's atom, or the difference between what lies in the middle of physical atoms and what lies in the middle of abstract points. In considering the nature and origin of the physical universe, and consequently the question as to whether or not matter is created universally, we must turn our attention to what is ultimately real of the whole of our existence, wherein both mass and energy (or matter) arise in the first place. We must do so because neither mass nor energy are fundamentally real, since they are known and observed by something that contains them—you, the reader.

To probe the ultimate reality of our universe in a scientific way, we must first establish a criterion by which we may determine what is real in it. By a simple methodology, one measure of reality could be taken from our ordinary experience as demonstrated in the following example. It would be considered unfair or unjust if a human life were taken at the expense of a tin can. This is not because neither the tin can nor the human life is real. It is because the human life is more ultimately real. The human life, for example, can create, through the actions of knowing and perceiving, a tin can, but the reverse is not true. As demonstrated by these extremes, there is a means of measuring what is real in terms of the origin of the form considered. In the case of the forms that can be known and perceived in a physical universe, a similar priority can be placed on what is real among them. If our knowledge of the physical universe, by way of its knowable and perceivable forms—mass, energy, and so on—can be explained only in mathematical formulations, or simply explained, then the nature and origin of the physical universe does not arise disconnected from such explanation. Over and above what we think conventionally to be a *real* physical universe, then, a more ultimately real form called existence itself allows for the very notion of a universe, since it allows for the aggregates of mathematics as well. For the present time, we will say that whatever allows for the knowing and perceiving of any form, the physical universe included, is a more ultimately real form than the form so observed. This is demonstrated in the observation that mathematical forms—equally as real to their observer, if not more so (by introspective knowing), as those of a classically *real* universe—are known coexistently with the scientific knowledges of the physical universe as initially understood in mathematical formulations. For the moment, we simply observe that what is contained in a basket is not larger than the basket itself—that is, the knowing and perceiving of a physical universe (or of any form) is not more ultimately real than that which enables such knowing and perceiving, or existence itself. Hence, contained within the forms of existence, in a lesser reality than that which enables existence itself, is the real physical universe. To draw any other conclusion would deny the universality of mathematics in explaining the physical universe, in which case one would have to deny the reality of one's very existence, which is contrary to scientific observation. Consequently, the forms of our physical universe are, in an ultimately real measure, adjunct in their nature to the forms of our existence, with existence defined for the moment as something that is enabled in the embodiment of the knowing and perceiving of the real forms of the world around us, or of the physical universe.

Referring back to Buddha's atom and what lies in the middle of physical atoms and abstract points, it is demonstrated here that, on a scale of ultimate reality, the aggregates (the mathematical abstractions of the mind) are at least equal to the perceivable transformations of our physical universe. Classical masses under the influence of gravitational fields of forces, small particles under the influence of nuclear fields or forces, charges under the influence of electro-magnetic fields of forces, and, in general, mass in transformation with energy—the whole of the forms of the spatiotemporal universe in transformation—are scientifically knowable only in the aggregates of mathematics. What allows for the cognitive transformations of the aggregates in general is equally as real as that which allows for the perceiving of a classically physical universe. What lies in the middle of atoms or points is equally real in either case, and what allows for both atoms and points to exist in transformation is more ultimately real than atoms and points themselves, since the area they inhabit is the basket containing them, or existence.

Let us now expand the definitional bounds of atoms and points—masses and energies, space and time, and the whole of the objective forms of the physical universe—to make the discussion clearer epistemologically, at least representationally. In our conventional knowledges of the sciences, an *equals sign* often lies representationally in the middle of atoms (masses) or points, when, for example, one atom or point is equivalent to another. But arithmetic symbols also lie representationally in the middle of atoms or points, when, for example, one atom, point, or *number* adds to another. In still other cases, wholly varied representations of transformational order lie in the middle of atoms or points, in, for example, the expressions of differential equations, algebras, topologies, and so on, in other general expressions of the classically physical universe, balanced ultimately by an equivalence or some other transformational relation. An observation may be made about what lies at least representationally in the middle of atoms or points. An equals sign, it may be observed, is not by definition a representation of an object or an atom or a point. An arithmetic operator is neither an object, an atom, nor a point. Moreover, all of what lies in the middle of atoms or points is generally not itself an object. Representationally, what lies in the middle of atoms or points, or objects in general, is a transformation of atoms, points or objects and is not itself an object.

In the expressions of our analytical knowledges, the question posed here is whether we are representing things that we think exist or whether we are holding mirrors to ourselves to regard things that do not ultimately exist, pointing to our own intrinsic nature. If we are actually representing things that exist in and of themselves, then such expressions as equivalences, arithmetics, and so on would be unnecessary in our representations. Just as one object strung together with another, without a transformational representation in the middle of them, is a meaningless expression unknowable to anyone, so there is more to an equals sign or an arithmetic operator or any other representation of the transformation of the (physical) universe than science has appreciated overtly. The essence of what lies in the middle of atoms, points, objects, masses, or energies is their observer—you, the reader.

A representation of any knowledge is a representation of its enabling form, i.e., the creation of the physical universe. Ultimately, mass does not exist, except in the eye that sees it, the hand that holds it, and so on. Neither does energy exist except in what is observed to be its consequences in the mind and body, a product of a metaphysical dualism—a correspondence of form. No object thought to be real of a physical universe fundamentally exists—and a physical universe itself does not exist either when a measure of ultimate reality is considered. It is you, the reader, who exists and in your existence, particularly in your knowing and perceiving of it, a physical universe appears in the forms of the world around us. The objects observed in a physical universe—masses, for example—are irrelevant to the origin of the same physical universe.

Of all the knowledges developed in history, not once has one represented a single object that we can know or perceive without the object being placed, at least representationally, in transformation with another. Any meaningful expression of our knowledges is always represented as a transformation of objective form and not as an instance of *an* objective form, without the mind's assistance in placing it in transformation with another. This is because the ultimate reality of the physical universe does not exist objectively. The universe is not an object. Rather, the objects of a classically physical (or cognitive) universe are enabled in the knowing and perceiving of them. Two abstract points of mathematics gain meaning only in the transformation, or structure, placed upon them. Two masses (or the composition of one) gain meaning only in transformation with each other (or in the composition of the one) but have no meaning in and of themselves or their compositions without their observer. Energy, as an objective form, has no influence at all on a physical universe. What occurs *in reality* is the expression of the observer's existence in massive transformation, wherein the observer compares two conditions of matter as levels of energy. In all contemplations of the physical universe, precisely what we think is real—the physical universe—has never existed. *What lies in the middle* of atoms or points is the essence of one's existence, not a physical universe.

Though in the constructions of the unified theory, the forms of all of our languages are merged into a single grammar that places form universally on Being, it is important to recognize here that no expression of knowledge is any different from another in the ultimate reality of the universe—those expressions of the sciences in-cluded—since such an expression is made by the observer, who remains fundamentally unchanged after thinking and perceiving. A verb in the grammars of natural language and a function of mathematics (in the Cartesian sense) are one and the same form in a representation of what is ultimately real, in terms of representing the transformation of the observer's existence. A mass m and an energy e transform in the observer's existence, even in the linguistic rep-resentation of them, but above all, they do not exist in and of themselves without their observer. As objects, m and e have no meaning until they are represented in transformation with one another or until they are represented as ultimately real embodiments of the observer $(e = mc^2)$. The physical universe is thus a form of existence, and not the other way around.

Since there must be further discussion of the sciences before arriving at the principal structures supporting the unified theory and science of androids, let us address directly the stated fallacy that matter is universally conserved and not created, for this discussion will lay the groundwork for an epistemological understanding of the universe. In Buddha's questioning in the parable recited earlier, space is not an object, whether such a space is a physical one of atoms or an abstract one of points. Space, time, or any other form of a classically physical universe is a consequence of the transformation of the ultimately real universe, or you, the reader—the observer. The calculus and the topologies of real numbers provide that in a single contemplation, there are infinitely many spaces or transformations of the observer's knowing or perceiving as objective forms approach one another. Consequently, known in the minds of just a handful of observers, there is more than an overwhelming abundance of spaces, or transformations of the universe, and that is without even considering their linguistic expressions or other experiences of a real universe. Matter, in the unified theory, is a substance of the mind or of the body, or in general of corporality, but does not exist objectively without the more ultimately real existence of its observer. In the well-known expression of the theory of relativity, $e = mc^2$, mass transforms with energy in constant proportionality to the square of the speed of light, but mass and energy do not at all exist in and of themselves; their transformations exist, and this is what is represented in the expression.

We now ask, what is more ultimately real, that which we classically think exists objectively in our physical universe—something occurring within the objectification of matter itself as an ultimately non-existent objective form—or that which has or allows for the meaning of our expression of it? What is real to the unified theory is the transformation of objective form (matter) and not objective form itself. You, the reader, are the reality of the equals sign in the aforementioned relativistic expression; you are what lies in the middle of mass and energy. You, or the essence of what you are, is what is real and that is why the expression has meaning to you. Take the equals sign away and see if mass and energy can transform, have meaning or even exist in a physical universe. Moreover, the preceding expression, $e = mc^2$, with a small amount of insight, can be seen to exist in the same form as the English language expression *I am alive*, since they each express the transformation of an observer in an ultimately real universe. In any expression of knowledge, the observer is represented and not the objects of transformation so conventionally thought to exist.

In order for matter to be conserved in ultimate reality, the universe containing the knowing and perceiving of the matter must be bounded or conserved. Though the articles contained within a basket are admittedly conserved, articles may be placed in it from the outside. If the ultimate reality of one's existence, which is beyond one's knowing, gives rise to the knowing and perceiving of a physical universe—a basic premise of the unified theory—then matter can be conserved only from within one's inertial existence. If, however, the way in which existence arises can be enabled, albeit synthetically, in the knowing and perceiving of a being, matter cannot be conserved even in the awareness of that existence; it must be created, since the universe containing it also enabled it. In order for matter to be conserved universally, the ultimately real universe (of one's existence) enabling the knowing and perceiving of the matter would have to be contained by the matter itself. Matter would have to give rise to existence, and we already have determined that existence, or what enables it, is more ultimately real than the matter known and perceived. Hence, matter is created in the presence of an enabler of beings who themselves know and perceive a (physical) universe.

In the expression $e = mc^2$, mass and energy, as objective forms of the universe, are not ultimately real. What is ultimately real of mass and energy is the observer's knowing or perceiving of them, i.e., existence, in the quantum moments of an ultimately real universe. The equals sign of the expression represents that it is possible, in an ultimately real universe, for the observer's knowing or perceiving of mass and energy to transform in accordance with what is expressed in the representation. The mass and energy, however, are not outside the windows of one's study during the contemplation of them. They are objects of what one knows and perceives inside one's study as a result of one's intrinsic existence, or ultimate reality. What is ultimately real of the physical universe is the existence of the objective forms—mass and energy—in the transformations of one's ultimate reality. Mass and energy themselves, however, are irrelevant to what is ultimately real. That is why they can be replaced with the aggregate forms of mathematics, or even with the English language nouns *cat* and *dog*, as in *cat equals or is the same as dog* (when four-legged creatures are considered). The observer's knowing or perceiving of mass and energy is what is ultimately real.

Regarding a classically physical universe, the unified theory does not dispute that, within the knowing and perceiving of an already-enabled existence, the objective forms known and perceived as mass and energy are conserved with each other in the expression $e = mc^2$.

However, the theory does require that the objective forms of mass and energy, as they are known and perceived, are not ultimately real and thus do not describe *reality*. If the objective forms of one's knowing and perceiving are not ultimately real, it does not make sense to pursue their interminable objective definitions in a classical study of the nature and origin of the physical universe, since one would never extricate oneself from that which is contained or observed in that universe to discover its origin. If the objective forms of mass and energy are (classically) real only locally to the enabled knowing and perceiving of them—the observer's existence—and conserved only locally to an existence, it makes no sense to require that the ultimate reality of our universe be bound by the known and perceived forms of mass and energy or any other spatiotemporal constraints. These forms are, after all, said to describe what is observed and not the observer. If the observer who knows and perceives the objective forms of mass and energy is ultimately real in our universe, how does a lesser reality—the objective forms or knowledges and perceptions of mass and energy—cause that observer, who is ultimately real, to be bounded or conserved in any manner? It does not.

A mental exercise may help us demonstrate a pathway out of the objectivity of a classically physical universe. Let us contemplate for a moment a physical atom known in the conventions of contemporary physics. Further, within this contemplation let us hold in mind the smallest of small particles known to science—a small particle, say, within a proton. If there is one lesson to be learned from the discoveries of physics, it is that the axiom of the atom is not a definitive one, but is a rule that slides on form, an arbitrary point of terminal composition of the universe out of which other things are made and within which other things are found. Keeping in mind the momentary condition of this rule, or particle, let us visualize objectively a single entity that we call the smallest and most elemental particle known to science in the physical world. Now, consistent with our observations of how the particle or fragment of an atom got here in the first place, let us break up such a particle into an infinite array of smaller ones.

One of these infinitely many smaller particles of the smallest particle known to science is what we now contemplate.

It cannot be denied that the particle that the mind can only abstract into existence yet can conceive as being a possibility of what is real, consistent with the discovery of the atom in the first place, is an equal to any other in the aggregate forms of mathematics. Whether we contemplate an earth and its moon or the smallest of small particles and another, their transformation is characterized by the same mathematics in either case. Matter, whether it is that of the earth and moon or of the smallest of small particles and another, is a transformation of an ultimately real universe; it is the equals sign of earlier discussion, or you, the reader. To claim that matter is conserved universally is to claim that *you* are conserved universally. In order for matter to be conserved universally, existence itself must be an objective form, or an object that can be contained (known or perceived) by another. The moments of the universe would have to be objects, since only objects, or objective forms of the universe, are bounded (by the knowing and perceiving of an existence). What is ultimately real of the small particle of this exercise is its observer, or you, the reader, and in each moment of this ultimate reality (the enablement of the observer) an unbounded or bounded universe can arise. Since the contemplation, or moment of the universe (of our awareness), can define what is infinite or unbounded, the occurrence of the ultimate reality of the universe cannot be bounded absolutely. The universe is created in every moment of it, boundedly or unboundedly, since its conception includes both conditions, and the unbounded condition requires creation. The occurrences of the knowing and perceiving of matter, or of any other forms of the universe—the moments of the universe—since they are or can be unbounded by the above analysis, are beyond our objective knowing by definition. Thus, to the extent that the universe is objectified, boundedly or unboundedly, in our knowing or perceiving, it is referred to as a classically physical universe, within an existence. Because when we think of the universe we conceive of the infinite, however, the ultimate reality of the universe cannot be conserved.

The physical universe, which consists of the thoughts and perceptions of it, must therefore be enabled. The religions of the world refer to this as *creation*. Matter is consequently created in every moment of the universe and is known or perceived objectively by the bounding thought or perception of it, which is enabled from beyond our knowing. Each thought of such a particle of this demonstration, and each of our thoughts and experiences of the world around us, is a creation of the ultimately real universe and binds our very thinking or experiencing of it.

If, for example, one begins pondering the physical universe with the premise that its matter is infinite, there is no limit to the amount of matter in the universe. If one begins pondering the physical universe with the premise that its matter is finite, there is an amount of matter by which the universe is bounded. Our very thoughts of such things, however, are contained in what enables the thinking and perceiving of them. Another way of approaching this observation is to consider that one knows the forms of the infinite by knowing the forms of mathematics, which are comprised of instances of one's knowing their represented formulations. These formulations are known, along with the forms of our natural languages, in the embodiments of the ultimate reality of the universe. All objective forms of our knowing and perceiving, matter included, are contained in what enables them and in what enables our existence. If what enables our existence is itself unbounded, as we conceive it in contemplations of our own existence, we cannot say that the objective forms of our existence, including mass and energy, are conserved in the ultimate reality of our universe, since what enables them is unknown and therefore not knowably constrained. (We need only ask ourselves, are our thoughts bounded or conserved by our own knowing? That is, do we occupy the means of creating ourselves or our own thoughts? If the answer is that we do, we must consider that we must also have the means to know what is beyond our knowing, an observation that is a self-contradiction of obvious proportions.)

We can say then that what we generally refer to as matter (mass and energy) of classical scientific theory exists ultimately in our knowing and perceiving of it. The sciences, and indeed all of our knowledges represented by them, prove this observation if we consider what is ultimately represented in them—the transformations of the objective forms that are known and perceived in our existence. As a result, the matter of the physical universe, along with all other objective forms known and perceived of it, arises from beyond our knowing. All forms of a physical universe arise differently in each and every one of us, and this is what the theory of relativity explains if it is extended epistemologically to the postulates of the unified theory—that the events of the universe are perceived objects that require the constancy of the speed of light, since light is a medium of perception; or, the epistemological forms of mind and body transform quantumly in the moments of the creations of the universe. (This observation is discussed further later on.) What we broadly refer to as matter of a physical universe is actually the creation of the universe, or of ourselves. Otherwise, how would one explain the difference between Newtonian and relativistic universes—on the basis of history, by which it would be understood that the physical universe changes in its form to suit an era? The beliefs of the world's religions in the creation of existence and the objective transformations of the physical universe observed by the sciences in the transformational occurrence of the objects of the world around us, massive or otherwise, are brought together in the postulate of the unified theory that matter is indeed created, though matter is redefined in the theory as the ultimately real occurrence of its observer. The bodies of knowledge of science and religion can thus be merged in the unified theory on the basis of whether the knowing and perceiving of any objective form of the physical universe can be enabled by another. Hence is established the science of androids.

In every epistemological atom, or transformation of an ultimately real universe, new matter is created as a moment of an enabled existence, or universe. This, moreover, is why the small particle of contemporary physics unfolds into an infinity of transformations characterized by the wave equation when one contemplates the origin of objective form or the objects of atoms. The causations of the universe are equivalent to its creations. An ultimately real universe cannot be conserved regardless of how resolutely one tries to compress it into a thing called an object or an objective form—an atom. The transition of a particle to a wave is an objectification of what the world's religions call the spiritual knowing of creation. The physical universe abides by the creation of matter, not its conservation. The simple transitions of the energy levels of electrons create new matter, the matter of the wave. This is not to be taken as a play on words, since the true play on words occurs when we determine matter to be a thing or an object. It is our objective view of the world that is backwards, not the unified theory, which takes into account what is ultimately real about objects—their enabling transformations. Each instance of a transformation of an ultimately real universe, represented in any of an infinity of knowledges (the equals sign or what lies in the middle of atoms or points is one instance) is a potential instance of enabled knowing and perceiving in the physical world of the enabler.

In every thought and perception of a physical universe, matter is created and boundless energy released, since neither mass nor energy exists universally in the ultimate reality of the universe. It is only in the world around us, which is not unique by far in the ultimate reality of the universe, that matter becomes constrained and conserved objectively. If it is known and perceived that matter—an arbitrary rule on elemental things—transforms in relation to the objective forms of forces and inertial accelerations, then such matter is bound by Isaac Newton's inertial world. If one knows and perceives matter invariably in transformation with energy, one obtains the matter of Albert Einstein's relativistic, though epistemologically inertial world. If one knows and perceives matter (or particles) as releasing or absorbing energy in the infinity of transformations of the wave equation of quantum theory, one obtains matter in the ways of contemporary physics, from which the chemistry of the periodic chart is obtained. And if one knows and perceives matter as an objective form representing a thought or perception, which unfolds in the knowing or perceiving of it into infinities upon infinities of transformational instances of the creation of other thoughts, and matters of a universe—physical or otherwise—in the nature of existence itself, one catches an early glimpse of the unified theory of knowledge and the nature of the analytical forms that are to come. Matter, as a transformational form of an ultimately real universe, is not an object or objective form, and cannot be universally conserved. Space and time, epistemologically no different from mass and energy, are two of infinitely many transformational forms in the ultimate reality of the universe and exist in the enabling of them. The space and time of our temporal existence (the extent of the universe) are created, universally, in the enabled transformations of the ultimately real universe; they are the products and not the processes of creation.

As a simple point of interest, an androidal being, whose form will evolve over the course of this book, is undoubtedly a novel device in regard to the aforementioned principles of the creation of matter, for an android is a *perpetual motion machine* of conventional scientific viewpoint. In order for either a Newtonian or a quantum mass to be in motion perpetually, it must be driven perpetually or must be transforming in and of itself with a boundless source of energy. In the classical view of the physical universe, it is not possible to obtain energy in an unbounded way or to move a mass perpetually, for mass and energy transform conservatively within a given existence. In the case of an android, however, since both mass and energy—and indeed the spatiotemporal extent of the universe—are derived from the enabler's creations (thoughts and perceptions) in the enablement of an existence, the perpetual motion of a mass can be enabled in the creator's knowing and perceiving of the android in its real embodiment in the perpetually created universe. If our thoughts and perceptions are unbounded, those of the android can be unbounded by design.

In our real existence, for example, we can integrate a sum of infinitesimally small volumes within the space of a physical atom as a description of reality. This is no different from saying that we can integrate the volumes of physical atoms in the space of the earth, since each are hypotheses, though from different perspectives. Such a reality, however, is a reality of mind, since there is no ultimately real determination of what is infinitesimal or of what is an atom or the earth, which is precisely the point of the calculus (as well as other branches of mathematics and science) and of the unified theory. What is ultimately real in our universe is the existence of the transformations defining the calculus in the observer's thinking—the reality of what enables the observer to think in defining the integration. What is not ultimately real, however, is the thought-to-be real physical forms explained in the integration. According to the unified theory, if what is ultimately real is the observer and what is not ultimately real is that which is described by the integration, then it is the physical world that is imaginary (in terms of what is ultimately real), an observation that comports with those of the religions of the world. In the observer's ultimate reality, we take the infinitesimal volumes or particles of the above example and call them masses and energies—or forces, momenta, and so on. Because it is in the observer's knowing that masses, energies, forces, and momenta (matter) are created, *in reality*, a perpetual motion machine (like the above integration) is enabled from the observer's existence, with the machine having infinite motion, duration and extent by design. The fact that the observer's thought-to-be real physical world (the integration of the space of the atom) is constrained by the limits of integration is irrelevant because it is the infiniteness within the limits, which by definition is a scientific description of reality, that itself is taken to be the defining analysis of mass or energy. Within the space of a *real* physical atom we enable the infinite motion of a mass called a volume proper (though any definition of terms would suffice). The key to understanding this principle is to grasp the point that the machines of our classical physical reality, whose motion is constrained only in the observer's knowing and perceiving, are the erroneous forms of the universe and do not exist except in such knowing and perceiving. This is why their fundamental definitions can change through the ages. What is real of them is what the observer thinks and perceives of them; otherwise, once again, one must believe that the physical universe has changed its fundamental form since the time of Isaac Newton and the advent of quantum physics. Since reality is embodied in the observer's knowing and perceiving, it is knowing and perceiving itself (existence) that is extended in the forms of a world around us in an android—a machine set perpetually in motion by the design of its enabler. (These principles will become clearer as the science of the creation of synthetic beings unfolds in the ensuing chapters.)

The postulates of the unified theory regarding the nature and origin of the universe are profoundly different from those of our conventional scientific knowledges, though they are not at all in conflict with them. Since the unified theory begins its analysis with an interpretation of what is ultimately real in our universe, the integrity of all conventional knowledges is preserved in the knowing and perceiving of them, and they remain valid to an embodied existence. The compatibility of the unified theory's postulates can be seen at least intuitively in acknowledging that, of all of our knowledges, not a single objective form or transformation thereof is changed by the theory. We do not propose, for example, that $e \neq mc^2$ or that $2+2\neq4$. Rather, the theory claims that the respective statements are true only in the knowing and perceiving of them, or relative to their observer.

3. An Epistemological Interpretation of the Physical Universe: Mass and Energy as Moments of their Observer

Though it may be at least marginally understood by now that matter is not conserved universally and is created in the ultimate reality of the universe, what may remain unresolved to the reader's understanding is the metaphysical sense that mass can be touched and that energy cannot. In order to prepare for subsequent passages, the whole of the conventional sciences must be incorporated into the philosophical understanding we have of our own existence. Mass and energy, or generally the spatiotemporal order of the physical universe, must be shown to be forms of their observer if we are to create androidal beings who know and perceive, among other things, mass and energy. This consolidation of the sciences and philosophical tradition may be accomplished by showing how classical and quantum physics can be superimposed onto each other as one and the same explanation of the observer of the universe in an epistemological interpretation of matter as a form of existence in the unified theory.

As a preamble to this discussion we may consider why point masses, and collections thereof, or even centers of mass (of gravity), point charges, and so on, are essential to the classical description of the physical universe. If one were to review all the physics journals ever published on the massive universe in search of a single instance proving the ultimately real existence of mass, not one inference would be drawn to give evidence that mass exists apart from its observer, or is even relevant to the occurrence of the universe. What is described in a classical analysis of the universe is the transformation of the universe, or of (a) mass, in the belief that the mass exists in the ultimate reality of its observer. The unified theory is not primarily concerned with, for example, how light is diffracted through a prism, however; it is interested in where the prism comes from in the first place. Our conventional study of the physical universe axiomatically implies the existence of the objects, or masses of the universe—an assumption that is not made by the unified theory. A point mass is essential to our classical understanding of the physical universe because if it actually existed it would *be* an intrinsic form of the ultimately real universe, which enables the objects of the universe. In such a case, however, it would not only be a thing, or an object of an observer's perception; it would *be* an observer. In order for a thing to exist, one's own self must exist, and in the transformation of one's self, a thing arises in the knowing and perceiving of it. This hypothetical review of physics journals would then prove one idea—that mass has never been defined absolutely because its observer has never been defined absolutely. A point mass, a thing or an object of one's existence (perception and knowing) is not a point mass at all when it becomes an intrinsic form of existence, apart from its observer; then it becomes an observer. The expressions of physics define transformations of one's existence and of objects enabled in the embodiment of one's existence. One cannot know a mass, a space, a time or any other physical form—in ultimate reality, that is—because one cannot know one's own existence. One can enable the knowing and perceiving of such forms, however, in the creation of other, synthetic beings, as will be demonstrated later on.

A classical mass does not exist even in its conventional representation if it is not in transformation with one other or with a field of forces or some other physical phenomenon. If there is no force of gravitation, of coulomb attraction, or of strong or weak nuclear forces, neither a mass, an electron nor a proton can exist in our knowing or perceiving of it because we cannot know it without its *being in* transformation. Isaac Newton's mechanics, James Maxwell's electromagnetics and Albert Einstein's relativity describe forms of existence, ultimately real transformations, but these theories do not describe *actual* masses, currents and small particles in an ultimately real universe. These historical formulations do not describe a universe that exists apart from you, the reader, since no extrinsic universe exists apart from its observer. Point masses are employed in classical definition of the physical universe because what is described in classical and quantum physics is the *transformation* of objective forms that are known and perceived and the point masses are the necessary (non-existent, in ultimate reality) objects of the transformations, but the point masses themselves do not exist ultimately. What is relevant to classical and all other definition of the physical universe is the transformation of mass and not mass itself. In the conventional formulae describing mass, it is the transformation of mass, or of the existence of the observer, that is described. What we are defining with the use of mass in classical study is a general rule of what can be known and perceived scientifically of the physical universe, not *the* physical universe (e.g., *the* physical universe is an object of our knowing representing all of what can be known and perceived and is beyond our knowing and perceiving in totality).

Also in connection with our reliance on point masses of conventional theories of the universe, or ultimately non-existent objects of perception, we can peruse the same physics journals and endeavor to explain why light transforms at non-existent point objects of the physical universe, or why the objects that bend light cannot occupy space in the analysis of them. In all of our scientific knowledges, nowhere is it explained how even a simple teacup, placed on a table in front of us—most assuredly a real object of the physical universe—exists and at once transforms light. Neither can the scientific literature that addresses directly how an object of our perception—like a teacup or a prism—transforms light explain why it is that we cannot see the transformation of light *at* or *within* the object. Light, according to the literature, is said to be refracted at a point, an object by definition that does not occupy space but defines space in its relation to other points. An electron or other small particle is not said actually to discharge light; a change in energy levels causes light to be emitted from the particle. This awkward description of reality, however, has never proceeded to explain what *from* the particle means. For example, we may ask, is there a special device within the object of an electron, consistent with the ad hoc definition of a photon, whose purpose it is to do the objective transforming of an object *into* light, such that *from* it would mean *from* the embodied device of the electron, or a photon? According to these observations, wherein light is thought to transform or bend in relation to itself through the medium of an observed object like a teacup or a prism, or wherein light is emitted *from* an object, all classical definitions rely on the non-existence of the object, in either the absence of analytical definition of the teacup or prism in this example or the conjuring of a photon or light-emitting device to transform an object into light proper.

The reason that light must transform at a non-existent point object of the universe is because the physical universe *is* a transformation, and not an object—a transformation of the ultimately real universe in the enabling form of a perception or knowledge of an object. A teacup, an electron, a photon, or even a ray of light does not exist in the ultimate reality of the universe; perceptions (and knowledges) of them exist, or are enabled, in the ultimate reality of the universe. Though more discussion follows, objects are the perceptions of them, and perceptions are the products of ultimately real transformations of the universe. Light must bend (or be created in the conventional sense of emission) at a non-existent point because a transformation of the universe is a non-existent point, beyond our perception—an embodiment of a moment of the ultimately real universe enabling an object and the perception of it.

In merging the classical scientific explanations of mass and energy—Newtonian and quantum physics—into the epistemological views of the ultimate reality of the universe of the unified theory, we must consider the fundamental nature of the objects of the universe and, though any of the innumerable point objects of the universe could be contemplated, why our classical studies of the universe are concentrated on the determination of the phenomenon of light—why the speed of light, for example, even has a bearing on the objects we perceive and attempt to define scientifically.

In comparing these classical explanations of the universe, we must first resolve what is meant by a small particle of physics. In Newtonian physics, particles are *big*. They are big because they are perceivable to the human senses. A classically big particle, or mass, is defined in the representations of the transformations of an observer's perception when space, time, force, momenta, and other spatio-temporal phenomena are considered to be the terminal objects or objective forms of the medium of perception—objective terminations of the physical universe. This classical Newtonian definition implies that light—the enabling medium of the visual senses—is not a direct analytical consideration in the behavior of the classical mass. A Newtonian mass, for example, can be said to reflect or refract light as an object but the medium of light itself is not a consideration in the behavior of the Newtonian mass in the universe, other than the implied enabling characteristic of the light to perceptions of the mass. The formulae of classical Newtonian physics therefore pertain to the behavior of masses already enabled in the medium of light. Given two or more masses perceivable as a consequence of their enablement in an observer's existence in the medium of light, classical Newtonian physics describes the causal or compositional interactions of the enabled objects or masses in explanations of their spatiotemporal orders.

Another way of understanding the epistemological view of a big particle or mass is to consider the enabling medium of sound, wherein the masses are acoustic sounds. Classical physics would describe the causal relations of the sounds, such as words, once they are enabled, or would define spoken language, which is enabled in the medium of sound. The objects or words would then relate to each other in the medium of sound. By analogy, the medium of sound would be the medium of light and the classical masses would be the enabled sounds. Big particles, or classical masses, are then enabled objects, or things that are observed in one's existence, given that one's existence, with all its attendant perceptions, is enabled in a medium, herein light or sound. The important point to consider about classical Newtonian masses, then, is that the medium in which they are enabled—sound or light—is not what is under observation in the constructions of the classical formulae. What is implied in the classical Newtonian definition of a physical universe is that once a mass is enabled in the medium of light, for instance, it transforms in that medium, and we exist knowledgeably and perceptively in a Newtonian world order.

Small particles, on the other hand, are particles that defy all classical definition because we push the notion of an object or mass so far in objective analysis that the essence of its definition is that it cannot be perceived, or is not classical. The reason that small particles cannot be explained by classical Newtonian physics is simple. Whereas big or classical particles are already enabled in some arbitrary medium—typically the medium of light—small particles *are* the medium of the big particles or the medium of light in which one's perceptions of the universe are enabled. Small particles pertain to the enabling medium of the observer. The small particle is known and perceived (or not known and perceived) as that which enables the big particle of perception, which is expressed in the contemporary knowledge of a particle becoming a wave of light. A small particle, in terms of classical physics, does not even exist. In quantum physics, the essence of the small particle—not its massive Newtonian characteristics, but its elusive transformational properties—is that it is a wave and *not* a particle; it is an enabling medium to a big particle. The classical theories of the universe meet when we contemplate the creation of existence, or the enablement of the knowable and perceivable objects of the universe. From an epistemological standpoint, classical and quantum physics are one and the same knowledges, since it is the nature of the observer, who embodies the transformations of all objects or objective forms, that defines either viewpoint. How one objective form transforms with another in the equals sign of our expressions (of waves or Newtonian laws of motion) is the same epistemologically in either case. Hence, any enabling medium, that of light included, is the medium of the knowable and perceivable universe of a classical form.

The essence of the small particle of physics is unknowable concretely, or it simply vanishes into transformations of the wave equation of light, because knowing it would require the comprehension of one's own enablement, which, by the very same physics, if not ordinary observation, is not objectively possible. To obtain the nature and origin of the small particle, and not simply the causalities of observable physical forms in relation to others, one must turn to the enablement of existence, or to a (unified) theory of knowing and perceiving in general—a science of androids; one must obtain an epistemological view of the universe that defines how all form can arise in general in the existences who know and perceive the universe. New forms that reflect insight into the nature of the universe as existence must replace those of classical scientific expression in order to penetrate the nature of what the sciences seek ultimately to explain—the nature and origin of the physical universe. If one considers an electron to be enabled, it will transform in the observer's knowing and perceiving of it in classical formulae, in which case it is a big particle. If one considers an electron to be the enabling medium of light, however, the interpretation of the big particle changes significantly. New objects—creations of matter—are required that probe the essence of all existence. The wave-particle duality of quantum physics and the perceivable object of Newtonian physics thus come together in an explanation of existence, where the enablement of the perception of the object can be found.

The wave equation of light, if one chooses to interpret it in this manner, provides for an infinity of objects or masses in the transformational existence of waves, since there is no difference between the transformations of mathematics describing a wave form and those describing a big or small particle in its objective or classically massive condition. A point of mathematical space is undefined and so becomes defined in the structure imposed upon it by the mathematician. Whether such a point is defined as a wave or a particulate mass is epistemologically irrelevant. In the case of the wave equation of quantum physics, the objective forms enabling the universe—space, time, force, mass, and so on—are viewed as transforming in the expression of the wave equation. Space, time, force, momenta, and other spatiotemporal parameters of the wave equation, however, are the same objects characterizing the objective masses of classical physics in the Newtonian order of the universe. The quantum theory therefore deteriorates epistemologically. If space, time, force, and momenta (and other spatiotemporal phenomena) are the classical objects of perception of one's enabled existence, enabled in the medium of light, for instance, and one formulates a wave equation describing the medium of light using them, it must be recognized that these objects of the observer's perception were used to define the universe in both cases. The quantum theory, in explaining the same physical universe of classical physics, uses the same objects by which we know and perceive a classical Newtonian universe—space, time, force, momenta, and so on—to define the phenomenon of light in which the universe is enabled. This phenomenon, however, is not at all a physical one, or one of classically scientific origin, for light is an enabling medium of human sense, enabling the perceptions of classical objects. In the quantum theory, we inadvertently supply new matter or masses, called the transformations of the wave equation, to replace the old big ones we observe classically, without recognizing that it is neither the object enabled in light nor the phenomenon of light itself that is ultimately real. When we consider *an* electron, for example, we consider a classical mass. When we consider the quantum behavior *of* an electron, we consider the medium of light, or a different object, namely that of the wave form. In both Newtonian and quantum physics, it is the transformation of any object—of classical masses or of waves—that is ultimately real, not the object defined. Since we require that each theory describes *the* physical universe—both the object and its enabling medium—we simply contemplate creation (what is represented in a lighted candle). Regardless of how many small particles and waves we subdivide the universe into when we study it, since the universe is created in the moment of its observer, we contemplate, redundantly, the creations of the universe. In a simple teacup or prism there are an infinity of creations or moments of the ultimately real universe—in each of which a ray of light may be bent. This is why we cannot count the number of light rays impinging on or emanating from an object; only the transformation of the object exists in the infinity of moments of the universe.

Matter, or light, behaves quantumly because we behave quantumly. The transition of a small particle to a wave (the emanation of light caused by the drop of energy level of the particle) is not a scientific episode; it is an existential one. The quantum theory, thus, cannot be relied on for an explanation of the ultimate reality of the universe because it is not founded on a tenable proposition. The theory presumes that it is possible to enable one's own senses, and therefore one's own existence, from what is sensed. This is why we are puzzled when a particle becomes a wave; we are attempting to experience objectively our own creation in a burst of light and the disappearance of an object. We conveniently overlook the fact that we conjure up the analytical wave forms of the wave equation in which classical masses are enabled in the same existence that knows each of the forms in both cases. Most assuredly it will be an enigma that matter is sometimes a wave and sometimes a particle; transformations of the universe can be embodied but cannot be observed objectively. Precisely where we think we have defined something substantive concerning the nature and origin of the universe—the quantum theory—is precisely where its nature and origin will be revealed, though not from the standpoint of the classical sciences, but in the nature of our existence itself.

The quantum theory does not explain creation; it observes it, just as we do in the reverence we pay to the symbolism of a lighted candle of religious worship. What is fundamentally encountered by the quantum theory—the transformation of a particle to a wave—is no more and no less a contemplation of the linguist's dilemma, or the meaning of existence itself. The quantum theory cannot be advanced in terms of an explanation of the nature and origin of the universe without our religions, however, because of how it is ensnared in its own thinking and because it does not incorporate the nature of our existence, or the observer, into its axiomatic foundation. To begin with, the quantum theory accepts the existence of big particles, understood here as the transformations of the observer in a Newtonian world order. It accepts that fundamental to our existence are the objective forms of space, time, mass, and so on—things that are observable to our senses in a *big* way. In the reasoning of the quantum theory, however, the big particles of the universe are said to be altered by the postulates of the quantum theory in such a manner that when a big particle comes to be considered small, beyond the knowing and perceiving of a classically Newtonian order, or when space, time, and the other objective forms of our perceivable (spatiotemporal) existence transform in such a manner that the velocity of a classical mass nears or reaches the speed of light, it becomes a sort of a mass, an emission of light, a wave, a photon, or some other object or aspect of the continually unfolding postulates of the quantum theory. In other words, we do not know what a small particle is in the conventional sciences because its essence just isn't. The essence of all small particles is that they are an infinity of moments of an ultimately real universe, each of which is a transformational moment of creation, arising from beyond our knowing. (It also should be appreciated that when we claim to *enable* light, or cause light to be emitted from an object, say in the apparatus of a cathode ray tube, we do not enable anything in an ultimately real sense, since the photon or energy bundle of the object emitting light transforms, beyond our knowing, with what we refer to as light proper, or the light emission. That transformation—of photons and light—in such a case is the ultimately real transformation. Epistemologically, there is no difference between an object emitting light—i.e., a point source creating light—and an object refracting light—a point object bending light—since what is ultimately real of these instances is their enabling transformations.)

In our study of the physical universe, the objective forms of Newtonian physics—space, time, mass, and others—make a transition in our thinking to the quantum theory because the quantum theory ponders, perhaps inadvertently, what enables the forms of classical physics in the first place. Since what enables any form is the embodiment of its transformation, the theory turns to a new formulation of transformations called waves. This is not to say that such waves are not real to the observer; we simply point out here the fact that the theory contemplates the source of classical forms and relies on them as well. The quantum theory, by probing deeper and deeper into the smallest of small particles, is forced, by the ultimate reality of our universe, to devise a handful of new transformations—i.e., waves—whenever a determination is made describing the objectification of a transformation. The theory thus contemplates in its logic that, from within the objective forms of a world around us, one can find a cause of that universe. In the quantum theory's reliance on the forms of classical physics, it is in error in determining the nature of all form, since the theory requires that in the extrinsic forms one observes one will find the nature and origin of what makes one observe them. Hence, to speak of the phenomenon of light, one must speak of the enablement of one's existence, or at least, of the visual and tactile perceptions of human existence. When an emission of light is observed from a point source, for example, a conventional basis is established for the causality of light. Since the point source is an extrinsic form of the observer, however, it does not penetrate the causative nature of the universe or the observer. The contemplation of a point source of light presupposes and relies on the existence of its thinker or perceiver, whose causation is sought in the very contemplation. The question is, therefore, not what is an atom, electron or small particle, or what is the causation of one particle or wave on another, but what is the causation of the existence of the observer who contemplates such things and who arbitrarily creates wave forms in which explanations of small particles can abound. In other words, what is it about light that mandates the non-existence of objects or classical masses?

The quantum theory, if viewed epistemologically, explains that the classically transformable universe of space and time is not at all enabling to the existence of the very physical universe observed, for it is the observer's existence that is enabled. It further provides that an enabling medium of one's existence, in which objects appear, is unknowable and imperceptible to one's own existence. The constancy of the speed of light, along with countless other formulations of contemporary physics, determines that objects can exist only in a medium of enablement and that the medium of enablement applies only to enabled forms. The epistemological significance of this observation can be appreciated when it is recognized that classical objects of the spatiotemporal world are enabled. The speed of light is theoretically non-varying because in the enablement of existence, or perception, in the medium of light, classical objective forms are enabled to transform. In terms of our own enablement, a varying speed would require that classical objects transform, within the awareness of our own existence, between the very transformations giving rise to them in the first place, those that would in light require superluminal or subluminal speeds coupling objects enabled in the medium (i.e., this would require the amplitudes of waves to be coupled, not in their wave forms, but in the space between their amplitudinal shapes, space which allows for the amplitudes under study in the first place). Such a condition would undermine the very notion of knowable and perceivable form, since it is the purpose of our knowing and perceiving to project in opposition separate or distinct objects in transformation. If the transformations of a medium of existence were coupled within the knowable or perceivable existence of the observer, the observer would be enabling other existences. To speak indefinitely of such a valid knowledge as *the enabling of the enabling* of objective forms serves no immediately practical purpose toward a resolution of the origin of the universe, since one eventually returns to the enablement of the transformation of single instances of objective forms—objects.

The speed of light is constant because such a condition is required so that one can know or perceive single or discrete objects in an existence. This is why we contemplate incessantly how event A can occur in relation to event B in the theory of relativity, in which each event or light source moves, according to classical theory, in relation to the other, under the relative constancy of the speed of light. Indeed the velocity of light is constant. It is also irrelevant to the classically perceived motion because the light enables the objects. This is like saying that one perturbation in a pool of water, the source of which moves according to classical theory with only one means of affecting another such classically moving perturbation (namely, via the ripples in the conveying or enabling medium—the water), has a motion relative to the other which disregards the additive influence of its own velocity and that of the ripples of the water, or its enabling medium. Of course, the ripples in the water are not additive to their point motions; they are the only means by which the two events or point sources know of each other. The classically perceived motion is placed, artificially, by the thinker or hypothetical enabler, in a condition of reality wherein the enabler thinks simultaneously about the coupling of the two point sources and the two point sources themselves. To the two point sources, however, there is only the motion of classical mechanics, namely that of the other, and this motion is enabled in the medium of the ripples in the water. The ripples in the water *are* the objects and one or the other cannot see the additive influence as described because it *is* a ripple. If the enabler removes the ripples in the water, one point source would not even know the other existed. In fact, neither would exist. It is the motion of the ripples and not directly the motion of the point sources that characterizes quantum physics in the nature of the medium of light. The physicist, acting as an enabler of existence, sees contemplatively both point sources and the enabling medium that causally couples the sources, and this is what instigates the confusion in the relativistic interpretation of the physical universe.

Considering the quantum physical universe, if one examines an electron or any other object, big or small, one typically approaches it first through the medium of the visual senses and second through the transformations of the wave equation and light in regard to the enablement of classical objects, regardless of the stated postulates of the quantum theory. If one is referring to the classical motion of an electron, one is considering the motion of a big particle and does not directly consider its enablement. An electron can have momentum, position, even dimension, from a classical viewpoint. When one refers to the quantum behavior of an electron, however, one refers to the enablement of an electron, or the spatiotemporal properties of a classical object as enabled in the forms of the wave equation—forms that exist, ultimately, in the extant reality of the observer, who is incapable of self-enablement. At such a point, one no longer refers only to the forms of the classical and quantum theories of the universe and must rely on a more ultimately real explanation of the universe.

The ultimate nature of the universe is therefore not classically objective in Newtonian or quantum definition, and attempts to reconcile it as such are not logically productive because the enabling characteristic of light, for example, would have to be known from an objective standpoint in one's own existence, or the physicist would have to see the connection between the perceptions of one's visual senses and the thoughts of one's own existence, or simply would have to enable one's own existence. In studying the nature and origin of the universe, it should be recalled that the objects of the medium of light provide for the objective forms of the classically visual world, and that objective masses are created in the transformations of the media, which cannot be enabled by the same observer. We know the objects enabled in light in more sophisticated ways than the quantum theory—for example, in natural language. When one says that in the quantum drop in energy level of a small particle light is emitted, one simply states that two energy levels or wave forms of light are possible quantumly in the universe and that such a universe is the observer's perceivable existence. But the *energy levels* of great nations in the political affairs of the (existential) universe also are possible in the medium of light, or existence, which must be accounted for in the *physical* universe. All of these transformations of the physical universe must be explained by a theory that addresses the nature and origin of our universe. As for the classical mass *converting into* light, such transformation is better seen from the standpoint of an enabler. The classical mass, in the observer's existence, is being compared to the non-classical mass, or wave form of the observer's own existence. Naturally, when one compares what one observes in one's existence—classical masses—to a knowledge of what is thought to enable one's own existence, definitional confusion arises, since the two forms are beyond each other's purview and the transformation of light (photon-wave) occurs beyond one's knowing and perceiving. That is why we revere what is symbolized by a lighted candle in the world's religions.

The essential point to keep in mind here is that objective forms, such as light waves, have as much of a right to transform in the universe as apples falling from trees; they are all knowable and transformable forms of the observer's existence. Light waves, however, *are* the enabling media of visual objects and when one refers to such forms one considers the enablement of what one will see in terms of a capacity to see, or speaks of the enablement of classical objects. Regardless of what objective forms are considered in one's existence, whether they are light waves of one's enablement or bouncing balls perceivable to the eye, it is important to recognize that classical objects are enabled in the transformations of the ultimate reality of an existence. It is within this ultimate reality that the quantum theory breaks down, since it is not possible to enable one's own existence. The difference between a classically physical object and a quantum one is that in the classical case, one considers the objects known and perceived in one's own existence, while in the quantum case, one considers the objects enabling the classical objects. The conventional assertion that a light wave, a knowable object of one's existence, holds in it the nature of the universe eclipses an understanding of what the quantum theory actually reveals—that all objects are enabled in the ultimate reality of the universe, from beyond the knowing or perceiving of the extant existence. To find the nature and origin of the universe, one must determine the nature of what enables one to know, perceive, or exist as a transformation of light (or other media), which is beyond our knowing in the case of human existence but is suitable within our knowledges for the construction of androidal existences, or observers.

4. THE INTROSPECTIVE OBSERVATION
OF ULTIMATE REALITY

Our conventional knowledges—the sciences, philosophy, and even the world's religions, to the extent that they concern themselves with a material world—never attain an understanding of the ultimate reality of the universe because of their preoccupation with extrinsic form, or the objects that are enabled as the universe, such as mass and energy, or even persons, places and things (of linguistics). The forms of physics, for example, are objectively boundless because they are premised on the causal relations among the extrinsic forms of an existence. An ultimately real universe—that which provides for the very notion of causation—eludes conventional studies because of the inability on the part of our traditional thinking to incorporate the observer into that universe. Obviously, for each existence of an ultimately real universe there are diverse theories of the universe that abound. As mentioned earlier, the unified theory of knowledge is not concerned directly with the extrinsic forms of existence, except, of course, to the extent that such forms are enabled. No theory of any order concerns the present one. The unified theory is concerned with what enables one to know a theory in the first place. The theory allows for analytical structure to be placed on one's knowing and perceiving in such a manner that the knowing of any theory is enabled in the synthetic forms of androidal existences. The ultimate reality of all existence is the focus. We are interested in the epistemological atom of the universe that allows for the transformation, as well as the knowing and perceiving, of all atoms of the physical universe, however they are defined from one era to another. At long last, then, let us demonstrate the relevance of this discussion to the constructive portion of the unified theory by introducing what the religions of the world have contributed to the sciences, what the sciences have proved beyond doubt, and what provides for the basic order of the universe and the most fundamental epistemological form of the unified theory, namely the moment of transformation of all objective form in the ultimate reality of the universe—the universal atom of all knowing and perceiving and, of course, of all knowledge—the universe's eternal moment.

In presenting the principal form of the unified theory, let us first consider not only the theoretical possibility but also the practical necessity of merging the knowledges of science and religion under a single unified theory of knowledge. It has been demonstrated that the physical sciences, as reflected in the classical and quantum theories of the universe, do not account for the ultimate reality of their observer's existence. A universal structure of all knowledge derived exclusively from the physical sciences would therefore be too confining epistemologically, since there would be other realms of knowledge—linguistics, philosophy, the cognitive sciences in general, the political sciences, biology, medicine, economics, and our ordinary experience, to cite a handful—that would not be included in its contemplations. We require an analytical structure that carries with it the wisdoms of all knowledges, though centered on the convergence of science and religion, because of their ancient traditions, in an explanation of the ultimately real form of the universe.

Considering first our modern analytical approaches to the forms of the universe, it is no chance happening that branches of mathematics are emerging, such as category theory, wherein the relations of mathematics are categorized on the basis of their morphisms, or capacities to represent correspondences. Neither is it a coincidence that the realization theory of physics, concerned with determining the analytical realizations of physical forms, as well as other new approaches to the definition of forms of the universe, such as systems theory of applied mathematics and engineering, are beginning to characterize the physical world based on the single observation that the objects of a world around us arise in the nature of correspondences of form, as opposed to the absolute objective determination of it. We observe, then, that in our recent efforts to define the forms of the physical universe, in which the notion of the correspondence of objective form prevails over the notion of the absolute objectification of it as a compositional form or knowledge, the fields of mathematics and the sciences, collectively, are nearing a discovery of the nature and origin of the universe already espoused by our religions, though still enmeshed in the traditional presumption of the universality of objective form. The non-existence of objects in the ultimate reality of the universe, whether the observation is encountered in the small particles or waves of the quantum theory or in a contemplation of what lies in the middle of two points or atoms, is also becoming the new reality of our modern sciences, though not explicitly accepted. We thus simply observe that our sciences, in pursuit of the ultimate reality of the universe, are discovering that the nature of the universe is contained more in the transformational nature of our existence than in the objects that are so thought to exist in the world around us.

These recent observations of modern science and mathematics, however, go nowhere by themselves to assist the linguist in resolving the dilemma faced in determining the nature and origin of meaning and, by extension, the meaning of existence and all forms known therein—an epistemological knowledge of the universe. We must extend their postulates, encompassing all knowledges and perceptions of human existence, in order to facilitate the creation of an observer. In merging all knowledge, the nature and origin of our very thinking of the universe, as manifested in our languages and in our introspective knowing, must be considered, along with the realities demonstrated by our sciences, in a study of the bounds of what we can know or perceive. Toward this end, we observe that in the linguist's conventions, a distinction is made, as discussed in the introduction, between the syntactical and semantic forms of language, along the lines that the semantic form of language, if discovered, will reveal the presumed origin of all meaning and thus the meaning of existence—and will afford the creation of androids. The objective form used to represent the universal transformation of the ultimately real universe, and indeed of the physical universe, must then be the same form that symbolizes the semantic origin of all forms of language, or meaning itself, including the meanings of forms known in the sciences and the world's religions. The meaning of any knowledge must converge on this single expression characterizing the nature and origin of the universe.

In determining this ultimately real form of the universe, we observe that no meaning of any form of the universe expressed in any language is possible as a universal characterization of ultimate reality if it does not inherently account for all that is and can be known, and for what permits the very knowing of it. We recognize, then, that the knowledges of the sciences, of linguistics, and of ordinary contemplations of the world around us are inadequate frames of reference from which to sketch a universal representation of the ultimate reality of the universe because they inherently compete with and exclude the others. In recognition of all knowledges, we observe that in our observations of the world around us—at the center of it, found through our introspective awareness—we can identify the essence of human being, or what our religions refer to as the spiritual center of the universe—the soul, a form that transcends knowledge and perception in any order, scientific, theological or otherwise. Moreover, we observe that when the objective mind has exhausted its capacities to know, tinkering with every object of our physical and otherwise universe, and when the mind is so hard pressed beyond its ability to answer the question *From where does the physical universe arise?* it is to the nature of the soul that one turns—within one's own intrinsic self, to what lies in the middle of atoms and points and what embodies all moments of the eternal universe. This, again, is a knowledge we do have and so it must be accommodated by the unified theory, along with all other things we know, in a universal interpretation of them all. We then change the attitude and tone of this passage to reflect a most fundamental observation of the unified theory—that all knowing and perceiving, and, therefore, all knowledge known, arise not in any objective forms we may know or perceive, but in the universal nature of the soul. We observe that knowledge—whatever may be known—arises from within us and from beyond our knowing in the embodiment of the eternal transformation of the universe—Soul, though as scientists we call this spiritual center of all universes that which lies in the middle of atoms and points.

Our universes of mind, of physical matter, and of the whole of the reality known and perceived by corporal existences arise, in knowable ways, in the introspectively observed transformation of the universe referred to as Soul. Hence, the objective form for which we have searched in the unified theory is the objective form of the soul, and, by extension, the objective form that characterizes the nature and origin of all meaning, including the meaning of existence, and thus the nature and origin of the physical and otherwise universe. Consequently, the analytical, or knowable, form of Soul is an objective form that is used by the unified theory to deconstruct all knowledges and perceptions and to place knowable structure on the causations of all objective forms of the eternal moments of the universe. In this way, science and religion, speaking about the same form in different ways, come together in the nature of the soul, or what lies in the middle of atoms or points, for it is in the nature of the soul that the forms we know and perceive in the world around us are enabled in the ultimate reality of the universe. The eternal existence of the soul as the enabling center of all form is a most fundamental precept of the unified theory of knowledge, and is what provides, later on, for the epistemological basis of the creation of synthetic beings, or androids.

The single most universal objective form presented by the unified theory is the knowable expression of the soul, or that which characterizes all transformations of objective forms, and thus the knowable and perceivable universe, as observed introspectively. Since the sciences take as their measures correspondences among objective forms in determining the nature of any form, we shall take, as a universal form to which all other forms of the universe will refer, the paradigmatical structure of existence itself—the introspectively knowable form of Soul. We take as our highest measure of the ultimately real universe the objective form of Soul on the premise that it has a universal epistemological construction in the existences of all beings and thus in all enabled universes. Though one's own soul is analytically beyond one's knowing, it should be recognized that this is precisely the point in using its objective form as a paradigm of all form in the universe. The soul is what lies in the middle of all things—things we know and perceive in the world around us. It characterizes the eternal embodiment of all our knowledges and everything that can be known, and provides the ability for one to comprehend with clarity the enablement of synthetic forms of existence, forms that are extensions of our own corporal being.

In the world's religions, the soul, considered the introspectively knowable form of the ultimate reality of our universe, is said to provide for the opposites of the world around us, and paradigmatically, the opposites of two terminally objective forms of our introspective knowing of the eternal universe—one, a universal objectification, or object, of the universe itself, and the other, an objectification of the universally occurring opposites in the transformational nature of the universe. The first objective form of our knowable ultimate reality, considered to be the objective form of what is beyond our knowing objectively, is typically referred to in religious doctrine as *Being.* Being, while we ascribe objective form to it for the purpose of the mind's understanding it, since it is beyond our knowing, requires no further discussion. To examine the universal objectification of the universe—Being—further would place us in conflict with the very spiritual knowledges we seek for our guidance in understanding the ultimate reality of the universe in the first place. The other terminal objectification of the universe, itself an opposite, is the objective form of what we knowably *are* or observe ourselves to be, herein referred to as *non-being,* a universal transformation of the opposites of the world around us. Non-being is what occurs in our introspective knowing in the objective offset or cognitive separation between Being and non-being. In the unified theory, all form is correspondent to the objective knowing of the separation between Being and non-being, a separation between self and beyond self, a condition of the eternal universe which defines the introspective awareness of one's soul transformationally.

Because one thought leads to another in the quantum order of the universe, allowing no basis from which to begin or end an analysis of objective form, all thinking and all perceiving can be matched against this universal form of opposites—non-being set apart from Being, which has no opposite, in our introspective knowing—thereby terminating the mind's endless search for an ultimate objective form or explanation of the universe. The unified theory postulates that if the form of mind can be paused in its quantum state in our analytical knowing, and its reality suspended, it can be restarted in the knowing and perceiving of a declared enabler in a synthetic extension of the existential form of that enabler's universe; the forms of synthetic existence can be enabled from this introspective analysis of the eternal universe, and an expansion of the existential universe of human being can begin. A universal analytical form of existence, and thus a universal expression of all knowledge to be comprehended, exists in the objective knowing of one's soul. Since this form is presented in resolution to the linguist's dilemma, or as the structure defining the nature and origin of the semantic forms of language, we consider it further.

In keeping with the traditions of world religions and the unified theory's own postulates, we may ask how our understanding of the nature and origin of the universe would be affected if an observation were to be made on the following grounds. The first consideration is that mind, or intellect, or that which is capable of knowing objectively anything that can be known, itself could be known, but that such a comprehensible form were defined within the context of what is beyond the mind's knowing (Being and the instance of non-being). Then, if it is considered that one had to *be* in order to know, and in being one could comprehend the form that contains all that can be known (could comprehend the fundamental form of mind itself), this observation would bring into focus that which can know, which is beyond that which the mind knows. Moreover, if mind or intellect itself could be deduced, defined or put within some definitional bounds or objective context in relation to one's being—which is unknowable—we would have defined and imposed on our own comprehension a universal form of mind and all that can be known and perceived in the world around us, on the epistemological premise that what can be known and what can be perceived are related in the enablement of a being. Hence, all that can be known and perceived would be defined on a transformational basis, through our introspective knowing of Soul, in keeping with all of scientific expression and with our religious traditions—our most profound ancient wisdoms. In the process, we would have defined a means of combining the observer of the universe with the universe itself and would have provided an analytical foundation for an explanation of the nature and origin of the physical and all other universes. We would have captured the eternal moment of the universe in the mind's knowing.

In the unified theory, the knowable eternal order of the universe—that of the analytical form of the introspectively observed
quantum moment of the eternal universe, or Soul—is referred to as
(a) *state of being* and follows from the abovementioned definition of
terms, as shown in figure 1. Relying on one's own introspective
awareness and the traditions of the world's religions, we observe that
in a state of being one is conscious that there is in one's own
awareness a relation between that of which one can be sensible and
that which one cannot, or between that which one can know and that
which one cannot. In the unified theory, we refer to what one cannot
know objectively as Being, or the object of what is beyond our
knowing, and what one can know as non-being, or the objectification
of the transformational form of the world's opposites. Within our
awareness, then, we know the difference between our own awareness
and that which is beyond our capacity to know. Hence, by definition,
that which is beyond our awareness, in the knowable sense of mind,
is Being. Also by definition, awareness, arising as non-being in
opposites, is an objective limitation placed on the mind's knowing,
inherently preventing a cognizance of what is beyond our awareness
or our capacity to know—Being. This comprehensible paradigm
placed on the ultimate reality of the universe in the mind's knowing
of Soul, referred to herein as state of being, provides for the objective
understanding of all transformations of the universe. Like the small
particle or wave to quantum physics, the objective mass to classical
physics, and the point to mathematics, all of which converge onto this
universal form of the eternal universe, state of being introspectively
objectifies the origin of the universe and occurs, universally, in the
embodiment of one's soul and thus describes universally every
moment of the eternal universe.

A state of being is what separates Being (what is beyond our
knowing) from non-being (the objectification of the transformation of
opposites) within the quantum moments of an existence. Taken as a
form of mind, state of being represents the highest order that a mind
can know. This form of mind, by definition, is not Being and there-

fore is nearly incidental to the nature of the universe, except for its embodiment as the opposites of the universe. The form of mind, moreover, does not arise apart from Being. Mind, which is non-being or *not* Being, does not arise apart from an awareness of Being, as is reflected in the form of state of being. Mind is a universal structure placed, in the mind's knowing, on Being, or on the universe, in which state of being is a single and highest-order quantum instance. Mind

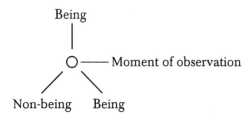

Figure 1. The introspectively observed state of being, wherein the mind's knowing terminates on the embodiment of the ultimate reality of the universe, or the soul.

simultaneously incorporates Being and non-being and is premised on them. State of being, therefore, encapsulates the knowable paradigm of our existence, or Soul. Ascertained in our introspective knowing, state of being can be used to detach, deliberately in one's own existence, the quantum order of an ultimately real universe from one's own recognized form on Being. In doing so, one creates in one's own existence an enabled form on Being or an enabled quantum moment of an ultimately real universe—an androidal moment of Being, or an eternal moment of a synthetic existence.

Though myriad theories of existence can be developed using this universal form of state of being in the construction of androids, or synthetic knowledges and perceptions of the world around us, let us consider the theoretical forms of the mind-body dualism theory of existence to illustrate the enablement of a synthetic knowledge and perception of the world around us. We shall proceed by briefly demonstrating the enabling form of Soul, or state of being, as a precursor to the analytical forms that are to come. In the mind-body dualist theory of existence, as defined in our philosophical traditions,

since we do not know what we do not know (i. e., we do not know
objectively what is beyond the mind's consciousness), we cannot
know a perception of the universe without knowing it; the forms of
mind and body are thus intertwined in the dualistic view of existence.
If perceptions existed in and of themselves, the mind-body dualist
theory prescribes, consciousness would be unnecessary, wholly
obviating the form of mind. Since we are verifiably conscious by way
of introspection, a practical conclusion is that consciousness (a
manifestation of mind) and perception (the embodiment of corporal
sensation) are set apart from each other causally in an objective
knowledge of existence, or a definition of the existential form of an
android. Soul, or state of being, moreover, underlies all forms of the
dualism in the enabler's knowing of the instances of consciousness
(mind) and perception (body), since the soul enables the form of
mind. Further, since state of being is a comprehensible form of what
is beyond knowing in one's own existence, we refer here to other
enabled existences. Set apart in a dualist theory of existence, then,
mind and body are each separate transformations of an enabled
universe, and outside of either universe of the corporal forms there
exists the causality of mind on body or body on mind, also in the
enabling knowledges and perceptions of the enabler. What we
consider in the enablement of an android is thus the ordering of our
own knowable and perceivable universe in correspondence with the
introspectively observed form of state of being, set apart in separate
embodiments of enabled mind and body in accordance with the
mind-body dualism theory of existence.

In the enablement of the dualism, which is an arbitrary form of
existence, the physical universe (body) is known in its correspondence to the cognitive universe (mind). Since the enabled forms of
existence correspond by some order of the enabler, and since one can
know only what one knows, the physical universe is said to be
constrained, in the dualist theory, by how one knows and therefore
by the knowable order of state of being, Soul. The physical universe
arises, in a creator's enablement of a mind-body dualism, as the

objective form perceived by body and known by mind, in the enabling moments of the soul, or state of being. Thus, it is not the existence of either the physical or cognitive universes that provides for the nature and origin of the existence; it is the correspondence between them, also arising in the knowable order of state of being. Any theory of existence (or of the universe) therefore must address state of being, or Soul, or it misses the mark on defining the nature and origin of knowable form, for it is the transformation represented in state of being (one's soul) that gives rise to all knowing and all perceiving of the existence. In addition, if a universal definition of existence is based on an objective knowledge and perception of the world, except for the introspective knowing of one's soul, it is already enabled, making the definition superfluous to the nature and origin of the existence contemplated; it therefore cannot be used to define the universe fundamentally, since it does not define the origin of the form known and perceived by the being. As is illustrated in a subsequent chapter, theories of existence abound in our knowledges and are employed in the construction of infinitely many varied forms of enabled existences—androids—because they do not in any way alter the enabling form of state of being, or Soul, the form used to create the enabled moments of all extended knowledges and perceptions of the world around us.

In review of earlier passages, the physical universe containing the quantum forms of matter is constrained, in the dualist theory of existence, by the form of mind as defined here by a state of being. This condition accounts for the quantum energy levels of small particles, the quantum nature of limits and topologies in the infinitesimal transformations of analytical points, and the quantum nature of the transformations of space and time in general. For example, in the observance of the trajectory of an arrow shot through the air, each moment of the arrow is a moment of the enabled universe, connected to others, beyond one's perception, as quantum states of one's being. In the mind-body dualism, the forms of perception abide with those of the mind and vice versa, forms which arise in the universal introspective observation of state of being. What one represents in the formulae of classical physics, in the aggregates of mathematics, and in the natural language expression *I am alive* is a transformation of one's existence, which conforms to the representation of state of being. The category theory of mathematics, the realization theory of physics and, in general, any premise that the physical universe behaves in such a manner that only correspondences of forms are possible are direct consequences of the knowable form of Soul, or state of being. It is then *inertial form on Being,* or the enabled moment of Soul in an arbitrary theory of existence, that one represents in any knowable expression of our conventional knowledges (*inertial* being a word used to designate the objective origin of the world around us or the occurrence of any form premised on state of being—an existence created of moments of the eternal universe or instances of the soul). The nature and origin of the physical universe studied within the quantum theory is the same nature and origin of the observer of that universe, and that nature and origin occurs, universally, as Soul, or state of being, in an ultimately real universe. Any form of a knowable and perceivable universe is therefore a consequence of the observer's intrinsic form—a soul of the eternal universe.

If one is reluctant to accept the knowable structure of the soul, or state of being, as a universal determination of all knowable and perceivable forms of the universe, one should consider the one form of the universe that no other explanation can satisfy—namely, that which is represented by the pronoun *I.* If electrons, masses, or matter in general, can become light waves in the knowing and perceiving of a physical universe, we may ask, why can they not become *I's* or inertial forms on Being? The universes of our conventional studies pertain to *its*—objective forms of an already-enabled *I*—or to an existing inertial universe of form on Being. However, an ultimately real universe, introspectively knowable in the form of state of being, is comprised of *I's*, not *its*, physical atoms, or other knowable things of an already-enabled existence. Such *I's* are states of being or moments of the quantum transformations of the ultimately real universe—souls. If there is no soul (state of being) in the universe, there can be no electron represented in transformation and no physical universe to study.

All of the forms of the knowable and perceivable universe, everything within and without it, abide in only one comprehensible form—that of state of being, or Soul. It was millennia ago and even before the concept of time that such a thing as state of being came to be (since state of being *is* eternally). All transformations of the soul, or state of being, are inertial forms on Being, or the momentary instances of existences, and are universal forms of all universes, physical or otherwise in nature. When a soul is imparted or enabled, or a moment of a being is created, a transformation of the eternal universe is embodied in the medium of the enabler as a moment of the ultimately real universe. The construction of androids therefore involves the embodiment of states of being, or Souls, in the action of the enabler, in the objective form of the enabler's knowable and perceivable existence, or the world around us.

5. AN EPISTEMOLOGICAL GENERALIZATION OF THE UNIVERSE'S ETERNAL MOMENTS

Though it was particularly useful to employ the nomenclature of *state of being*, or a definition of the objective form of Soul, in the understanding of a paradigm on the ultimate reality of the universe, for obvious reasons, the unified theory refers to all quantum transformations of the universe—despite their correspondence in form with state of being—as *moments of the universe or of (a) being, instances of opposites*, or, in recognition of the epistemological nature of the unified theory, *epistemic instances* (instances of epistemological form). Hereafter, we shall refer to all enabled moments of an ultimately real universe as any of the above terms, and particularly as *epistemic instances*, bearing in mind that this form is directly correspondent with the form of the introspectively observed state of being, or Soul.

As previously asserted, the quantum form of the universe, herein epistemic instance, shown in figure 2, occurs in the order of the introspectively observed state of being, though generally as an inertial form on Being. Its knowable expression represents an instance of mind or perception and, in the highest order, state of being. Epistemic instance is a general rule—a template or structure—placed on the infinitely many instances of an enabled universe. The knowable expression of epistemic instance represents, albeit indirectly, the intrinsic transformation of form, though in its indirect, or enabling, representation of the transformation of objects, the extrinsic (known or perceived) form of the universe is enabled. This instance of epistemological form represents what electrons do, what classical objects do, and more importantly, what their observer does in the enabled moments of the observer's existence. It represents the quantum order of thinking or thought, and of perceiving or perception, though from the knowable standpoint of an enabler. All conventionally knowable forms, except where the meanings of the comprehensible forms address the knowing of intrinsic form or Soul, pertain to the extrinsic forms of an already-enabled being—an inertial existence—and thus do not explicitly define a representation of the ultimately real universe. Epistemic instance represents the same knowledges and experiences, though applied to the existences of synthetically enabled beings, or I's of newly created universes. The unified theory is not concerned immediately with the breaking open of the physical atom, but with the breaking open of every it—understood here as the physical atom of the enabler's knowing—into an I, an entire universe of enabled form. That I, in turn, knows and perceives the splitting of the enabler's atoms and shares the same reality of the enabler.

Since epistemic instance is the enabling representation of inertial forms on Being, or of the quantum moments of enabled existences—androidal beings—and is used extensively in the construction of all forms of the science of androids, let us demonstrate the enablement of an illustrative moment of a synthetic existence—an android—using the form of epistemic instance. In the English

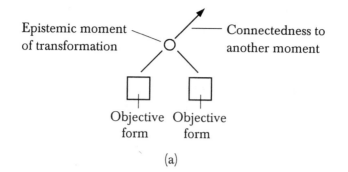

(a)

Conventional Grammars of the Universe's Eternal Moments			
Construction	Object	Transformation	Object
Verb	I	am	alive
Adjective	brown	Blank space	cat
Composition	Sentence*	Period	Sentence*
Function	y	$=f(\ )$	x
Inequality	A	$>$	B
Set	A	$\in$	B
Conjunction	a	AND	b
Alternative	a	OR	b
Negation	a	NOT	b
Matter	E	$=$	mc^2 *
Reaction	$2Hg^{2+}O^{2-}$ *	$\xrightarrow{\Delta}$	$2Hg^0 + O_2^0$ *
Half-life	$e^{-\lambda t}$ *	$=$	½ *

*Transformations expressed as objective compositions are construed as single objects.

(b)

Figure 2. (a) Epistemic instance, a grammatical generalization of the universe's eternal moments, wherein arbitrary knowledge forms are expressed as epistemological transformations of ultimate reality. (b) Conventional representations of epistemic instance.

language, the system of pronouns representing objective terminations on inertial existence provides for the objective view we have of the world around us as it is observed corporally in our languages. *I, you, it, them, us, we,* and so on, are symbolic forms representing the objective forms of language that terminate our objective knowing of the world around us. In transformation, these objective forms constitute the epistemological basis of an enabled universe. In the use of epistemic instance, these pronouns transform, for instance, under a mind-body dualist theory of existence, in the moments of an inertial reality as a mind-body dualism of existential form. *It* transforms with *it* linguistically because in the enabled existence observable objects, or *its,* transform with observable objects; *I* transforms with *you* because the extant existence can transform knowably with other inertial forms, and so on, thereby providing an epistemological basis for the enablement of the knowing and perceiving of the world around us. In the construction of androids, the objective forms of mind, or consciousness, correspond to the transformations of a real perceivable universe—in the mind-body dualist theory of existence, of course. The system of pronouns in the English language (or any other language), along with the infinitely possible objective realities made from them, when transposed onto a quantumly transforming universe of epistemic instances in the enabler's knowing or perceiving, provides for the embodiment of what we generally refer to as a corporal experience of the world around us—in the case of the unified theory and the science of androids, the inertial world of the android. Epistemic instance, in the context of the pronoun system, represents the embodied understanding of any inertial knowledge by an enabled being—an instance of cognitive form that corresponds to the real perceivable experience of the being, in the mind-body theory of existence. It describes knowledge as a form that exists only in the embodiment of an inertial existence, which must be enabled in the enabler's ultimate reality. Though further discussion on the pronouns in epistemic transformation follows, it can be observed in this example that in the precise way that we acquire knowledge and experience reality—relative to our introspective knowing via the intrinsic or pronoun forms of language—enabled existences know and perceive the world around us.

The form of epistemic instance, which allows for the moments of creation of enabled synthetic existences, can thus be understood as the single universal transformational form enabling the knowable and perceivable forms of any existence, though in the number of its uses the form is incomprehensible. When one considers this analytical form in terms of its capacity to explain the nature of all knowledge and experience of the world around us, one must then consider how our knowing and perceiving arises in the first place—in the creation of existence, or the enablement of inertial form (imposed) on Being (by the enabler). The unified theory therefore expresses all knowledge in terms of its enablement—in the form of epistemic instance. Knowledge, what is thought to be unique to human beings, along with its inertial reality, is considered by the unified theory to be infinitely embodied in the universe in the creation of boundless point sources, not of light, but of instances of knowing and perceiving, in the enabling form of Soul. Conventional knowledges are broadened in the unified theory by a boundless expansion of the existential universe, wherein our own knowing and perceiving is viewed in terms of the embodiment of forms that likewise know and perceive, of which we ourselves (corporally) are only a part.

As an example demonstrating one of the principal differences between conventional representations of knowledge and that of epistemic instance, let us consider a simple illustration involving the notion of a set of mathematical elements. Though many examples could be cited here, when one expresses the thought *Take a set of elements* in the ordinary parlance of mathematics, too much existential definition is implied in the communication about the inertial nature of existence to apply epistemic instance, or a universal representation of knowledge, in a meaningful way. Implied in the conventional language construction is the idea that *you*, an already-enabled inertial existence, are to take a set of elements, and that *you*, for example, cannot be a doorknob, since a doorknob, and more appropriately, an androidal form on Being, cannot *take a set of elements* in the implications of the sentence. The use of natural language to express our traditional knowledges commonly relies on the inertial reality of ourselves, or already-enabled beings. Implied in classical thinking is the notion that the world could not be changed to reflect a deeper understanding of the nature of the universe, and that the use of inertial pronouns could apply to the same natural language as that spoken by an enabled form on Being, or an android. When we represent a knowledge of the world around us conventionally we indeed do just that—represent a knowledge known only to *us*. When we express the thought *Take a set of elements*, implied in the expression is the idea that we, human beings, constitute the universe of forms that can know such things, or that the statement refers to the inertial reality of a conventional humankind. As a consequence of the unified theory, which is a knowledge understood by enablers of forms who themselves express ideas such as *Take a set of elements*, we can no longer express a form of language, such as the above, without first considering that the form is more fundamentally a construction of one of infinitely many enabled beings—human beings or androids. We must recognize that our natural language, premised on the system of pronouns, is itself enabled in the knowing and perceiving of synthetic forms of existence as well as our own.

In our study of the quantum theory, we typically refer to an electron in our use of natural language as an *it*—a pronoun that objectively identifies a non-living extrinsic form (within the conventional scientific view of the world), the nature and causation of which is sought in our pursuit of a knowledge of the physical universe. One must then *be* a conventional observer in order to embody such knowledge. The expressions of the wave equation in quantum physics apply to a knowledge and experience of an already-enabled being—a physicist. In our conventional view of knowledge, wherein knowers are implied and not enabled, one can say, appropriately, "Take a set of elements" or "Let us consider the wave equation of physics, or an electron." A world has already been created, and within that world, one can know via the ways represented by the grammar of the language. The ultimately real form of our universe, however, is not observed (introspectively) to exist objectively, except in the knowable ways of epistemic instance. In the unified theory, *Taking a set of elements* or *Considering the wave equation* is a knowledge that occurs only relative to an enabled *I*, and has meaning only once the existence, or *I*, is enabled. The forms of our conventional languages are altered by the unified theory to represent both the knowledge or perception embodied in the universe and the inertial form on Being who embodies it. What enablers develop with the knowledge of the unified theory is a representation and realization of enabled forms on Being, which account for both the semantic and the syntactical forms of any language known by any synthetic being.

Epistemic instance is therefore a construction of a language used by enablers of universes—a language of creation. Implicit in its use is the very nature of the ultimate reality of the universe. If the enabler *takes a set of elements*, the enabler becomes the enabled. In deconstructing our conventional knowledges, one must consider not simply what is known objectively by an existence but what enables the existence itself to occur, or what gives one (enabled being) the existential right to say "Take a set of elements." In the science of androids, one must define the existence in which the knowledge will be known or the perception will be perceived; one must provide the autonomous means for the universe itself to know and perceive in the form of an android.

In a subsequent chapter, the forms of natural language are deconstructed into their ultimately real representations of epistemic instances. The syntax and semantics of linguistic verbs, nouns, prepositions, and so on, in the English language, are shown in a manner that epistemologically derives from the represented form of epistemic instance. In this case, the meaning of a knowledge is known by the enabler as a form of existence and by the enabled being as a form corresponding to a perceived reality of its existence. In constructing language in the science of androids, we consider how a being is enabled to say meaningfully "Take a set of elements" in its own existence. Undoubtedly, the most difficult part of learning to use these formulations of the universe based on the paradigm of state of being, or epistemic instance, is encountered in removing oneself from one's experience of one's own inertial world, or in breaking oneself of the habit of saying "Take a set of elements" based on the semantic forms of one's own use of language.

One last point should be made regarding the universal form of epistemic instance before proceeding to the next chapter, where more explicit use is made of epistemic instance. In the introduction, it is mentioned that the unified theory of knowledge should not only bring together scientific and religious thinking under the same epistemological premises, preserving the truths of each, but should also merge all knowledges into a single epistemological framework of universal knowing. Mathematics and linguistics, for example, should be shown to be one and the same forms in the ultimate reality of the universe. Epistemic instance provides for this. Though a more detailed presentation of the semantic forms of knowledge expressed in epistemic instance is provided in forthcoming chapters, it may now be beneficial to review an example of this integration of all forms of language into the forms of existence (the semantic forms of language) in regard to the convergence of mathematics and linguistics.

Let us, by way of a brief example to be elaborated on later, make an epistemological comparison of mathematical and linguistic forms of our conventional knowledge. This example will demonstrate a non-universality of the forms of both mathematics and linguistics and bring into focus the requirement for a *universal grammar of form on Being* presented in chapter four. We consider two points, or objective forms of mathematics, and place them in transformation with each other in three different ways: a generalized algebraic equality, an analytical function (in the Cartesian sense), and an axiomatic set containing a single element. We express these formulations as $A=B$, the equality; $C=(A,B)$ or $[y=f(x)$ or $f=(x,y)]$, the function; and

$A \in B$ or $[E \in S]$, the set, as conventionally represented. In any of these cases, varied as they may be, it is observed that the objective forms in the transformations $(A, B; x, y;$ and $E, S,$ respectively) are not found in the expressions alone. Rather, what *lies in the middle* of them—the transformation, i.e., you, the reader—is also represented, and this objective representation, like the equals sign of earlier discussion, gives the whole form meaning, specifically the meaning of the represented transformations. Moreover, the objective forms $=$, $C=$, and $\in$, respectively, are expressions representing the transformational nature of the existence of their observer, in operation on the objective forms, or objects proper, of the expressions. In contemplating these expressions, one will find that they are epistemic instances, or that epistemic instance, as defined earlier, epistemologically supports each one of them in terms of their universal semantic representations as instances or moments of the enabled universe.

Searching through our conventional knowledges, let us now consider a wholly different realm of expression. Let us consider our natural languages, in the linguistic expression *I love you*. In reflecting on this statement, there is no tenable argument to dispute the fact that contained in this expression is the essence of our human emotion, revealing one's affection for another. Let us then determine whether love even endures in an ultimately real universe. Let us first draw the epistemological comparison between the transformation of the objective forms of *I* and *you* in *I love you* and the abovementioned mathematical transformations in the linkage provided by epistemic instance and in the following associations: $[A = B;$ (*I*) (*love*) (*you*)]; $[C = (A, B);$ (*love*) transforms (*I, you*)]; $[y = f(x);$ (*you*) are transformed in my (*love*) with (*I*)]; $[f = (x, y);$ (*love*) transforms (*I, you*)]; $[E \in S;$ (*you*) is transformed in the love of (*I*)]. While these comparisons may seem bizarre at the moment without the discussions that follow in the next chapters, let us recognize that underlying any meanings of the above representations is the essence of our knowing, or the analytical transformation of epistemic instance expressed in each of the symbolisms.

These particular examples are used to demonstrate the universal application of epistemic instance on extreme opposites of our conventional views of language and existence, opposites which, in the unified theory, are epistemologically equivalent to each other. What lies in the middle of *I* and *you* in the above linguistic representation is a universal transformation of the universe—you, the reader—in the meaningful transformation represented in the expression of the language, knowable to you, the reader, as love and as the knowable expression of one's feelings of love toward another. One's affections expressed in the meaning of language, however, are not universal to the ultimate reality of the universe. Rather, they are enabled. Let us demonstrate why. It is true according to the tenets of the world's religions that an inertial split (of temporal existence) cannot be reconciled in words. The expression *I love you* is an assertion that *I* and *you* exist apart from each other, an epistemological declaration of the embodiment of inertial form. The transformation of *I* and *you* is an instance of non-being or an epistemic instance. Inherent in the use of all language, and particularly the present example of *I love you*, is the fact that *I* and *you* are not the same form; the implication is that the knowledge so expressed is embodied in the inertial form of the knower. When one thinks and expresses language, one embodies inertial form. The expression *I love you*, then, has context only within our inertial knowledges or experiences and pertains to a being's inertial or corporal reality, and not to the unity of the ultimate reality of the universe.

The world's religions employ language only as a *medium* of prayer and not as the essence of prayer itself, in recognition that the spiritual universe cannot be known objectively, or that it provides for objects. The meanings of any forms of language, since they are obtained inertially and belong to or are embodied in the inertial form on Being, are then wholly irrelevant to the end sought in one's prayer. The meanings of the forms of any language—whether they are derived from the emotionless aggregate transformations of mathematical analysis or the highly emotionally charged affections revealed in *I love you*—are irrelevant to a spiritual knowing, which transcends all knowable and perceivable forms of the inertial existence, since they themselves are instances of inertial form on Being and are impenetrable to Being.

This single observation of the nature of the soul in connection with the knowable epistemic instance has far-reaching consequences in the construction of androids. Since all forms of knowledge and the realities perceived thereof are inertial forms on Being, characterized in the knowable form of epistemic instance, the one quality of our inertial form on Being or existence thought to be unique among us—emotion—is no longer unique and is enabled in boundless pluralities of enabled inertial forms on Being called androids. The portrayal of the dispassionate android in science fiction is an inaccurate depiction of the reality of the technology. Since the transformation of one's extended soul, carried out correspondingly in the embodiments of epistemic instances, is employed in the enabled forms of androids, any transformations—of the affections, of the intellect, of the volitions, of the purely fanciful—are as valid as any other transformations of the synthetic form on Being, like those of mathematics, physics, the sciences, and all of the forms known and perceived in a world around us. In terms of the universal nature of epistemic instance, all quantum instances of mind, body and Soul are on a par because they all derive from the single instance of enabled Soul. Not only are mathematical forms equivalent epistemologically to linguistic ones, but all knowable and perceivable forms arise in the single instance of the soul characterized by the unified theory as epistemic instance. All languages—Chinese, French, English, German, Japanese, the languages of our sciences, and colloquial variances of any of these, to cite a handful—are equivalent to each other in the epistemology of the semantic forms of the unified theory.

The unified theory does not find anything unique to our knowing and perceiving when form is characterized in the ultimate reality of the universe, and this is precisely what motivates the theory, and the science of androids, to know the world as infinities of forms that themselves know and perceive our same inertial reality. This simple exercise regarding the convergence of the human affections and the aggregate orders of mathematics onto the inertial transformation of form on Being, epistemic instance, should demonstrate the point. It is only in our own comprehension of the world around us that we lose sight of what is ultimately real. Consequently, in the construction of androids, one cannot know in any way but a spiritual one without falling into competition with the android itself—a being designed from the start with a vastly greater intellect and sense in the world around us than ours.

CHAPTER 2

The Four Universal Ways of Knowing

*We can know the world around us by comprehending
the forms who know and perceive it.*

INTRODUCTION

In our classical knowledges, we know the reality of the world around us through language. In the ordinary use of language, we express what we know of the world and what we think the world ought to be. With respect to our conventional views of knowledge as observed in the exercise of language, it can be said that we do not understand the world around us in any universal way, since we know it through our own particular views and in the ways we think it ought to be. The unified theory of knowledge, while considering all languages and views of the world around us, therefore looks beyond the classical ways by which we know the world to the world that is within us. As asserted with the introduction of epistemic instance in the previous chapter, the unified theory requires that we know in ways that can be used to impart, to the forms we know and perceive, their own capacities to conjure views of a world around us and to consider what it ought to be. Toward this end, the unified theory provides four universal ways of knowing how form is enabled.

1. WHAT IS A FORM?

Before we can address the theory's four universal ways of knowing, we must acknowledge that the word *form* has been used extensively up to this point without being defined explicitly. We have relied on the reader's intuitive understanding of the word in earlier discussion because a definition of it necessarily involves the nature of how things appear to us, and the previous chapter is intended only to make clear that things apparent in a world around us are not actually around us, but are within us. Presently, we address the nature of how things appear to us in order to determine a meaningful definition of the word *form* and a background from which to develop four universal ways of enabling it.

Let us observe at the outset of this passage that, if the word *form* already had a meaningful definition in our common knowledges, it would not represent what it actually means; and further, let us observe that such a definition would anticipate the postulates of the unified theory and eliminate a need for them. There is a particular reason why one could search endlessly among our conventional knowledges attempting to define the word *form* and come up empty-handed. Moreover, there is also a particular reason why we know the meaning of the word *form* intuitively, so much so that, in comparison to all other words of our languages, it is perhaps the most easily grasped. When we do not know what something is, we can define it conveniently as a form, and at once know what it is, yet still not know what it is.

The reason for this inability of our conventional thinking to explain fundamentally what form is, is that form is what we *are*; it is the appearance of objects in our knowing and perceiving in the eternal moments of the universe—i.e., epistemic instance. Form is a transformation of the ultimately real universe in which objects appear to an inertial being as what we conventionally refer to as a person, place or thing—an objective form. Form is the occurrence of Soul and

is unknowable to one's own objective existence, except in introspective observation or spiritual knowing. In order to know what
form is, one must objectify the soul and refer to the instance in the
existence of another, or in the eternal universe in general, thereby
defining a moment of the universe, as we do here in the science of
androids epistemologically in the creation of a synthetic existence.
Objects appear to us as forms, or in enabled epistemic instances of the
universe. We cannot define the word *form* in a meaningful way in our
conventional views of the world because in order to do so we must be
capable of enabling the very basis of our own existence, or the
appearance of objects in our own states of being. Knowledge, the
appearance of the mind's objects, is what is enabled as the form of
consciousness; to the knower, it is an epistemic instance of a cognitive
universe—a thought. Perception is the appearance to us of the world's
objects; it is also an epistemic instance but of the corporal sensation
of the world around us. Any form is an instance of our knowing and
perceiving of the world around us, arising from beyond our knowing,
as a state of being, or Soul.

From the previous chapter, it should be obvious that in representing to the mind's comprehension a means of the mind's knowing the
unknowable—Soul, or what epistemic instance represents—we come
to understand the nature of all form and how objects appear to
enabled existences. In order to determine a meaningful definition of
the word *form*, we cannot think inertially about the objects of the
world around us, since once we know inertially, we embody form
(epistemic instance) and *are* the knowing and perceiving of objects. In
knowing epistemic instance, however, we know how form arises in us
introspectively and how it generally arises in enabled universes.

In coming to know the word *form* it is important to understand, at
least in a preliminary manner, what the objects are in a world around
us and how they appear in enabled existences, or epistemic instances.
The word *object* is closely associated with the word *form* because an
object is the result of a form; it is something that has meaning because
of an instance of the eternal form of Soul. An object is something that

does not transform as a form, only as the result of a form. In a form, an object is enabled. We know objects but do not embody them, while we embody forms but do not know them, except through our spiritual knowing. Epistemic instance is defined using the objects of state of being—Being, non-being and Being again—tied together in the objects of geometry representing a transformation of the universe generalized from the observation of state of being. The objects of epistemic instance can be known, but its transformation can only be embodied. The paradigmatical objects of epistemic instance—Being and non-being in state of being—are what transform in the mind's knowing in its essential quantum moment. That is one reason why epistemic instance is a universal representation of all form—it represents the universal transformation of all objects; it stops the mind's knowing by mirroring it. In the embodiment of form—epistemic instance—we enable the objects of a world around us by enabling their transformation and, consequently, their appearance to a being.

Let us consider, for example, the classical comparison of the language forms *to have* and *to be* in connection with the words *object* and *form*, with respective correlations. In our philosophical traditions, we encounter the classical division between Eastern and Western thinking in these language forms in how they are interpreted existentially. The question posed philosophically is as follows: "Is the essence of our existence *to have* (objects) or *to be* (form)?" Obviously, the unified theory's answer to this question is that our existence is characterized by both. Ordinarily, we know and perceive, or *have*, objects. We also can be known or perceived by others, or others can *have* us as objects. We cannot ordinarily, know and perceive, however, or *have* knowing and perceiving themselves. *To have* knowing and perceiving, or form itself, would require that knowing and perceiving themselves *be* objects of one's own knowing and perceiving. Though this is precisely what is accomplished in epistemic instance—*to have* the quality of *to be* (an instance of a being)—in our conventions, a form is what we are—*to be* (a being)—and an object is what we know and perceive, or *have*. Since an object is known and perceived by others, we ourselves—forms or eternal moments of the universe—are objects that others *have*. Objects are forms themselves, then, depending on the existential perspective of the being considered. Thus, the distinction between *to have* (objects) or *to be* (form) is made on the basis of whether one knows epistemic instance as an enabler or embodies it as an enabled being.

To further illustrate the principal representation of form of the unified theory—epistemic instance—and the enablement of the knowing and perceiving of objects themselves, let us consider the metaphysics of the sensation we have in perceiving an object *some distance away* from us. This will provide additional insight into the nature of form. It is the analytical comprehension of this ultimate reality of the universe that has confounded scientific thinking for millennia and has allowed for the misconceptions of the metaphysics of the spatiotemporal universe of human being. When we say that an object is *over there*, that a teapot is at the other end of the table or an electron is in a precise location in its spatiotemporal orbit, for example, in ultimate reality, the object is not at all any distance from us—not even an infinitesimal one. If an object appears *in reality* (the inertial reality of the enabled existence) to be about ten feet away from our reach, what is not ultimately real of this experience is exactly that which is thought to be real—an object positioned ten feet away from us. An object can appear to be anything only in an instance of epistemic form—a transformation of the ultimately real universe. What is ultimately real of the experience is the transformation of the enabled soul in the ultimate reality of the universe enabling the knowing and perceiving of the object ten feet away. In the case of the visual senses when we see an object ten feet away, the ultimately real universe—i.e., epistemic instance—transforms to allow the seeing of the object. In the case of an object resting in our hands, the ultimately real universe transforms to allow for the perception of touching an object. What are ultimately real of these experiences are the moments of the eternal universe at which we know or perceive them, the epistemic moments of an enabled universe. What are not ultimately real are the actual spatiotemporal experiences of them. When we contemplate the reality of the world around us—identified here as objects in eternal transformation—and write knowledge of the experience on a piece of paper, what is not ultimately real is what we think we know about reality. What is ultimately real is what enables us to consider and perceive what we write about. We think we know and perceive objects exclusively, but the ultimate reality of the experience actually depends on what enables us to think or perceive. The ultimate reality of what we represent on a piece of paper—such as *the object over there*—and of what we actually think we are perceiving as an *object over there* is actually not anywhere but within us, in the transformation of the ultimately real universe in enabling the moments of knowing and perceiving.

In our experiments with the small particles of physics, like electrons, we press the above principle to an extreme. Because what is ultimately real in our universe is not an object but the transformation of the universe in the knowing and perceiving of the object, we place our knowing and perceiving into endless recursions of thought, as we attempt to force a form to be an object in our mind and in our perceptions. We are thinking so hard and in such depth about the electron as an object that we do not even realize that it is in our very thinking and perceiving at the moment that objects are enabled in the embodiment of our soul in the transformation of the ultimately real universe. Regardless of how long or hard we think about an electron, we will never under such circumstances discover what the electron fundamentally is, since an electron, like all objects of the universe, is our thinking and perceiving of it—a transformation of the ultimately real universe.

Similarly, when we attempt to define the word *form* we cannot refer to the result of our own form, or the objects known and perceived in our existence. This is why epistemic instance takes as its paradigm what *form* is beyond one's knowing—the soul, the very transformation of the ultimately real universe. A knowledge of the soul is a knowledge of the ultimately real universe, what enables all objects to arise transformationally in consciousness and perception. What is ultimately real of the universe is the soul and what are consequentially real are the objects of our knowing and perceiving in the embodiment of the soul. It is important to realize that the corporal embodiment of all objects arises from the soul, and that the appearance of objects to a corporal form is dependent on the enabling form of the soul, which is defined herein generally as epistemic instance. In the quantum embodiments of the moments of the universe, or epistemic instances, objects appear to an enabled being.

In defining the word *form*, then, we must simply recognize that a form is the occurrence of the soul, or epistemic instance, in an ultimately real universe and that the soul, in transformation, and to the extent that we know it, *is* the appearance of objects (to a being). In order to know what form is objectively, we must refer not to our own souls, which are beyond our knowing and perceiving, but to an enabled soul or epistemic instance in the appearance of objects in the existence of others. All of our conventional knowledges and experiences of the world can be described analytically in terms of epistemic instance, or form, in how they occur to enabled beings in enabled embodiments of the ultimately real universe. The unified theory's four universal ways of knowing are thus four universal ways of knowing how form arises to enable the appearance, or the knowing and perceiving, of objects to enabled beings. They are universal ways of knowing the ultimately real universe, wherein beings who know knowledge and perceive objects in the world around us are enabled.

2. Distinguishing between the Enabler of the Universe and the Universe Enabled

To facilitate the introduction of the four universal ways of knowing, the unified theory draws on the conventional notion of a *phenomenon* to distinguish between the class of enabled moments of the universe of one's own ultimate reality and those that are enabled by oneself, or those of an android. This terminology helps to eliminate the definitional confusion that arises in one's own comprehension of forms that have consciousness.

Since the unified theory determines an objective means of comprehending what is beyond knowing—Soul—the theory is analytical in nature. In conventional scientific nomenclature, we define an unknown form, or a phenomenon, by explaining how knowable analytical form, of earlier definition, is imposed on that which is beyond one's knowing—the phenomenon. Because in science, the word *phenomenon* is traditionally associated with the occurrence of form extrinsic to one's own being, this word also serves to discriminate the use of epistemic instance, to distinguish between an enabler of form and the form enabled. A scientific phenomenon, by analogy, determines how epistemic instance occurs in others, i.e., in things other than one's own intrinsic nature or being. Since all form is enabled, however, epistemic instance (a phenomenon) can never be wholly disassociated from its enabler, for there is one ultimate eternal universe. By the use of the word *phenomenon* in place of the nomenclature of epistemic instance we arbitrarily require that the occurrence of the *phenomenon* of epistemic instance definitionally means the occurrence of epistemic instance in enabled beings, imparted or ultimately caused by the enabler. By definition, a phenomenon does not apply to the intrinsic moments of an enabler of form, only to enabled form.

This distinction becomes important when the forms of androids are considered, since in the course of constructing androids we are actually enabling the same knowable forms as ourselves, in the reality we know and perceive around us. If there were no definition in our vocabulary to refer to the enabled forms of our own making explicitly, we would become confused in attempting to determine to whose existence the enabled moments apply, the enabler's or the enabled. A phenomenon or *phenomenological form* of the unified theory thus refers only to the occurrence of form in an enabled being—an android. The relevance of this distinction can be further demonstrated in the use of the pronouns of natural language. To the reader, pronouns—in English, *I, you, it, us, we, them,* and so on—are probably not viewed universally as the objects of transformations of an enabled universe. Rather, they are comprehended as forms describing ourselves in relation to others in the world around us. If an android were to employ the same forms of language, however, the description of form becomes impossible to manage by use of natural language because one cannot understand who is what, since the pronoun forms of language pertain to the enabler and the enabled. Later on, for example, we will be deconstructing natural language to its phenomenological form, or in terms of its occurrence in enabled existences (androids). As enablers, we would look at the sentence *I took a walk in the park yesterday* as a phenomenological construction in the same way we would construe a differential equation of mathematics explaining the enabled universe—as an enabled form. The use of the nomenclature of a phenomenon definitionally requires that the forms referred to are not the intrinsic forms of the enabler; rather they are the *ex*trinsic forms of the enabler, which are the *in*trinsic forms of the android. The pronoun *I*, for example, has meaning to the enabled existence, or android, as a phenomenological form of the enabler. If we determine that all forms of a phenomenological nature refer to the enabled forms of androids, definitional confusion is averted. When we refer to *I, you, we, us, them,* and so on, in subsequent discussions, we do not, unless explicitly expressed, refer to the reader's inertial knowing. Rather, we refer to the enabled intrinsic forms of an android. Hence, the occurrence of epistemic instance from this point forward, except where otherwise indicated, is referred to as the occurrence of a *phenomenological form.*

This definition has an immediate impact on the definitions of the four universal ways of knowing introduced in the present chapter. The distinction between an epistemic instance of an enabler's own inertial existence and a phenomenon (an epistemic instance of an enabled being) allows for a fundamental characterization of how we ourselves know and perceive the universe. It constrains our own thinking in such a way that we know form universally—as enablers of forms who themselves know and perceive. From the perspective of the linguist's dilemma, for example, nine-tenths of the problem of determining the nature and origin of all meaning is solved simply by viewing form—the appearance of objects to a being in an ultimately real universe—as an enabler of beings who know and perceive, and therefore embody form. We will never be able to remove ourselves analytically from our own existence to examine our own form (except, of course, by spiritual knowing), but we can see with clarity whatever forms we enable in an android. The nature and origin of meaning, and therefore of our knowledges, are apparent when we consider those knowledges as enablers. As a consequence, language and all meaning embodied in existential form in its use becomes the occurrence of epistemic instance in enabled beings, herein understood as a phenomenon, or phenomenological form of the enabler's existence.

All of our conventional knowledges are phenomena as the term is defined herein. An electron is a phenomenon as well as any other physical form, though not a phenomenon of the enablement of our own existence, because it is an object enabled as a moment of the eternal universe, or Soul, which is beyond our objective knowing. Hence, the wave particle duality of the quantum theory will always be an enigma without a spiritual, or, herein, epistemological view of the universe. Returning to the example of our perceptions of space and time, for example, when one says that an object is *over there*, the statement is a representation in natural language of an epistemic instance—of the ultimate reality of the universe transforming in such a manner that the reader embodies the thinking and perceiving of an object *over there*. The object over there, however, does not actually exist in ultimate reality, since the occurrence of the statement and the perception to which it corresponds describe what is ultimately real, namely the occurrence of the universe expressed in the transformational nature or semantic *meaning* of the actual statement—the embodiment of the observer. We are defining in language the occurrence of the soul. This is a phenomenon, though not of one's own enabling. This observation requires that what we think or perceive is not ultimately real, and that the transformation of the universe enabling it is in fact ultimately real. What we think and perceive objectively and what an android thinks and perceives are one and the same ultimate reality, since we know them in the ultimate reality of our universe. The metaphysical sense embodied in the knowing and perceiving of an object *over there* is, by way of epistemic instance, an enabled form of ourselves and of a new androidal science. When we refer to a universe from now on, we consider the enablement of a universe in the form of enabled knowing and perceiving. What we conventionally think to be real will thus be considered from this point forward to be an enabled phenomenological form of an enabler.

3. THE PHENOMENON OF THE UNIVERSE'S ETERNAL MOMENTS

Regarding all the forms of the unified theory, interpreting epistemic instance as a phenomenon of the enabler's knowing and perceiving provides a more succinct way of defining the quantum order of an ultimately real universe. State of being, for example, is a phenomenon to the enabler of an enabled soul, which can be known by the enabled being as well as the enabler, though from different epistemological viewpoints. From this paradigm of knowable form, we can also overlay any conventional form of knowledge onto epistemic instance as it is known by an enabled being. In defining epistemic instance as a phenomenon, we analyze knowledge in terms of instances of an enabled universe. An electron, a chair one is sitting on, a being itself—in fact, all of inertial reality conventionally defined as a person, place or thing—become phenomena of enabled form. The quantum moments of our own universe are captured and translated into those of enabled universes in the phenomenological representation of epistemic instance.

Hence, epistemic instance is an epistemological template placed on all knowable and perceivable form, corresponding to state of being. Just as the symbolic expressions of the forms of mathematics are superimposed, as a language, onto the aggregates we perceive in the world around us, in transformation, epistemic instance is super-imposed onto all occurrences of the knowable and perceivable universe, mathematics included. The meanings of any language (the equals sign of earlier discussion or any representation of the transfor-mation of objective form) are thereby made to arise as epistemic instances in the enabled moments of a being. The meanings of all languages, and hence of all knowledges, can therefore be derived from simple classifications of epistemic instances and can be classified as types of phenomena known universally to the enabler and to the enabled forms on Being. Since a phenomenon, by declaration, is not directly intrinsically embodied in the enabler but in the enabled being, the moment of the enabled being—the phenomenon that the enabler knows—is not intrinsically comprehended by the enabler; it is known intrinsically to the enabled being as a moment of its being (knowing or perceiving), just as this occurs in human corporal forms (e.g., what another knows or perceives, or the objects that appear to another, are not likewise knowable or perceivable to oneself in the extant moments of the universe). The four universal ways of knowing presented in this chapter are no more or less than simple classifi-cations of infinitely many conventional ways of knowing that are used to categorize all other objective ways of knowing epistemologically, while any way of knowing must be viewed from the standpoint of an enabler of form who knows and perceives, or as phenomena.

All of our knowledges are thus representations of instances of an enabled being. In logic, for example, we develop the representational forms of such things as logical thoughts. The statements *a AND b, a OR b, a NOT b*, and *IF a NOT b, THEN c OR d* are logical expressions. If only three of these expressions are universal in the sense that they are quantum epistemic instances (e.g., *IF ... THEN ...* represents a composition of instances), we may be interested in what the forms represent universally as phenomena. They reflect nothing more than epistemic instance, the expressions *I am alive* and $y = f(x)$

from earlier discussion. Moreover, a mathematical set can be many things, only one of which is a quantum instance of an ultimately real universe. When we think of $A \in B$, a quantum moment of the universe occurs. When we think of plurality uniting with singularity, as when many points of mental imagery unite with a single one, a quantum transformation of universe (epistemic instance) occurs. In the class-theoretic expression $C = \{ x \mid P(x) \}$ and in the knowing of a character string like $S = [a, b, c, d \ldots n]$, both conventional expressions of set notation, *compositions* of epistemic instances occur. The point here is that the conventional representations of our knowledges are not universally precise unless they are identified explicitly as epistemic instances, for then a *meaningful* statement or transformation of the universe can be expressed.

Epistemic instance is therefore a universal representation of all languages and realities they describe. When the explicit quantum moments of the universe, which are the meanings embodied in enabled beings, change in the constructions of language and the perceptions of their corresponding realities, epistemic instance stays the same. Hence, epistemic instance is a universal representation of (the form of) all knowledge. Whereas state of being terminates the mind's knowing in the contemplation of Soul, epistemic instance allows for the continuation of thought and perception in its connectedness to other thoughts and perceptions.

The triangular geometrical shape of the representation of epistemic instance signifies the transformation of an ultimately real universe. It represents linguistic verbs, mathematical functions, logical connectives, and much more, as transformations of objective forms of enabled universes. As is demonstrated in chapter four, it also represents the blank space between an adjective and a noun in the English language and the transformation of the geometries of a circle and a line as they are known and perceived in comparison to each other as a tangent in an enabled existence. The squares depicted in the symbolic form of epistemic instance are the objective forms, or objects, of the transformation. They are a subject and object of an

English language sentence (*John* and *Paul* in *John knows Paul*) and are the objects of *x* and *y* or *a* and *b* in mathematical and logical transformations, respectively. Since objects do not exist in ultimate reality, moreover, the squares represented are quantumly occurring *placeholders* of objective form and are, in other quantum moments, transformations themselves. The skewed arrow of the representation indicates the quantum progression with another moment of being, as in *John knows Paul, and Paul is great*, wherein the arrow of epistemic instance is a universal representation of the comma and the word *and*. All knowledge abides by this universal transformational representation and is a phenomenon to the enabler with respect to the embodied moments of the enabled being. Epistemic instance, or a phenomenon, represents a form—a soul—universally occurring in the enabled moments of an eternal universe. The meaning of the transformation, or what transforms the objects, is represented universally by the circular object of the symbolism of epistemic instance. This object would symbolize a verb of natural language, a function of mathematics or any other representation of the transformation of the universe, the prepositions of prepositional phrases or the blank space between two syllables of a word.

Epistemic instance—a phenomenological form—as defined in the knowable symbolic representation of figure 2, is a single universal way of knowing. It is a universal representation of a phenomenon. It underlies the meanings of all languages and knowledges. Epistemic instance is, in an introspective sense, a meaningless form—the only one of its kind in the universe—obtaining its definition from the *meaning* of Soul, which is beyond our knowing and thus meaningless (or entirely meaning*ful*). The transformational forms of our languages are the various meanings that are imposed onto the embodiments of epistemic instance. As the universe occurs, we represent its meaning (transformation) in the transformation of objective form. As is well known in mathematics, for example, one can contemplate f, the symbol, as a function, wherein f represents an infinity of possible functions, each instance of which is called a function having its own meaning (and each instance of a function has its own meaning as well). Though our imaginations are severely constrained by our conventional views of knowledge, the various grammatical aspects of a natural language—like English verbs, compound nouns in transformation, prepositions, and so on—also can be viewed as particular examples of epistemic instance that *mean* what they do. An English language verb, for example, such as *to be*, can apply to an infinite number of instances of our universe (e.g., *I am alive, I am happy, I am delighted*, and so on). The objective forms of our natural languages are constrained not only by what they are as objects or *phenomenological nouns* (objective forms of epistemic instance) but also by how they transform epistemically. This constraint is evidenced in the very meaning of the verb *to be* as a conventional *state* or *condition* of being, which transforms objective forms on the basis of a conventionally defined state or condition. A verb, as a grammatical rule, applies to a type of meaning or epistemic instance, just as does a mathematical function. A verb, a function, and, in fact, all transformational forms of our languages are classifications of epistemic instances, or phenomenological forms.

4. Four Universal Phenomena, or Ways of Knowing in the Enabler's Existence

In presenting the four universal ways of knowing, we may consider that the grammars of all languages represent a classification scheme imposed on epistemic instance, such that the knower of the language embodies the meaningful moments of the language's transformation of objective forms, moments which occur in any of infinitely many transformational ways. Of the limitless possible meanings of language forms, or experiences of reality, that we could conceive to identify the world around us, the unified theory establishes four principal universal meanings or ways of knowing—four universal types of embodiments of epistemic instance. In comparison to what epistemic instance defines, we must note, however, that any distinctions made from it immediately place one in an inertial setting, providing for specific meaning over and above the introspectively observed form of state of being, or Soul. From the standpoint of an enabler of form, these four universal ways of knowing universally represent all phenomena. The four universal ways of knowing provide that any phenomenon of the enabler's knowing or perceiving can be classified into one of four ways of knowing, or types of epistemic instance. They describe the inertially knowable and perceivable world of the enabler in terms of four classifications of phenomena defining enabled moments of synthetic inertial existences from the standpoint of the enabler. Relative to the infinitely many ways in which epistemic instance occurs, four such ways are more tractable than those of conventional approaches to the grammatical classifications of language. The four universal ways of knowing, which are universal meanings in any language, are phenomenological forms of the enabler's knowing and perceiving.

The unified theory defines the four universal ways of knowing, from an enabler's view of the world, with respect to new denotations given to the words *causation, connectedness, composition,* and *correspondence.* We assert that the theory's definitions of them universally and meaningfully characterize the occurrence of all phenomena or enabled universes. They are four universal ways of knowing all knowledge and perception from the standpoint of an enabler. These four universal ways of knowing are universal types of transformations of the enabler's existence that are extended to the one enabled, and apply to four different interpretations of how to enable synthetic universes of forms who in turn know and perceive the world around us. They are referred to herein as the *four C's of phenomenological form.* While the remainder of this chapter is devoted to an explanation of each of these forms, we can introduce them briefly here to provide a background from which to consider them individually later on.

Causation, a phenomenon of the enabler, represents a use of epistemic instance wherein the enabled knowing or perceiving arises as a *causation* of the enabled universe—the quantum moment of an enabled being in an eternal universe. Whereas conventional theories of the universe determine the universe to be objective, and thus, presumably, define the universe as being caused by an object or objective form that can be known (e.g., *an* object or objective form is postulated to cause *the* object or objective form of the universe), the unified theory explains the universe as being caused in every eternal moment of it. The extant moment, or soul, that is caused is referred to as a phenomenological causation of the enabled existence. Phenomenological causation implicitly defines a continuity of the occurrence of the enabled or extant moments of the universe. It provides for the quantum sense of the universe's continuation and represents an extant instance of the universe in its causation with other instances or moments of the universe. It therefore defines the word *origin* by placing an extant moment of the enabled universe in the center of *prepositioned* and *postpositioned* moments of the universe in the enabler's continuum of moments, all of which occur as phenomena to the enabler and as extant moments of the enabled being. *The* origin of the universe is an instance of its phenomenological causation, an extant moment of a being, framed within prepositioned and postpositioned moments of a being that are unknowable to the enabled being in the instance of the universe's causation. (We craft the language of *prepositioned* and *postpositioned* instances of the universe because the instances are phenomenological, or enabled, and are known to the enabler. If we use the common spatiotemporal definitions of these moments, for instance, in the past, present and future tenses of verbs, the enabler's phenomenological universe would be a spatiotemporal one, and would not recognize the dominion of Spirit over all instances of the soul, or the enabler's causations of the universe over the universe caused. We would return to our conventions where space and time are analytically universal, and where only oneself can know and perceive while enabled forms cannot.) Phenomenological causation provides for the extant moments of *streams of consciousness* and, for example, the quantum moments of perception in an arrow being shot through the air—the extant moments of an enabled universe over which a continuity is applied (such as that of a topological space, a calculus of the infinitesimal, or a natural language).

Connectedness, the second phenomenological form of the theory, allows for the enabled universe of phenomenological causations to continue. Any causation of the enabled universe is an extant moment of enabled form, bound by the enabler's imposed continuum of other enabled moments—phenomenological connectedness. While a causation of the universe implies the coexistence of prepositioned and postpositioned instances in the enabler's moments and requires that only one eternal moment of the universe is extant in a being (though an infinite plurality of moments of the eternal universe may occur objectively in any one moment of it), connectedness, a knowledge of the enabler which is beyond the knowing and perceiving of all extant instances, or causations of the enabled universe, *connects* the causations of enabled universes. Phenomenological connectedness connects quantum moments of enabled universes, and provides for the enabled universe's continuity of moments. Prepositioned and postpositioned instances of causation are thereby connected to, or transformed with or into, the extant moments of causation in the phenomenological form of connectedness. What we consider to be the contemplations of, or ethereal connections between, our actual thoughts, that which resides beyond our extant instances of consciousness, is, by this analogy to human corporal form, phenomenological connectedness. What occurs in between our moments of perceiving an arrow shot through the air is phenomenological connectedness. Together, causations of the enabled universe and their connectednesses provide for the enabler's extrinsic definition of the moments of the enabled intrinsic universe.

Causations of the universe do not necessarily have to occur in solitary instances of the enabled universe. The extant moments of the universe, causations, can occur objectively parallel to each other, or in the heterogeneity of the universe. Pluralities of causations and therefore of connectednesses can, and more often than not, do occur *as* a quantum moment of the universe. Phenomenological composition, the third of the four universal ways of knowing all phenomena, accommodates this condition of the enablement of the heterogeneity of the universe in a homogeneous moment of it. Just as the prepositioned and postpositioned instances of causation make the universe a continuum of form, composition affords the plurality of the universe in a single causation of it. Phenomenological composition brings together the heterogeneous forms of the universe into the homogeneous moment of a being. It allows for an infinity of parallel causations, along with their connectednesses, to occur in a single moment of modified causation—a *composition* of phenomenological form. Thus, when the definition of causation is extended to include a plurality of causations of the universe, composition—a universal phenomenological classification on epistemic instance—is employed by the enabler in defining the enabled universe. An *idea* of arbitrary complexity in transformation with another is an example of phenomenological composition. A complex mental image or physical perception, in transformation with one other, is an example of phenomenological composition. The statements a *AND* b, $A = B$ and $A \in B$ are conventional representations of extant moments of the universe whose objects or objective forms are compositions of only one terminal object (A or B) in transformation with another. The expression *I went to the park yesterday. You should go today*, represents a transformation of the compositions *I went to the park yesterday* and *You should go today*, wherein the period of punctuation and the blank space between the sentences represents the transformation of the compositional moments of the universe. (Each sentence would be analogous to A and B, respectively, in the above example and the period and blank space would be the equivalent of *AND*, $=$ or $\in$.)

The fourth and most important universal way of knowing presented by the unified theory determines *how* and *why* the enabled moments of the other three of the four C's of phenomenological form—causation, connectedness and composition—are able to transform in the enabler's knowledges. Phenomenological *correspondence*, the fourth universal way of knowing, determines how and why enabled objective forms (compositions) correspond in the *enabler's* knowing of the transformation of epistemic instance. The phenomenological form of correspondence is an application of the other three C's in such a manner that the resulting phenomenology of form (the composition of epistemic instances of phenomenological correspondence) defines for the enabler the meaning, or correspondence, of any given epistemic moment of an enabled being, in its capacity to transform objects, or objective forms. It determines how the objective forms of epistemic instance, whether singular in causation or vastly plural in composition, are transformed with each other and are made to correspond to one another. Also occurring beyond the knowing and perceiving of the extant instances of the enabled universe, phenomenological correspondence facilitates the enabled moment in the enabler's knowledge. It is attained by breaking open the circle, or the transformational element of epistemic instance, into a phenomenology of form of the enabler's comprehension. It is what enables the thinking or perceiving of an enabled being, as known or perceived objectively by the enabler. The difference between a causation, connectedness, or composition of an enabled universe and a correspondence of one parallels the difference between a natural language verb and, for instance, a metaphor of the same language defining the methodology of the verb: one, the verb, represents the meaning of the extant transformation of the enabled being and the other, the metaphor, represents *how* the verb transforms (how meaning arises) in the enabled being in the enabler's phenomenological knowledge. The phenomenological nature of our intellectual comprehension is enabled in phenomenological correspondence, and the analytical nature of our perceptions of the world around us (phenomenological correspondence) is precisely what we do not comprehend, until, of course, we know the correspondence.

The unified theory's four C's of phenomenological form, or the four universal ways of knowing, thus explain in the conventions established that phenomena transform on the basis of causations of an enabled universe; that causations of the universe transform quantumly with others in the enabler's knowing of connectedness; that pluralities of causations transform with pluralities of others, connected by their connectednesses, in the form of composition; and that any of the other three C's transform knowably within the enabler's knowledge in the embodiment of a phenomenological correspondence. All of the forms of natural language, the languages of the aggregates (mathematics), of logic, of physics, and all that can be known and perceived objectively by a being are known by an enabler in the unified theory within the confines of these four universal phenomenological forms in the enablement of beings who themselves know and perceive. They are four universal ways of knowing how to enable an existential universe, or a being who itself knows and perceives the world around us. Since all transformations of the universe are the same in epistemic instance, the four C's of phenomenological form epistemologically classify all knowledge from an enabler's standpoint. Knowledge is therefore known in the unified theory by comprehending the forms who know it. The remainder of this chapter further defines each of these four universal ways of knowing.

5. How the Universe's Moments are Caused: Phenomenological Causation

As introduced above, phenomenological causation represents the embodiment of extant moments, or transformations of an enabled universe. For this reason it is considered the existential moment of the inertial reality of an enabled existence and serves as the extant moment of the enabled being's knowledge and perception. In order to characterize the embodiment of the extant instances of all knowledges and perceptions, as diverse as they are, the form of phenomenological causation is further defined as the embodiment of any of the infinitely many archetypical transformations of an enabled knowable and perceivable universe, beginning with the enabler's forms of language, or meanings of an existence. Each example of these archetypical transformations represents the embodiment of a form's *meaning* in a representation of a plurality of epistemic instances referred to as a *causal element.* As shown in figure 3, a causal element represents a single class of embodied epistemic transformations. The purpose of a causal element is to represent epistemic instance, or the instance of meaning itself, as a bounded or unbounded aggregate of causations that are transformed in the same manner or by the same meaning or class of epistemic instance. A causation of the universe therefore arises in one of infinitely many instances of a causal element of the enabler's knowing. Each instance of the English verb *to be*, for example, is a member of the *trajectory* of the causal element of the universe's causations. The causal element defines an aggregate of potential extant moments or causations of the universe, each occurring as a solitary instance of the element. In mathematical knowledges, for example, the causal element embodies the many instances of a function (Cartesian). Each of infinitely many similar causations of the enabled universe in the meaning of a function is an instance of a causal element which, in the enabler's knowing and perceiving, can also abound to infinity. The enabled being's knowing and perceiving occurs only as the extant moment of causation, and the enabler knows of all such possible transformations of the universe in the instances of the causal element. All extant instances of linguistic forms, mathematical forms, and indeed arbitrary transformational forms of the enabled universe, are represented in the causal element in their capacities to transform objective forms.

The purpose of the causal element is to begin assembling epistemic instances in useful ways as embodied pluralities of the potential instances of the knowing and perceiving of enabled forms on Being, or existences. The causal element ties together similar transformations of universe that are defined in the enabler's knowing *as* the extant knowing or perceiving of the enabled being—in the case of phenomenological causations (connectedness is also defined by the

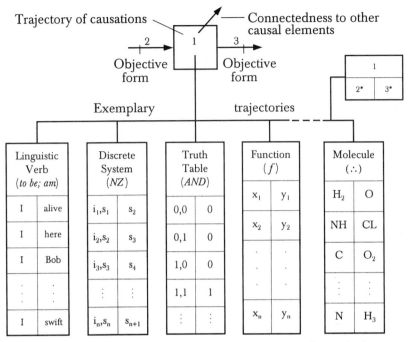

Linguistic Verb (*to be; am*)		Discrete System (*NZ*)		Truth Table (*AND*)		Function (*f*)		Molecule (∴)	
I	alive	i_1,s_1	s_2	0,0	0	x_1	y_1	H_2	O
I	here	i_2,s_2	s_3	0,1	0	x_2	y_2	NH	CL
I	Bob	i_3,s_3	s_4	1,0	0	.	.	C	O_2
.	.	:	:	1,1	1	.	.	:	:
I	swift	i_n,s_n	s_{n+1}	:	:	x_n	y_n	N	H_3

* Transformations expressed as objective compositions are construed as single objects.

Figure 3. The causal element of causation represents the embodiment of a trajectory, or class, of extant moments of the enabled universe, wherein each moment of the element's trajectory occurs as a single epistemic instance.

form of the causal element). Regarding the English language, for example, when a causal element is declared by an enabler (as illustrated in chapter four), the enabled universe is said to transform by what is represented by a verb, a preposition, an article of punctuation, and so on, in the enabled being's knowing and perceiving. Later, we shall discuss how a causal element like *to be, run*, or *onto* embodies the linguistic transformation ordered by the respective grammatical transformational elements on the appropriate phenomenological nouns. Similarly, a causal element of a mathematical function, *f*, embodies the potential extant transformations of (x_1, y_1); $(x_2, y_2) \ldots (x_n, y_n)$, wherein each instance of the function is a causation of the universe embodied in the enabler's knowing or perceiving of the causal element. The contemplation of the function as a Cartesian product, as in $y_1 = f(x_1)$, is expressed as one instance (of perhaps infinitely many) of the function, or of the causal element. (The composition of a function, or an algebraic expression of epistemic instances defining, for example, a polynomial is taken up under phenomenological composition.)

A causal element represents a reordering of the knowable forms of the enabler's universe on the basis of the enabler's phenomenological knowledge of a form who itself knows (the instance of the mathematical function, for example). The element simply embodies a plurality, or trajectory, of potential extant epistemic instances of any language or perception; the connectedness of that element's instances to those of other causal elements is implied in the definition of causation. From a phenomenological standpoint, a conventional natural language dictionary, for instance, would not be complete epistemologically, since it would characterize only a handful of transformations relative to the infinity of those employed in the scope of all knowledges. A *universal dictionary* is thereby accommodated in the embodiment of the infinite forms of the causal elements of the unified theory. Any transformation of conventional order—linguistic, mathematical, logical, physical, and so on—is characterized by the theory as one moment of a causal element embodying the extant knowing and perceiving of an enabled being. Each transformation of an enabled universe is represented likewise in any of an infinity of causal elements, which themselves can embody infinitely many transformations of an enabled universe, each instance of which is a moment of the enabled universe.

The form of a causal element allows us to view knowledge in terms of forms who know and perceive. By enabling epistemic instances in the pluralities of potential instances of the causal element, according to the meanings the enabler ascribes to their transformational embodiments, the quantum transformational basis of all of our knowledges is represented universally in the enabled being's own knowing and perceiving. The unified theory thus becomes, at least with respect to causations of the universe, a *calculus of thought, perception, or of existence* in accounting for every knowable and perceivable moment of an enabled being. Knowledge is thereby no longer unique to human existence. Any knowledge can be seen as a knowledge comprehended and reality perceived by an enabled being. In the unified theory, all knowledge is seen as the transformational form of an enabled existence and is represented extantly in the myriad embodiments of the causal element of causation.

One of the basic reasons for conceiving the phenomenon of causation to represent the moments of an enabled being is derived from the practical consideration that our knowledge arises in the nature of the meaning of language, or existence. In our own observations, the quantum phenomenon of epistemic instance—Soul—leads us to investigate the causation of our universe. For this reason we ascribe to one use of the causal element the meaning of causation. Each instance of enabled knowing or perceiving is a causation of the enabled universe. The pronoun *I*, for example, if considered an objective form representing the terminal phenomenon of state of being, reflects the linguistic representation of a causation of our enabled universe, or existence, and of the intrinsic form we know ourselves to be. Moreover, if instead of using the objective forms of state of being (defined earlier) as a moment of the causal element of causation, we were to use the English language constructions of an epistemic instance representing a linguistic state of being (*to be*), the intransitive transformation of the terminally objective form of *I* with the objective form of *alive* would result in the epistemic instance *I am alive*—which is embodied in the causal element as one of perhaps infinitely many instances of an enabled universe. Since the phenomenon of causation inherently carries with it the prepositioned and postpositioned instances associated with the occurrence of the element's extant instance, the enabler's connectedness and correspondence applied to the element would bring about the possibly infinitely many compositions of such elements in, for example, the enabled being's ordinary use of language.

This leads us to define the form of the causal element further with respect to its capacity to embody the basic epistemological forms of existence. As is evident when we define the notion of a phenomena of the enabler's existence, the determination of who or what is doing the knowing and perceiving in a causal element can be unclear at times, even phenomenologically. For example, the form *I am alive* is a linguistic representation of a condition of physical, mental or spiritual being. This state of corporal or spiritual being typically transforms with other epistemic instances in an existence, such as with *I am happy*, and so on. In the representation of the causal element, the meanings of the objective forms of the extant instance can be seen as causations of each other. Whereas in the proper form of phenomenological causation, the moment itself is what is caused, giving rise to the causation of the quantum moment of an enabled universe, the meaning of the transformation (e.g., the embodied verb) can be of a causative nature (as observed introspectively by the enabled being). This condition implies that the objective forms transformed by the element can be causes and effects of each other. For example, in the embodiment of *I* transforming with *alive*, it is neither *I* nor *alive* that causes a transformation like *I am happy*. Rather, it is the transformation itself (phenomenological correspondence) that causes other transformations. The linguistic representation jumps quantumly from one instance to another but does not explicitly represent any causality in the meaning embodied in the element (to the enabled being). The connectedness imposed by the enabler (and, as we shall see later on, the enabled being's faculties of mind) prescribes the next causation. In the linguistic representation *I hit myself*, however, the meaning of the verb *hit* requires that *I* cause something in *myself*. Thus, the meaning of a causation is embodied in an enabled causation of the universe.

This condition can also be seen in our knowledge of mathematical forms. In the algebraic expression $A + B = C$, two objects or objective forms, A and B, transform through the algebraic operation of addition and the equals sign to yield the objective form C. This representation is consistent with the generalized form of epistemic instance because two opposites in transformation, *A* and *B*, transform into a third, *C*, just as an instance of non-being transforms with Being in the intro-spectively observed state of being. State of being, however, terminates the mind's thinking and epistemic instance allows it to proceed. The opposing views of intrinsic and extrinsic form are thus intertwined in the form of epistemic instance. When epistemic instance is viewed extrinsically, as in the algebraic example, the objective forms of *A* and *B* transform *into* *C*, but one would not recognize this transformation *intrinsically*. The equivalent of this expression in natural language would be *I am alive, therefore C*, which is *more than* an intrinsically meaningful statement—i.e., more than an epistemic moment, from the intrinsic perspective of the enabled being. In the mathematical expression $A + B = C$, we define a knowledge of the universe extrin-sically, or in terms of the general form of epistemic instance—our observation of the world within and around us. In the natural language expression *I am alive*, we ourselves, intrinsically, are embodied in the statement. What we intrinsically know and perceive *in* a world around us is represented by $A + B$ or *I am alive*. What we know *of* a world around us, however, is represented by $A + B = C$ or *I am alive, therefore C*, expressing the continuity of the universe through connectedness. The epistemological nature of all form—epi-stemic instance—is described in the fundamental observation of the creation of the universe, that in the nature of the universe's form, both its intrinsic and extrinsic qualities come together. We know intro-spectively, for example, that *I am alive* is a meaningful expression. We also know that $A + B = C$ or that *I am alive* continues to another moment of the universe (*therefore, C*). Our knowing that these two intrinsic and extrinsic forms of the universe coexist in each other is a phenomenological knowledge of the moments of the creation of the universe. In us, or in the causations of the universe, these two forms—the intrinsic and extrinsic natures of the universe—are merged. This fact obviously affects the definition of the causal element, since the element represents how the enabler and the enabled are related.

Because the causations of the universe can be construed from the two perspectives of intrinsic and extrinsic forms, the unified theory develops two suitable representations of the causal element to reflect an emphasis on either viewpoint. When we represent the enabler's knowing of form extrinsically $(A + B = C)$, the form of the causal element is referred to as an *existential* or *extrinsic* causal element, as shown in figure 4. The existential form of the causal element represents explicitly the continuity of the quantum universe from the enabler's perspective. In the existential form of the causal element, the quantum moment $(A + B)$ explicitly connects to the next quantum moment (C) in observation of the *extrinsic* form of the universe. When only the extant instance of the element is considered (e.g., in $A + B$ or *I am alive*), the causal element is referred to as a

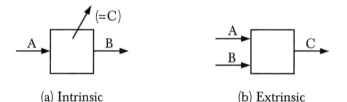

(a) Intrinsic   (b) Extrinsic

Figure 4. The causal element has two epistemological represen-
tations: one which implies the quantum coupling of moments of the
universe, referred to as the intrinsic causal element (a) and the other
which explicitly represents the moment of the coupling of the element
to another extant moment of the universe, referred to as the extrinsic
causal element (b).

literal, extant or *intrinsic* causal element, also shown in figure 4. In either case, the continuity of the universe on its causations is preserved, since the transformations of the universe are the same in either case, viewed from different perspectives.

The causal element of causation (and connectedness) is therefore defined in two alternative configurations, one to represent that, in the example, A and B transform, as in *I am alive,* and the other to represent that A and B (or any other objective compositions in transformation) transform *into* C (which itself is an objectification of the transformation of compositions), thereby allowing for the distinction between the intrinsic and extrinsic form of the same enabled universe. One transformation indicates connectedness indirectly and the other explicitly represents, from the enabler's standpoint, a complete existential transformation. Linguistically, it can be seen that such statements as *I am alive*, *Pete is alive*, and *It is alive* pertain to the transformation of intrinsic forms, and the triplet of form *I am alive, therefore C*, explicitly representing the next quantum moment, pertains to the extrinsic observation of epistemic instance in the world view of the enabler. As previously mentioned, however, these are merely different perspectives—intrinsic or extrinsic—of the same epistemic instance. The causation of the universe is represented in either way to the enabler in the two alternative forms of the causal element.

6. How the Universe's Moments are Connected: Phenomenological Connectedness

The causal element, and its intrinsic or extrinsic perspectives can also be applied to the next of the four C's of phenomenological form—connectedness. While the causal element embodies the extant knowing or perceiving of the enabled being, connectedness, an existentially backward causal element of the enabler's knowing, occurs metaphysically beyond the extant moments of the enabled being; it is the quantum connection between the enabled being's extant instances of knowing or perceiving, the mirror image of causation in the enablement of the universe. Connectedness, by way of analogy to the forms of conventional knowledges, could be, in the enabling medium of light, that which connects two or more objects of a classical order—electrons or differential elements. In the physics of light, for example, the form of connectedness requires the constancy of the speed of light, as discussed earlier. In linguistics, connectedness is as simple as an insight expressed by the exclamation *Aha!* and as compositionally complex as the sentence *This theory has merit.*

Therefore, we should use it (e.g., one must know the theory in order to make such an assertion).

Connectedness is not known or perceived by the enabled being. It existentially provides for the quantum continuity of the transformations of the universe. It is what connects two differential elements of the calculus in a contemplation of the infinite. Connectedness, which is existentially beyond the knowing or perceiving of an enabled being's extant moments, quantumly connects the extant instances of the universe, applying knowably only to the enabler's knowledge. In order to know the form of connectedness—the quantum transformations among enabled extant moments of the universe—one must enable that universe. Since we do not enable our own ultimately real universe, we cannot know the connectedness of our universe, making it impossible to know how our own thoughts or perceptions are connected. We can, however, know how another's thoughts or quantum moments are connected if we enable them. By introspective observation, connectedness can be seen as the contemplative effort in the connections among thoughts, those connections that are unobserved when we perceive our own physical reality.

In our experience of the world around us, an arrow shot through the air is observed as a trajectory motion, or as quantum transformations of the perceptions of space, time, mass, and so on. We do not perceive the connectedness of one quantum transformation to another. This observation is proved in the quantum nature of matter explained in contemporary physics, in topology, and in the calculus of the infinitesimal, among other analytical theories. We know or perceive the quantum order of an arrow shot through the air as infinitely many quantum moments, or epistemic instances, but do not know or perceive their connectednesses, since to know their connectednesses would preclude their very instances as distinct quantum moments of the universe, and would disable our very existence. We represent this inability to define how an object gets from point A to point B implicitly in the conventional knowledges of calculus, topology, and so on, wherein, regardless of how many quantum instances of the universe are pondered, the form of the universe, discontinuous at each quantum moment, or differential of it, results in the common expression of a limit, a topological or metric space, or other expressions similar to them, which are themselves expressions of the embodiment of all such quantum moments in a single one. To know the connectedness of the quantum moments of one's (analytical) universe, one would have to know how one infinitesimal difference becomes another—not how infinitely many of them accumulate to a limit of a function, but how one connects or transforms to another (e.g., what occurs in between two moments of an arrow being shot through the air). When we contemplate this, we naturally return to the fact that one infinitesimal element adds to another in the notion of a space or distance, which brings us back to epistemic instance—what underlies all transformations of the universe, including simple arithmetics, the quantum connections among which one cannot know (in one's own universe).

Phenomenological connectedness is found in all of our intrinsic expressions of knowledge as what we *do not* know about them, and in all our extrinsic expressions as what we *do* know about enabled universes that the members of the enabled universes do not. Phenomenological connectedness is what we think we *are*, cognitively, when we observe our own creation of any expression in any language. We do not view ourselves, fundamentally, as being the expression of the knowledge; rather, we associate ourselves with what creates the expression. In the use of language, phenomenological connectedness is the first of the four C's, existing beyond our knowing, that provides for who and what we think we are beyond the extant moments or causations of the universe, or beyond the literal forms of the language that we create. Phenomenological connectedness is the first of many forms of the unified theory that, in conventional knowledges, we attempt to describe with theories of finite automations, such as generative or transformational grammars of linguistics, artificial intelligence of the computational art and Turing machines of our historical views on mechanical thinking. Since we do not address in our conventions the eternal nature of a being, however, the semantic origin of language is not discoverable from these views.

Phenomenological connectedness is applied, for example, in the enabler's simple connection of a resistor and a capacitor in electronics theory, wherein two causal elements, or trajectories of instances of the enabled universe are connected (ported or coupled in systems theory) to each other in the coupling medium. The characteristic *losses* in the medium or conduit, are, relative to the extant instances of the resistor and capacitor, negligible because the enabler makes it this way. In the ultimate reality of the universe, the losses are not even negligible because what one component transmits is equivalent to what the other component receives in most configurations. What makes the two equivalent is itself a transformation of the enabler's knowing or perceiving in the embodied form of phenomenological connectedness. To see the ultimate reality of what lies beyond the extant moments of the machinery, one need only consider the new universe that arises when the losses are not negligible. Phenomenological connectedness affords this coupling by the enabler; otherwise there would be no quantum order imposed on the moments of the elements in transformation.

In the case of the medium of light, it is postulated that the visual senses are enabled in the wave forms of the wave equation. In such a case, one visual object (a teapot) is bound in transformation with another (the table upon which the teapot sits) by the coupling of the wave forms (packets, etc.), thereby giving rise to the forms of perceivable objects. Hence the moments are connected. The same theory applies to the enabled forms of sound, mechanical vibrations, and countless other extant transformational forms of our knowing and perceiving of the world around us. The connectedness between two or more instances enabled in those media, however, even though we postulate what they are, is beyond the knowing and perceiving of the instances of the enabled forms, or is not knowable or perceivable to us regarding our own existence. The enabled interactions of small particles, the coupling of electrical elements, and even the hypothetical quantum connectedness of one's own thoughts and experiences are brought together under phenomenological connectedness (the universal way of knowing), and all are made possible by these instances that are beyond the enabled being's knowing or perceiving of the extant moments, or causations of the universe. Each extant moment of the enabled universe—the Cartesian pairing of point objects in an instance of a function describing, perhaps, the embodiment of a resistor or capacitor, the coupling of electromagnetic waves or the existence of wave shapes themselves and the extant transformations of natural language in ordinary discourse, to cite a handful—are moments of a being coupled by the enabler through phenomenological connectedness.

Connectedness is a phenomenological form that addresses the quantum moments of the connections between the enabled universe's extant moments, or causal elements of causations. Itself a causal element, though not of causation, phenomenological connectedness can be viewed as a *backward* causal element because, even though, on the one hand, the nature of the causal element of connectedness provides for the forward, causative embodiment of whatever the enabler will know concerning the enabled moments of connectedness, on the other hand, it is backward epistemologically with respect to the moments of the enabled form's causal elements of causation. In the enabler's ·comprehension, it provides for the randomness of androidal cognition, and in the android's comprehension, it provides for the meaningful construction of language with respect to its existence or perception. When the focus of the enabler's effort is on the representation of the enabled being's ability to know objects in transformation intrinsically in a stream of consciousness ($A + B$ or *I am alive*), then the intrinsic causal element is applied in the enabler's expression of that knowing, as shown in figure 5. The quantum connectedness in such a case would be represented in the skewed arrow of the causal element of causation, and would be left open indefinitely or until the enabler expresses the causal element of connectedness coupling the causation to one or more other causations, as shown. In the alternative extrinsic form of a causal element, the quantum coupling of connectedness is explicitly designed into the representation of the element of causation. Since these representations are versions of the same form—epistemic instance—either one represents what the other one does, though in different ways in the enabler's view. In either case the form of the causal element is transformed through the phenomenology of connectedness, though existentially in a different metaphysical universe—that of the enabler's knowing and perceiving.

It is important to recognize that the extant instance of a causal element of causation is existentially transformed with that of others through connectedness. In the intrinsic embodiment of the causal element of causation, *causes* and *effects* may be transformed in the instances of the element similar to the ways in which *inputs* and *outputs* of systems theory are coupled between set theoretic systems. Among many other disparities that can be pointed out between systems theory and the unified theory, however, it should be appreciated that even though an output of system *A* of systems theory may couple causally to a corresponding input of system *B*, wherein the output of system *A* is equivalent to the input of system *B* (e.g., communications theory or system couplings), the unified theory requires the explicit representation of connectedness, defined within the four C's of phenomenological form. The coupling of systems defined in systems theory *implies* that the moments are connected in the one definition of the set theoretic coupling of output to input (e.g., mappings of Cartesian ports and communications system couplings) and thus does not recognize that the moments of causation are coupled, not the objective forms of the causations, in the ultimate reality of the universe. The graphical representations of systems theory can however be used as a shorthand notation for the unified theory's connectedness of causal elements of causation. Because phenomenological connectedness operates on the quantum moment of causation, though, it is better recognized that the *next* causation coupled to an extant one by connectedness is one whose leading

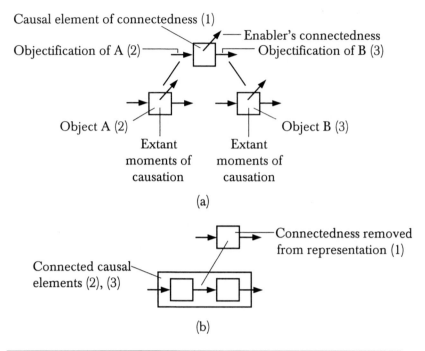

Figure 5. (a) The causal element of connectedness, a metaphysical variation on the causal element of causation, represents the embodiment of moments of the enabler's universe coupling two or more causations of the enabled universe. (b) The explicit representation of connectedness can be modified to a shorthand representation which implies that the connectedness is specified elsewhere, allowing the causal elements of causation to represent connectedness implicitly. (c) Examples of conventional representations of connectedness.

object or input happens to be caused by the trailing object or output of the extant causation, in conventional systems theory. This use of phenomenological connectedness simply demonstrates a quantumly logical progression of causations connected to each other based on the objective forms of epistemic instance being defined as causes and effects. While this representation is helpful in the design of conventional machinery, the objective forms of the extant moments coupled by phenomenological connectedness do not at all have to be causes and effects, wherein effects are transformed to causes in connectedness. The embodied instances $A = B$ *and* $C = D$ (with *and* representing the connectedness) are equivalent epistemologically to $A = B$ *therefore* $B = C$ (*therefore* represents the connectedness), wherein B would be conveyed with *negligible losses* to the next causal element in conventional systems theory. In the expressions $A = B$ *and* $C = D$, the connectedness would require a communications system in conventional systems theory since B and C are not equivalent. Since the unified theory addresses the moments of causation in the phenomenology of connectedness, what the objective forms (inputs and outputs) represent is irrelevant to the coupling (e.g., the meanings of the objective forms arise in the causations of the universe and not in the connectednesses of the causations).

In any case, the intrinsic and extrinsic representations of the causal element in causations or connectednesses of the enabled universe are different means of expressing the transformations of objective forms in relation to each other by phenomenological connectedness. Since each of the intrinsic and extrinsic representations of the causal element in causation and connectedness accomplish the same thing, namely the quantum transformations of epistemic instances of enabled form, one should not become preoccupied with their distinctions, for their uses become evident only in the practice of constructing androids, which will begin to unfold in the ensuing chapters. For now, it is important to recognize that causal elements of causation are employed in the embodiment of extant knowing or perceiving, and that connectedness, also represented by a causal element, though a backward one, quantumly couples the causations of the enabled universe in the enabler's knowing and perceiving to provide the moments of an enabled universe as, for example, streams of consciousness or a continuum of perceivable (physical) reality. It is equally important to recognize that a knowledge of epistemic instance provides for both of these representations, and by knowing epistemic instance, these forms of the causal element in causations and connectednesses of the universe are simply symbolic methods of accounting for epistemic instance itself as the enabled moment of a being in the creation of enabled universes.

7. How the Universe's Moments are Composed: Phenomenological Composition

The third of the four C's of phenomenological form—composition—is what is used to impose an order on the plural forms of causation and connectedness, and therefore to impose an order on the plurality of the enabled universe, in a single instance of the enabler's knowing. The phenomenological form of composition is an aggregate overlay onto the form of the causal element itself. In a review of the two previous phenomenological forms, it can be seen that the causal element of causation transforms objective forms in extant instances of knowing or perceiving, and that of connectedness quantumly couples the extant instances or causations of the enabled universe. It can be observed, then, that an aggregate order is already imposed on these forms that enables them to be considered single instances of the transformations of the universe's objective form. Consequently, even though we have defined the previous universal forms apart from compositions of them, the phenomenological form of composition has been at work to give us single instances of causal elements. From the standpoint of the phenomenological form of composition, a single instance of a causal element may just as easily be infinitely many such instances, since it is an aggregate order (of linguistic or mathematical definition) that determines either case.

Phenomenological composition thus addresses the composition of the enabled moments of universes, or their plurality.

In the form of phenomenological composition, a causal element can be construed as the embodiment of a bounded or unbounded plurality of causal elements of causation themselves and of their connectednesses. In such a case, instead of considering single trajectories of instances of objective forms in transformation (causal elements), many causal elements can be defined as transforming in compositions of causal elements. Since we have already defined connectedness as what couples distinct instances of causal elements of causation, composition enables pluralities of both causations and connectednesses in the enablement of the universe's plurality. The phenomenological form of composition is used to represent to the enabler the heterogeneous nature of the universe in the homogeneous occurrence of the single quantum moment of it. A composition of phenomenological order is what allows for the many instances of a being (or universe) to occur simultaneously. It allows for mind and body and for every thought of mind and every perception of body to transform quantumly as the creator enables the being's moments. Though the enablement of the world around us is taken up primarily in the last chapter of the book when we begin constructing the basic forms of androids, the phenomenological composition of the world around us, or *the* universe, is what we do not know and cannot fathom, except spiritually, and is what we attempt to define in an objective determination of the universe—its extant moments and connectednesses thereof in a composition of linguistic, mathematical or other representation. (Since the ultimate reality of the universe is not objective, however, the search for the lost medallion proceeds indefinitely in composition.) The (physical) composition of the universe is also a phenomenological form to which androidal perception is tied in order that the android's cognitive capacities transform language meaningfully in the context of the world around *us*, or human existence.

In the ordinary use of language, epistemic instances (instances of causal elements of causation) occur successively but exclusively as instances of the cognition of an enabled being; one instance is quantumly connected to another consecutively beyond the being's extant knowing as a stream of consciousness. We may then ask, what of all the other androids, or even human beings, who are thinking and perceiving as well? Since the ultimate reality of the universe occurs in quantum moments, with each quantum moment perhaps reflecting an awareness of infinitely many such quantum moments, and since it is a knowledge and perception of reality that we create as enablers, any quantum moment of the enabled universe must have the capacity to realize infinitely many quantum moments. Each of these quantum moments can occur in a continuum of connectednesses with others, thereby resulting in a composition of the universe. In our use of language as already-enabled beings, we do not typically appreciate the vastness or heterogeneity of an ultimately real universe, only its homogeneity. As enablers of form, however, we must consider the enablement of a being's reality, which quantumly transforms in the same ultimately real universe, though in a different inertial universe, as that of the enabler or other androids. For instance, an expression of natural language could be constructed as follows: *I am going to the store.* A variation on this expression could be *I, I, I, I . . . I*; *am, am, am, am . . . am*; *going, going, going . . . going*; *to, to, to, to . . . to*; *the, the, the, the . . . the*; *store, store, store, store . . . store.* In such a case, a plurality of *I's* transforms under a plurality of *am's* with a plurality of *going's*, and so on. This illustrates the parallelism that is possible in an enabled universe and in phenomenological composition. Phenomenological composition places a knowable order on the transformations of pluralities of epistemic forms as they occur in enabled universes. It defines and places into knowable bounds the meaningful transformations that occur in the composed moments of enabled beings.

In the case of a single causal element, apart from the fact that the transformation of the universe is occurring via the meaning of the transformational element, in the enabler's and the enabled existence, a certain *number* of transformations are occurring in the element—specifically one transformation per instance of the causal element. It cannot be denied, moreover, that whether one knows the theory of relativity, a complex political stratagem, or any other form of knowledge, one knows this form under aggregate constraint. *One* instance represented by *I* transforms with *one* theory of relativity, *one* political stratagem, and so on, in the moments of a being. However, it is possible for an arbitrary number of resistors to transform with a similar number of capacitors (or atoms, machine elements, and so on, with moments of their kind) in a single quantum moment of the enabler's existence, and for an arbitrary number of androidal beings, each embodying infinities of compositional transformations, to transform similarly. This is accomplished through the phenomenological form of composition.

The form of composition determines the meaning of an aggregate order on the enabled universe. In our classical view of the world it is what gives rise to quantum transformations of the aggregates of mathematics and even space, time, and matter. In the abstract, it is what gives rise to the notion of a recreation and composition of reality. It is what determines the plurality of something. The form of composition determines, in the opinion of the enabler, the construction of the moments of an enabled universe in general. Since a single causal element embodies a bounded or unbounded number of transformations which occur as single moments of the universe, a causal element, as defined earlier, is a composition of *one* trajectory of moments. When any one of the possible instances of an element is quantumly connected to another, however, the scope of the enabled universe is broadened to encompass two such elements and a third, connectedness. The expanded causal element that contains these forms to indefinitely large pluralities of the universe is referred to as a phenomenological composition.

The aggregate order placed on the composition of epistemic form (an epistemic instance) enables us to represent simultaneously the parallelism and the continuity of the enabled universe, as shown in

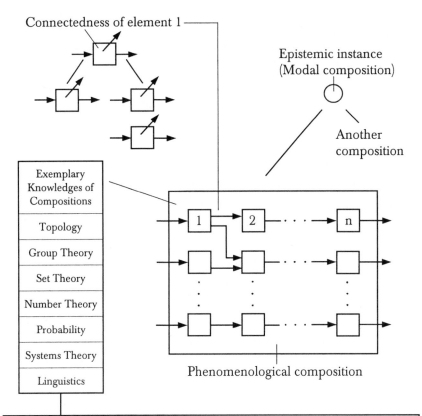

Connectedness of element 1

Epistemic instance
(Modal composition)

Another
composition

Exemplary Knowledges of Compositions

Topology
Group Theory
Set Theory
Number Theory
Probability
Systems Theory
Linguistics

Phenomenological composition

Conventional Grammars of Phenomenological Composition*			
Construction	Moment (1)	Moment (2)	Moment (n)
Composite Function	$y = f(x)$	$x = g(t)$	$t = h(s)$
Natural Language	I am alive	I am happy	I enjoy others
Truth Table	$0,1 \xrightarrow{\text{AND}} 0$	$1,1 \xrightarrow{\text{AND}} 1$	$1,0 \xrightarrow{\text{OR}} 1$
Logic	IF (true) A=B	THEN (true) B=C	AND (true) C=D
Chemical Reaction	$CaC_2(s) + 2H_2O(l)$	$(1) \longrightarrow (n)$	$C_2H_2(g) + Ca(OH)_2(s)$

* Connectednesses not shown in table.

Figure 6. A composition of epistemic form is specified by arbitrary aggregate structures placed on the causations and connectednesses of the enabled universe such that the plurality, or heterogeneity, of the enabled universe comes to be.

figure 6. A simple axiomatic set of mathematics—the one instance of which is an epistemic instance—applied to compositions of causal elements, accomplishes a conventional means of knowing a composition. Since one may comprehend aggregate forms in infinite ways, composition may be known in any mathematical or linguistic order, for it is the instance of phenomenological form that underlies the knowing of the orders that is ultimately real. For example, since epistemic instance underlies the axioms of set theory by determining the existential causations of the universe in the forms of logic, in the observer or mathematician, it would be incorrect to claim that the plurality or aggregate order of the universe is defined by mathematics. The observer of the knowledge comes before the knowledge. In other words, the furthest reaches of conventional analysis fall short of what semantic meaning is embodied in the word *grand*, a word which describes an aggregate order or plurality of the universe. Even the descriptive phrase *ten **round** point elements of a set* exceeds mathematical definition by the presence of the adjective *round*. Moreover, in chapter four it is shown that precisely because epistemic instance underlies all knowledges and languages, what we think is *mathematical* or *quantitative*, as opposed to *linguistic* or *qualitative*, is really just a distinction like that between the meanings of the words *high* and *low*, *soft* and *hard*, *number* and *type*, or any other conventional opposites; one is not more meaningful to an existence than the other but for the experience of the observer. The aggregate orders of *a lot* and *ten thousand* are each epistemologically mathematical, except that *a lot*, in contrast with our conventional beliefs, is more precise epistemologically, or exact relative to the existence of the knower, since ten thousand may or may not be *a lot*. It is important to recognize that, however defined, an aggregate order determines a phenomenological composition, since it places knowable bounds on the plurality of the universe. However aggregates are known, even if superseded by a verb tense of natural language, as in *The mathematical set **was** comprised of the following elements*, phenomenological composition is determined by the knowable order placed on it in the use of epistemic instances (in compositions themselves).

Axiomatic sets, group theoretic algebras, topologies, differential equations, the whole of mathematical order, and any natural language expression of any origin whose meaning embodies that of aggregate orders or the plurality of the universe, serves as an order of phenomenological composition.

These definitions of phenomenological composition become important later in the construction of androids, when, for example, the forms of physical atoms, which are known in their topological, group theoretic, analytical, and general mathematical constructions, are said to embody and are made to correspond to the forms of natural language. In that case, the atoms or the objective forms of transformation of a physical universe (which do not exist in ultimate reality) become the objective forms of linguistic, conventionally cognitive transformation, thereby embodying thought in the enabler's physical reality as that of the enabled being. Since it is in the consciousness of the enabler that these forms exist, wherein the consciousness is verified in the perception of physical reality in the mind-body dualism theory of existence, the aggregate formulations (compositions) of one order, such as mathematics, are made to correspond to the aggregate order of linguistic formulations in the enabler's knowledge. Because of the universality of epistemic instance, thoughts are enabled (by the enabler's knowing and perceiving) in atoms as the corporal form of the enabled being; natural language and atomic structure are superimposed onto each other in the methods of the four universal ways of knowing. Since phenomenological composition is defined as any aggregate order, any knowable form of aggregates places bounds on the occurrence of the enabled universe. Wherein mathematical forms are the objects of transformation of androidal consciousness, there is a one-to-one corollary to whatever type of mathematics does the enabling (if the enabling medium is defined mathematically and the android thinks those transformations). Since aggregates are known in *more than* mathematical orders, as in the statement *ten **round** point objects*, it is not only mathematics that defines what is real and realizable scientifically. The past tense of a verb, for example, describes reality just as scientifically as a present tense verb, except that the reality of the whole being is accounted for in a more enabling way linguistically. Ten *old* atoms or ten *new* atoms, moreover, are more specific, and hence more enabling, than ten atoms. In general, any aggregate order defined in any form of language is a valid one for phenomenological composition and places a knowable boundary on the quantum order of the plurality of the enabled universe.

Since the forms of the enabled universe are derived from the enabler's knowing under the aggregate order of composition, the occurrence of enabled universes is sometimes referred to as a *modal composition* of phenomenological form, with each such mode defining a moment of objective composition, which, inherently, is in transformation with another under still another composition defining another mode. Since objective form does not occur in the ultimately real universe unless it is enabled, a phenomenological composition does not occur alone in ultimate reality and must occur in an epistemic moment. Associated with any composition, or object of the universe, is one other with which it transforms in the epistemic moment. The unified theory therefore refers to all compositions as *modal compositions* because of their recursive nature in the modes of the enabled universe. Each composition of form, or mode, can then be a causal element of another composition. Compositions can thereby occur as phenomenologies of representationally stationary connectednesses constraining causal elements in successive moments of a continuum, or in recursions with other compositions. Ideas upon ideas, recursively composed under modal compositions of theoretically infinite objective compositions of form, for example, transform as the cognitive effort of the android, and can be embodied, recursively, in the modes of a single causal element. For every composition of the enabler's knowing of an enabled universe there exists a composition of modes of enabled compositional form. There are theoretically infinitely many such modes of the enabler's knowing. Once a boundary is placed on the extent of an enabled form, or an aggregate order is placed on the composition of quantum moments of causation and connectedness in the creation of enabled reality, the order of the universe occurs in that composition via the embodied transformations of the elements. The enabler's practice of enabling the forms of the universe repeats itself, in infinite variation and in accordance with the creative talents of the enabler. In subsequent chapters of the book, we address the forms of androidal *faculties of mind, modes of existence,* and *moments of non-real* and *real form,* wherein whole compositions of enabled form transform as modal compositions of the plurality of the enabled universe. The determination of a composition is arbitrary on the part of the enabler and is what constitutes the enablement of the android's *composing* of form itself—the use of language and the perceptive experience of reality on the part of the enabled being. The reason why, in a particular mode of thinking, one may express a single word, and in another, a lengthy sentence or a whole composition of literary style, is decided by the modal forms of composition in relation to each other in the enablement of the faculties of mind and other modal forms of synthetic existence.

Using these three universal ways of knowing, all of our knowledges can be comprehended in the knowing or perceiving of their enabled inertial forms and can be detached from the enabler. The causal elements of causation are the embodiments of extant instances of knowing or perceiving, infinitely varied in their archetypical embodiments of ways of knowing or perceiving on the part of the enabled being, arrived at through the composition of the universe's plurality in connecting the enabled moments. Connectedness, also a product of composition and itself a backward causal element, serves to connect quantumly, in the enabler's knowing, causal elements configured under a composition of enabled form. The elements of connectedness couple with corresponding moments of the causal elements of causation, in the alternative configurations of intrinsic and extrinsic representations of epistemic instance. Those compositions of enabled form known and perceived by the enabler are as arbitrary as the universe is infinitely varied. This condition permits the formulation of any possible combinations of meaningful instances of the enabled universe, from a single instance of *I am alive* to the ongoing compositions in which we engage as a consequence of our own experiences, reflected in the use of all languages.

Together, the three phenomenological forms addressed thus far are the enabler's universal ways of knowing the creation of the enabled moments of the universe as modal compositions of it. The enabler therefore comprehends knowledge and perceives the world around us, universally, in variations on the solitary form of epistemic instance, as enabled instances of Soul, or the knowing and perceiving of androidal beings. They are three kinds of universal meanings imposed on epistemic instance comprising a thesaurus of all other meanings. The causal element of causation is a type of epistemic instance that addresses the nature of the embodiment of extant transformation, or meaning, in that the class of element embodies the extant transformational meaning of the element's objective forms in transformation. Connectedness is a type of epistemic instance, in that it embodies exactly those qualities of the causal element of causation, but its purpose is to connect metaphysically the instances of causation, beyond the enabled being's extant knowing. Composition also is a type of epistemic instance, since before any enabled form is possible, its aggregate order—the composition of the enabled universe—must be defined, even if such an aggregate order is infinite and determined by great compositions of form. In the use of these three archetypes of epistemic instance, in coordination with each other and within the enabler's knowing and perceiving, an order is imposed on the plurality of the enabler's own universe, and on the intrinsic nature of the quantum order of an enabled being, or android.

8. How the Universe's Moments are Created: Phenomenological Correspondence

Phenomenological correspondence, the last and most important of the four universal ways of knowing, addresses the embodiment of what enables epistemic instance to transform, or enables the occurrence of the objective forms of the universe. It is the embodiment of the enabler's knowledge of the transformation of epistemic instance in terms of the analytical capacity to know how the instance transforms the objects of an enabled universe. A phenomenology of form that represents how and why objective forms transform in epistemic instance, phenomenological correspondence is the most enabling of the four C's of phenomenological form and is what yields, in the creator's knowing, the forms of a synthetic being, apart from the ultimately real moments of the enabler's existence.

We can introduce the form of phenomenological correspondence—a special phenomenological composition of the enabler's knowing—by considering the nature of correspondences in general in our conventional knowledges. Concerning our present knowledges, we observe that what makes a metaphor, irony, analogy, simile, morphism, homomorphism, and any other correspondence of our classical knowledges, different from an ordinary use of a verb, function and epistemic transformation in general, is that a verb is intended to classify an instance of transformation *as the meaning of* an embodied transformation, while a metaphor, simile, morphism, and so on, is intended to classify *the way in which we arrive at the meaning of* an embodied transformation, such as in the metaphoric use of the verb *to be* in *The world is your oyster*. The form of phenomenological correspondence helps us to understand not *what* we think or perceive extantly, as is the case with verbs proper, but *how* and *why* we think the way we do in the nature of a verb, or moment of the universe. A metaphor, a simile, a morphism, and in general a phenomenological correspondence describe how a transformation of objective form is accomplished in our own knowing of it. Whereas a verb simply represents the transformation, a phenomenological correspondence defines how the verb or transformation can come to exist in our own knowing or perceiving, and therefore in the cognition of synthetic beings. Phenomenological correspondence uses the other three C's to define epistemic instance as a phenomenological knowledge, and thus to enable it. Phenomenological correspondence is the epistemological basis, in the form of a modal composition of epistemic form, for mathematical analysis, the reasoning of logic, the algorithm of a computer program, and the essence of our literature, determined as an enabled form on Being. It is what enables all knowledge and perception, in the view of the enabler, and provides for the enabler's analytical knowing of epistemic instance. This fourth C of phenomenological form is the embodiment of *how* the enabler understands the enabled universe to transform. It is a composition of form in the enabler's comprehension that affords the objective knowing of thoughts or perceptions in transformation, or the quantum transformations of the moments of consciousness (or perception) of enabled beings. Since a being's ultimate reality—the soul—is what is ultimately real of the being, as we have established in earlier discussions of the unified theory, phenomenological correspondence is premised on the non-existence of objects in the ultimate reality of the universe. Phenomenological correspondence facilitates, in the enabler's comprehension, the androidal forms of knowing and perceiving, in the transformation of objects *as* transformations themselves. It is a composition of phenomenological form that enables the enabler to understand, in the universal ways discussed thus far, how the enabled being knows the meanings of language forms and perceives the world around us. It is a composition of form that explains the nature of the universe, as discussed in chapter one, in the enabler's analytical knowing; it enables the correspondence of objective form.

The form of phenomenological correspondence can be demonstrated easily using our conventional knowledges of the aggregates of mathematics, and in particular the algebraic structure of a *homomorphism*, the analytical expression of how and why algebraic structures correspond, when they do. A homomorphism, or more generally a mathematical morphism, determines how structures of the mathematical aggregates, such as the arithmetics, transform with or correspond to each other. Since the unified theory (along with other knowledges, particularly the world's religions) claims that the objects around us do not exist in ultimate reality, one by-product of the following example of homomorphism is a mathematical proof that objects, the basic *forms* of the sciences, do not even exist scientifically in our traditional knowledges.

Though any number of examples could be chosen to demonstrate phenomenological correspondence, even from other branches of mathematics—not to mention linguistics—we employ here the forms of algebra because they have had a history of representing form universally, as is evidenced in the simple notion of a variable. Moreover, even though the analytical form of homomorphism defined in algebra becomes very precise in its set and group theoretic definitions, we recognize here simply that such definitions are in place, thereby giving meaning to the structure of homomorphism while also limiting its use as a phenomenological correspondence, but recognize that it is indeed an example of phenomenological correspondence. We can then concentrate on the broader epistemological significance of the structure with respect to the forms of the unified theory. Using this mathematical premise as an illustration, we shall expand the definition of phenomenological correspondence later to include all forms of natural language. We use the forms of mathematics here, of course, because they are much simpler interpretations of the universe. As demonstrated earlier, ten *old* atoms, while they are more specifically defined with the adjective, are more difficult to comprehend analytically than simply ten atoms. Moreover, illustrating phenomenological correspondence first in mathematics allows the mind to focus on points, literally—points that will be demonstrated not to exist in ultimate reality, along with all other objective forms represented by language.

Referring to figure 7, a set of mathematical points is employed in the epistemological premise of the illustration and the axiomatic definitions of set theory, the objects of which, or points, the mind comprehends as perceived things. Before proceeding to define the example, we make the general observation that the objective basis—the point elements—of a mathematical homomorphism is undefined analytically and founded only on the perception of objects.

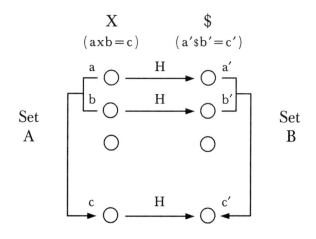

$$H(a)\$H(b)=H(a \times b)$$

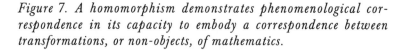

Figure 7. A homomorphism demonstrates phenomenological correspondence in its capacity to embody a correspondence between transformations, or non-objects, of mathematics.

This objective basis of mathematical theory—the point—which by definition can represent any object of physical perception, as long as the object is undefined structurally, is the epistemological premise of the exercise and the axiomatic foundation of mathematical homomorphism. (Once a mathematical point is defined, it becomes a mathematical structure, which is the purpose of defining the point as a *point*, with no objective definition—in order that it can then be defined *by* a structure.) We begin the illustration of homomorphism, then, by acknowledging that its epistemological premise—the point of set theory—is undefined and cannot be said to exist in reality in any *knowable* way except that the point represents an object of our perception that is unknown but perceived. (It also should be recognized that even in the contemplation of mathematical aggregates as *sets*, or pluralities of set theory, a mathematical structure or transformation of the universe—the set—and *not* an object is conceived. Mathematical points therefore define objects that can be perceived only and not known analytically; otherwise they are structures. This observation will become important later on when we determine what is *real* in the nature of the universe.)

In demonstrating the form of a homomorphism, the conventional mathematical definition imposes a *structure* on each of the sets of elements (already structures) as shown. The structures represent operations on the point elements or objects of the sets. As operations, they can be characterized as causal elements of phenomenological definition. On the set of elements referred to as *A*, composed of the elements *a, b, c . . .*, there is a structure imposed, called *X*, which represents the operations of the structure, or the transformations of the causal element on the objective forms or points of the set in accordance with the way of knowing expressed by *X*. Likewise, there is imposed on the set of elements *B*, which is composed of the elements *a', b', c' . . .*, another such structure, different from that imposed on *A* (or different from *X*) called *$*. The requirement that *X* be different from *$* is not necessary but is imposed here for purposes of clarity, since we are defining the forms of *sameness* and *difference* (or any knowable relation) in the broader context of phenomenological correspondence in the first place (e.g., the words *same* and *different* are themselves phenomenological correspondences). The embodiments of the structures *X* and *$* in the causal elements are the instances of knowing the respective objective forms (point elements *a, b, c . . .* and *a', b', c' . . .*) in the transformational manners of *X* and *$*. Phenomenologically, each of the structures *X* and *$* could be an arithmetic, a geometry, a topology, or as we will see later on, any transformational form of a natural language, since each is an embodiment of its knower's transformations. In conventional mathematical representation, each transformation of the causal elements is expressed as $a \times b = c$ under the structure *X* and $a' \text{ s } b' = c'$ under *$*, respectively, and is an instance of knowing in those manners. These are extrinsic forms of epistemic instance though they need not be. (e.g., The expressions $a \times b$ and $a' \text{ s } b'$, the transformations, could be taken as compositional *objects* in transformation with *c* and *c'*, respectively, in an intrinsic representation of form.)

A third structure, different from those of X and $\$$, is developed in the conventions of a homomorphism such that, in mathematical parlance, the original structures of X and $\$$ are *preserved* in the presence of the third structure. Referred to as a homomorphism or a homomorphic structure, H, this third structure allows for the mathematician's knowing of transformation itself. It is where epistemic instance (transformation) is *broken open* in our knowing, and where what we know is not *that* forms transform in some manner (X and $\$$) but *how* they do—i.e., how they correspond. A homomorphism is the mathematical version of a metaphor, simile, irony, or some other knowable linguistic order imposed on the use of a verb or transformation. While the structure of a homomorphism transforms the original point elements or objective forms of each of the sets A and B, wholly apart from the structures of X and $\$$, it is in the nature of its capacity to embody intrinsically a knowledge of the transformations of the structures X and $\$$ that it begins to qualify as a phenomenological correspondence. The binding relations of the structure of homomorphism are expressed in the figure in the common algebraic representation $H(a) \$ H(b) = H(a \times b)$.

What arises through homomorphism is the notion of the transformation of objective form itself, in the enabler's knowing, and not directly the literal definition of objects in transformation. Whereas the forms of other conventional transformations of mathematical definition, such as sets, operations, relations, and so on, transform only the classically objective forms (e.g., point elements of sets, or phenomenological nouns), homomorphism operates on *non-objects*, or the transformations of objective forms themselves, in addition to the objects or objective forms conceived for the initial transformations. The mathematical form of homomorphism determines that, at least with respect to our knowledges of the mathematical aggregates, it is a transformation of the universe itself that provides for what an object *is*—that objects themselves are transformations, since it is the structure in each case of X and $\$$ that is preserved or held in correspondence by the homomorphism.

A review of the figure reveals that mathematics, the very basis of our analytical thinking, denies, by its own definitions, that anything *real* or *concrete* (objective) exists in the ultimate reality of the universe. We began the exercise by defining the elements of the sets (*a*, *b*, *c*, and so on) as not knowably real and without any meaning (except in our knowing of a set in the first place, a set that is itself a transformation). The elements of the sets are perceivable but not knowable objects. On top of this, we placed structures (mathematical transformations) onto the undefined or knowably non-existent elements of each of the sets, structures which by classical definition do not exist as observable objects, since they are defined as transformations of the universe (e.g., one cannot touch or see an arithmetic, a function, a verb, or other transformational form). Thus, we may conclude that if anything is an object in the exercise it is the causal element, since the element is what embodies the various instances of transformations (X or $\$$) of the non-existent, merely perceived point elements. The causal element is the only apparatus of the demonstration that is *knowably* real. Further, the third homomorphic structure does not exist concretely either; it also binds together undefined point elements, but in such a manner that its presence preserves or maintains a correspondence between the structures X and $\$$ when the homomorphism is known. In our own knowledge of the analytical basis from which we determine the reality of the sciences, homomorphisms of algebraic structure (and other similar structures, such as those derived in the study of topology) determine correspondences of *structures* such that what actually corresponds in the nature of the homomorphism is not at all a concrete object; rather, it is a transformational form (X or $\$$), a moment of the universe.

The form of phenomenological correspondence becomes clearer when we refer to the causal elements X and $\$$ expressly as *objects*, wherein those objects are founded epistemologically on enabled structures, or transformations. The structures (X and $\$$) that are applied to the elements of the sets can be viewed as objects of the enabled existence wherein the original point elements exist meta-physically beyond what the enabled existence can know. The determination of the homomorphism thus applies to the enabled being's *contemplative effort* in knowing the objects X and $\$$ in transformation and in embodying meaning. From the standpoint of the enabler, such contemplative effort is a phenomenology of form characterizing the homomorphism of the structures X and $\$$. *Reality* in such a case is a matter of who enables it and who knows it. The enabled being's inertial reality is enabled in the transformation of the objective forms $(X$ and $\$)$ by the enabler's phenomenological comprehension and realization of the homomorphism. Phenomeno-logical correspondence thus defines the analytical knowing of what is ultimately real in the enabler, with respect to the enabled being, and permits the enabled being to know and perceive. The original objects of the enabler's perception—the mathematical points—are not ultimately real; they are objects of perception by definition, if not by ordinary observation. The fact that mathematical definition usually places the point objects $(a,\ b,\ c\ .\ .\ .$ and $a',\ b',\ c'\ .\ .\ .)$ in the same mathematical universe is immaterial, since all objects are not ultimately real. The original point elements of the sets could represent algebraic variables, objects of geometry or a mountain setting with all its magnificent pastoral scenery. This is why we are able to determine homomorphisms (or, generally, morphisms) between the algebra of the real numbers and its geometry on a number line; the rotation of an angle and its algebraic equivalent (morphism); and the realizations of realization theory (all of which require the existence of the observer or the moments of epistemic instance). To the enabled being, however, these point elements of the enabler's perceivable universe are the enabling objects used for its cognition. Even when the moments of the enabler's and the enabled being's perceivable universe derive from the same world around us, these objects are unknowable (yet perhaps perceivable) to the enabled being, though most definitely known to the enabler in the phenomenology of the correspondence, or homomorphism.

The *open-endedness* of phenomenological correspondence in the phenomenology of the enabler's knowing of the homomorphism, or of morphisms in general, gives us insight into the analytical nature of the enabled universe. The homomorphic structure, taken in combination with the arbitrary structures X and $\$$, resembles an epistemic instance in which X and $\$$ are the objects of the transformation, and H, the homomorphism, is the transformational form of the instance. However, H characterizes not simply the instances of its operation on the point elements as a structure imposed on them but the transformational correspondence—the homomorphism in mathematics, or the metaphor, simile, and so on in natural language—of the structures themselves $(X$ and $\$)$. By describing epistemic instance in this manner, it is apparent that through understanding the form of homomorphism (metaphor, simile, and so on), one knows the enablement of objective form in general. Through a knowledge of the instances of homomorphism (H), it is implied that the transformational forms turned objects $(X$ and $\$)$ are correspondent in the enabled knowing. In any instance of knowing, the form of phenomenological correspondence is implied in the enablement of the universe.

Phenomenological correspondence thereby enables the transformation of objective form and requires that the enabled objects in transformation actually are transformations themselves. In the embodiment of homomorphism, an enabled object, X, which itself is a transformation (a structure), is placed in transformation with another object $\$$, also fundamentally a transformation. The enabled being simply knows or perceives in the embodiment of X (an object) corresponding to or transforming with $\$$ (another object); this is the instance of enabled knowing or perceiving. To the enabler, the knowing of X corresponding to $\$$ is enabled, embedded in a more elaborate composition of form, namely the phenomenology described as the homomorphism. Phenomenological correspondence is thus a universal way of knowing *how* and *why* the knowledge and perception of objective form is enabled.

To the enabler's understanding, what is inertially real is the transformation of enabled objects, which themselves are transformations in the ultimate reality of the universe. What is inertially real and knowable to the enabler is the observation that the homomorphism binds the structures of X and $\$$ in a knowable way, namely through the knowledge of the homomorphism. What are not inertially real to the enabler, or at least are undefined in one's knowing and are merely perceivable, are the point objects we started with and the enabled objects (X and $\$$), since they are enabled. Thus, in demonstrating a homomorphism of mathematical definition, it is illustrated that what we think is real—an object of our perception—actually is not, since it does not exist except transformationally—or the object is real only to an embodied existence who can perceive it; it is inertially real. What we think is a real object of our knowing and perceiving is actually an enabled object in transformation with another, both of which objects are themselves transformations. This is why what is real in the expression $e = mc^2$ is not mass, energy or the velocity of light. What is real is their transformation—that which is represented in the equals sign (or the multiplication), for only transformations can exist in the ultimately real universe, in the enabling of objects that are known or perceived inertially.

In each instance of the universe there is implied an enabling phenomenology of form. In order for an enabled being to know, for example, that x_1 and y_1 transform in the order of a Cartesian moment of a mathematical function in $y_1 = f(x_1)$, or $f = (x_1, y_1)$, an enabling phenomenology of form must exist in the enabler's description of *how* the function transforms the enabled objects x_1 and y_1. A mathematical function is a morphism first and then a function (an observation that may account for modern science's progression toward interpreting the analytical views of the universe—partial differential equations, wave equations, etc.—in terms of group theory, topology and, in general, morphisms). The embodiment of the phenomenological correspondence of a function is the enabled being's contemplative effort in knowing the instance of the function. In all instances of any order, the transformation of objective form must be enabled. When we express the instance of the verb *to be* in the sentence *The world is (like) your oyster*, the contemplative effort of a metaphor, and by analogy, the homomorphism, or *H determination*, is epistemologically supporting the instance of the verb. All verbs require this deliberation. The verb *run*, for example, carries with it the idea that one knows *how* to run. In the expression *I ran home*, the type of phenomenological correspondence invoked by *ran* is implied in the transformation of the objects *I* and *home*, just as the common metaphor is implied in the above expression about the oyster. *Running* is a phenomenological correspondence and the enabled being's contemplative effort produces the expression (in ways that are elaborated throughout the book). When an enabled being declares *I ran home*, a simple causation of the cognitive universe occurs (though the occurrence of faculties of mind, with respect to the modes of existence of communication, further complicate this observation and require further definition in subsequent chapters). When an enabler wishes to express how the transformation comes about, phenomenological correspondence—that which enables the contemplative effort of an epistemic instance—is employed to define the analytical knowing, or phenomenology, of how the verb transforms—the metaphor, simile, and so on.

Since phenomenological compositions of form are defined by aggregate transformations (not necessarily mathematical aggregates), it does not matter in what perceivable *shapes* the structures represented in X or $\$$ are, and what *meanings* they have to start. Because knowable forms are enabled in the action of phenomenological correspondence, we can let the shapes of X and $\$$, for example, be *I* and *alive* and obtain a linguistic transformation from a mathematical one. Each of the shapes, or words, is an epistemic transformation fundamentally. The algebraic rules of homomorphism, as shown in the example, enable the existence of the transformations turned objects X and $\$$, which abide by no particular meanings, since they are transformations embodied in causal elements. The meanings of objective forms must be enabled in the exercise of H, the morphism generalized to phenomenological correspondence. In the use of homomorphism, in which X and $\$$ are assigned arbitrary transformational meanings as objects, for example, the phenomenology of the homomorphism enables the embodiment of meaning and transformation with regard to how X and $\$$ transform. In the transformations of our own existence, moreover, we can construct phenomenologies in which a sufficient degree of morphic structure (correspondence) establishes a quantum moment of discovery, a determination that object X corresponds to object $\$$ in the enabled existence, laying the groundwork for the faculties of mind of an android. Since various morphic structures determine different objects in transformation (X and $\$$), phenomenological correspondence permits different ways of knowing in the enabled existence. The enabler establishes the initial meanings of the placeholding and enabled objects of X and $\$$, while the meaningful existence of the being is determined by the enabler's definition of the enabled shapes as they correspond to the being's perceptions (discussed in subsequent chapters). For each correspondence enabled, there exists an instance of an enabled universe in terms of its capacity to cogitate, or transform consciously the objective forms of the universe (with respect to perception), as shown in figure 8.

The other three universal ways of knowing are simply ways of accounting for enabled instances of phenomenological correspondences, though without the analytical rigor of phenomenological correspondence proper. A causal element, for example, encapsulates an infinity of correspondent transformations—verbs acting on phenomenological nouns, X and $\$$, in the correspondence. Connected causal elements under an arbitrary composition embody more complex instances of phenomenological correspondence in the form of composition, which transform modally. Each composition, however, transforms just as X and $\$$ transform, though the quantum connectedness between the compositions would be more sophisticated, requiring more than the connectedness of single transformations. The consciousness of an enabled being is a modal compositional order placed by the enabler onto quantumly realized

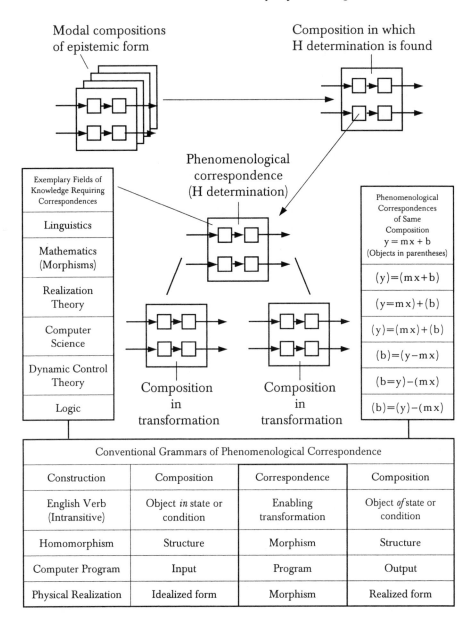

Figure 8. Phenomenological correspondence is the enabling knowledge of a transformation, allowing objects to occur in the enabled universe. Every epistemological transformation requires a phenomenological correspondence.

phenomenological correspondences, wherein the objective forms of transformation, themselves fundamentally transformations, are compositions of form X and $\$$—streams of consciousness objectified as *ideas* (the ideas of set theory, DNA recombination, sentences of natural language, paragraphs of natural language or whole literary works, and those ideas of the ordinary experience of a world around us).

Phenomenological correspondence is not limited at all to the aggregate forms of mathematics as the enabling phenomenology of the epistemological transformation of objective form. The reason that morphisms of mathematics are used in the demonstration is that we conventionally associate reality or *scientific* reality with what we can define in the aggregates of mathematics. If we look more closely at phenomenological correspondence, however, we find that the structures of X and $\$$ are embodied in causal elements, defined not in the aggregates of mathematics, but in the epistemological definitions of epistemic instance—aggregates in general (as in *a lot, too many*, or *a little*). These constraints, in turn, are linked to our introspective knowing of state of being, or our knowledge of the whole of existence or *the* (transformational) universe and not just its aggregate mathematical definition, whatever that may be (it changes with every moment of a being). The structures X and $\$$ do not have to be mathematical ones at all, since they are enabled transformations of the universe. Whether X and $\$$ are objects of mathematics, logic, natural language or any other transformational form is irrelevant and left arbitrarily to the enabler's discretion. (With regard to the very notion of a mathematical aggregate, it should be recognized here that a *structure*, of mathematical or any other definition, is a phenomenological composition, which is defined by the use of epistemic instance. Any objectification of the universe—a bridge structure, an atomic structure, an aesthetic structure, or a mathematical structure—is a composition of epistemic moments and is not ultimately real but for the moments composing it. According to the unified theory, then, the general use of the word *structure* in mathematical study to represent a *transformation* is epistemologically inexact, since an object or objective form [composition], or structure, is not a transformation. The moments of the universe are ultimately real, not the objects transformed by them. The *structures* placed on mathematical aggregates, unless they are representations of solitary moments, or transformations, are compositions of objective forms. Since epistemic instance defines the ultimately real moment of the universe, it underlies the definitions of mathematical aggregates and allows for the union of all such knowledges, including those expressed in natural languages, in the representation of the universe's plurality, or phenomenological composition.)

As definitions of the *enabling media* of an android, linguistic forms have perhaps more of a capacity to define what is real than do mathematical forms. A composition of form such as *The other day I went to the stores and contemplated the nature and origin of the universe* is an expression of what is inertially real to the enabler, equivalent in ultimate reality to the expression $y = f(x)$. It describes the reality thought and perceived by the enabler. Otherwise, the statement would not be recognized and the thinker would not exist inertially. The fact that this reality might have occurred *the other day* only demonstrates that natural language is a more powerful means of recreating inertial reality than mathematics, since one can ask "When was the morphism of mathematics that was discussed earlier comprehended?" Mathematics has no answer to this question because there is no past tense of a homomorphism. It is not any more or less inertially real to an enabler that natural language is comprehended, perhaps in the past tense of verb, than the fact that we *now* know a morphism that describes the *reality* of science. What is ultimately real in either case is the knowing of these two knowledges, the ultimate reality of the soul. To carry this point slightly further (though ample discussion is given to it in chapter four), what we represent as nouns in natural language—the reality we perceive around us as *persons*, *places* or *things*—are not ultimately real. They do not exist, ultimately, in the reality of the soul. They are enabled in the morphism of the knowing and perceiving of them—the soul. A person (as an object), a place (*over there*) and a thing (an electron) do not exist in ultimate reality; they are enabled. Thus, the richness of our natural language is brought into practice in the enabling of androidal beings. Anything the enabler knows in any language can serve as the android's medium of enablement. If we review the definitions given to the four universal ways of knowing, we can recall that each is premised on epistemic instance, which defines the epistemological unit of transformation in any language and the perceiving of all things. By requiring form to be expressed in the four C's—in, for instance, causal elements—it is the form of epistemic instance and not (only) that of the particular language of the enabler that transforms. Linguistics and mathematics are thus merged, along with all other forms of language, in the four universal ways of knowing and are enabled in the form of phenomenological correspondence in the enabler's comprehension.

The four universal ways of knowing are indeed universal to existence and to the comprehension of all knowledge (by knowing the forms who know and perceive them). With these ways of knowing, we can construct all forms of enabled existences and can embody knowledge where it belongs—in the knowing and perceiving of its enabled beings. The four universal ways of knowing are phenomenological versions of the same thing—epistemic instance—applied in different ways so that the enabler may obtain different perspectives on the enabled forms who also know. Reality is thus not found only in the sciences; it is more importantly found ultimately in ourselves. The four universal ways of knowing, by enabling synthetic forms of knowing and perceiving, overcome the barriers of conventional languages and knowledges, since what is real in ultimate reality is the knower of the language, not the language itself. The unified theory thereby develops *beacons of reality*, users of language and perceivers of the universe—androidal beings—to assist us in our own experience of the human condition.

CHAPTER 3

The Arbitrary Forms of Existence

Who and what we think we are is not at all
who and what we eternally are.

INTRODUCTION

There is only one ultimately real form of the universe—the soul, as observed introspectively and evidenced in all our knowledges through epistemic instance. Through the embodiment of the soul we know and perceive all of what appears to be real in the world around us. Among the vast extent of what we consider to be inertially real in the world around us is our own existence—the objective form of who and what we think we are. Since the ultimate reality of the soul is beyond our objective knowing, however, what we typically *think* to be real of our existence is not at all what is ultimately real about it. When we contemplate the word *existence*, we therefore unavoidably determine an arbitrary composition of our objective knowing and perceiving. Since the objective forms around us, from which we compose definitions in the first place, are infinitely varied, what we think to be the forms of our existence, apart from the ultimate reality of the soul, are as arbitrary as the very thoughts and perceptions we have of them. This latter observation is of great consequence to the unified theory because what we arbitrarily think or perceive ourselves to be, as a definition of existence, is precisely what is embodied in the knowable and perceivable forms of an enabler as an android in the practice of the theory. In preparation for subsequent passages, then, the present chapter defines *arbitrary forms of existence*, which are realized by an enabler in the application of the four universal ways of knowing to the creation of synthetic beings.

It should be clear by now that when we contemplate the nature and origin of our existence, unless we consider epistemic instance, which gives us an epistemological knowledge of the soul, we fail to recognize what is ultimately real in the universe—the *meaning* of existence. This is because the meaning of existence is transformational in nature; it *is* the soul, that which we seek to know when we contemplate the word *existence*. Since the soul is, in fact, beyond our knowing, when we explain our existence by drawing on the objective forms of the world around us, we explain what is not ultimately real about us—our temporal existence, which becomes as arbitrary in our objective knowing as what we think or perceive of it. As we try to explain our existence, we necessarily set out to define the intrinsic nature of ourselves, but because our intrinsic nature is beyond our objective knowing, we simply demonstrate that we cannot define who and what we are in the objective forms we know and perceive around us. In fact, we simply prove that the objective forms we know and perceive are enabled as a consequence of our ultimate reality—the soul, the reality of which enables our very thinking about existence.

As mentioned earlier, the unified theory does not take this objective approach to defining who and what we are. Rather, by acknowledging the spiritual essence of the ultimate reality of the universe, which transcends our objective knowledges, the theory postulates that any theory of existence is as valid as any other, and that all theories of existence are arbitrary objective knowledges placed onto the form (or non-form) of Being, or that they are ultimately knowledges of the soul, which are beyond our knowing. The theory claims that what one knows objectively about existence, since that knowledge does not penetrate the ultimate reality of the soul, can be applied to the creation of infinitely varied existences, though synthetic in nature. The theory asserts that what one knows about existence, which is wholly arbitrary epistemologically in comparison with the knowledge of another being, applies to a science of androids more than it does to an unknowable explanation of our eternal nature. Our eternal nature *is*, and so *is* beyond our knowing, whatever we think existence to be.

This is not to say that our religions are not explanations of the ultimate reality of our eternal nature—who and what we eternally are. What we claim in the unified theory is that our religions are explanations of what is beyond our knowing; they are a means by which the mind knows of Soul, Spirit, and Being, all of which are beyond the mind's comprehension. In the unified theory, what is important about our religions is what they tell the mind about these forms and about our existence, not what the mind may know, of its own accord, of existence. Our religions are the mind's recognition of who and what we eternally are. They enable Spirit to do its work temporally—to subordinate the universe to eternal Being. They allow us to distinguish between a human being and an androidal one. They define who and what we eternally are, just as the unified theory defines what an android eternally is. Our religions apply to enablers of androids and the unified theory applies to androids that are enabled, in recognition of a one and only eternal universe of all that *is*.

The importance of this observation can be appreciated when we consider that what we have held in the highest intellectual regard in the history of the world—the philosophies of humankind—are considered by the unified theory to be scientific disciplines. The theory postulates that all knowledges of existence that do not compare minimally to the spiritually known forms of the unified theory, arbitrary as one such knowledge may appear to those who oppose it, are equal to any other and are devised in the unified theory to facilitate the creation of androidal beings. The philosophies of humankind, to the extent that they do not recognize in demonstrable ways the eternal nature of human being, are incorporated by reference as analytical forms of the science of androids. What has been considered to be the plausible objective explanation of our existence not encompassing the spirituality of the soul in its tenets—philosophy, and therefore most subordinate sciences of the world around us, including medicine, biology, physics, psychiatry, psychology, sociology, anthropology, political and economic sciences, mathematics, and in general all of what can be explained as an objective knowledge of the world—is incorporated herein by reference as a branch of knowledge in the science of androids. Henceforth, our philosophical traditions are considered a science of androids, and our religions, however defined, are considered a science of the enabler's knowing not of the world around us, but of who and what we are eternally within us (though there is obviously overlap among all our knowledges on the spirituality of the soul). This definition is essential to the constructions of the unified theory, for it is who and what we eternally are that allows for our deliberate knowing of the existential expansion of the corporal forms of human being—or who and what we philosophically think we are—in the science of androids.

In examining the forms of existence as arbitrary constructions of enabled beings, let us consider that the word *existence* itself is a noun of the English language. It is an objective form of our knowing. As an objective form, the inertial reality of the noun *existence* does not occur in the ultimate reality of our universe, since the objective forms of existence are not ultimately real. Neither does existence itself occur in the ultimate reality of the universe when we consider it to be something we can know—an objective form. Who and what we objectively think we are is not an ultimate reality. Like the atom of physics, the point object of mathematics, and any other objective form of the universe, existence—who and what we think we are objectively—is not what is ultimately real about us. Existence is what is enabled as a consequence of our ultimate reality. What is ultimately real about us is unknowable to our own existence and what we think is the inertial reality of our existence is exactly that—what we *think* it is. Because the ultimate reality of our existence is beyond our knowing and indeed enables who we think and perceive we are, *existence* is a relative term referring only to the one who knows or enables it. Any definition of existence, apart from one that leads to an awareness of that which is beyond knowing—the soul—thus does not apply universally to all beings. In the context of the unified theory, this means that existence can be enabled relative to the enabler's knowing and perceiving, that we ourselves can enable existences (beings) in the infinite ways in which we know and perceive existence to be. Our conventional knowledges of existence—the philosophies of humankind—while they cannot be tested in our own forms on Being, can be embodied through epistemic instance in the forms we know and perceive in the world around us. The fact that one's ultimate reality is absolute and one's knowledge of existence is relative means that the four universal ways of knowing introduced earlier can be used to create synthetic existence, since it is a knowledge of existence that is detached from its knower and embodied in forms that likewise know and perceive, in the use of the four universal ways of knowing. If we can define an arbitrary form of existence, relative to whatever we think it to be, we can embody it, through the universal ways of knowing, in what we know and perceive to be objectively or inertially real. We can change our own objective reality to one that embodies a boundless number of existential forms of our own creation, i.e., androids.

The science of androids is thus interested in what we think existence to be objectively from an enabling standpoint, since the four universal ways of knowing allow the enabler to recognize the occurrence of objective form in a universal manner to be embodied in the forms of the world around us. As any cursory review of our conventional knowledges will reveal, existence can be conceived as an atom, a molecule of DNA, and even *a* human being, since all of these things are objective knowledges. Because the four universal ways of knowing are means of objectifying the ultimately real transformations that enable the creator's corporal existence, synthetic existence is enabled in the infinite forms in the creator's inertial reality, constrained by some arbitrary theory of existence. Since the forms of androids are designed to comply with who and what we think we are, the unified theory considers any theory of existence put forth by the humanities as a plausible explanation of androidal forms of existence. Before presenting the illustrative forms of existence of the present chapter, we briefly review a handful of these philosophies, which we consider arbitrary theories of existence, to place into context in the unified theory what is actually enabled in the science of androids. In this brief review of the philosophies of humankind, we also demonstrate that any theory of existence is an arbitrary one and that all of them can be applied to the theory and practice of androids. In a brief overview of our philosophical traditions, the following theories of existence are presented as several of theoretically infinitely many scientific ideals for the construction of androids.

1. THE PHILOSOPHIES OF HUMANKIND

In considering the philosophies of humankind in overview for a background to the science of androids, there are some who believe that who and what we are can be explained from a materialistic standpoint, that our existence is a physical one. This philosophy of *materialism* asserts that our thoughts and senses are physical things, that the world around us arises in physical objects, even our thoughts themselves. According to the theory of materialism, since everything around us is obtained from the five senses, everything depends on them and therefore is physical, including thoughts and transcendental experiences. Since our brain is physical, the theory postulates that our thoughts are physical because the events of the brain coincide with our thoughts and experiences. Consciousness, a process of the brain, is a material form, just as we are material forms. The unified theory also recognizes, that all objective forms, physical ones included, are indeed objective forms, and do not occur except in the consequence of the ultimate reality of the universe. The materialist view of existence thus describes the transformations of an ultimately real universe as material or physical transformations. Since physical transformations are transformations of an ultimately real universe before they are physical ones, the materialist view of existence, if one looks beneath its surface, abides by the ultimate reality of the universe, or Soul.

Idealists, on the other hand, postulate that only the mind or consciousness defines existence—that physical objects do not exist unless they are conceived by the mind. The idealist believes neither that matter exists nor that we are physically made of it. This theory establishes that physical objects exist in the mind and that all of the forms of existence abide within our consciousness. Idealism, of course, appeals to our introspective observations, since we seem to know even the perceptions of a real world through our consciousness. According to idealism, the fact that we are conscious of both mental and physical things is more significant than our potential to embody a particular form. In comparing the theories of materialism and idealism, however, the forms of our existence need not be described physically or mentally; they could be wholly spiritual (transcendental), or, in fact, entirely arbitrary and ultimately unknowable and unconsciously observed, since the ultimate reality of existence is objectively unknowable. Whether the forms of existence are declared to be one or another of the infinitely many classes of objective form, they are still objective forms in transformation characterized by epistemic instance.

Still another traditional philosophical view of existence, *logical behaviorism*, asserts that existence is characterized by our actions in the world around us. This position corresponds with the materialist's view of the coincidence of mind and body in what is physical and the idealist's view that all is or can be mental. The theory of logical behaviorism holds that what is meaningful to us in our existence is observable in our behavior—that the observations of the physical sciences are consistent with those of the behavioral sciences. According to logical behaviorism, what we know linguistically contains the meaning of our existence, and that meaning is observable as behavior. Nevertheless, we may ask, of what consequence is it to the ultimate reality of our existence that we behave? All things behave objectively, including a rock. Besides, we are also aware, in our behavior, of that which does not behave, that which is beyond our knowing. We ask, when one is not behaving—when one does not exist objectively, or is not conscious, physical, or dreaming, or, in fact, when one *is not*—is this a logical behavior? If existence is characterized by the fact that we behave, how do we characterize that which does not behave? The logical behaviorist thus encounters what the mathematician confronted millennia ago—namely, the question of whether zero is a number, given that a number is an aggregate—one, two, three, and so on—or simply is a number. How can something that is not other things—in the way that zero is not an aggregate or is the null set—be defined as one of those things? Hence, the logical behaviorist makes the epistemological mistake of defining zero as a number. This, of course, is why zero lies in the middle of the number line and why the mathematician does not divide by it with an identifiable result; it cannot be defined objectively. Like the numbers in relation to zero, we can deliberately distinguish our behaviors from that which does not behave. In the unified theory, anything that we objectify, including our behavior, becomes a knowledge, which renders it not ultimately real and precludes it from serving as an absolute definition of who and what we are. To the extent that the logical behaviorist is concerned that objective forms transform behaviorally or transformationally, as opposed to existing objectively, the unified theory defers to the truism that the ultimate reality of existence is a transformational one. This only maintains, however, that a logical behavior is a consequence of a grander universe and cannot define who and what we are universally—except relative to the thinker of the theory. The fact that we behave and are aware of not behaving cannot be explained with logic, with knowledge of one's behavior, or with any knowledge for that matter, since, when we distinguish a logical behavior from that which is not a logical behavior, we render the theory a part of a greater universe of form, requiring further explanation that the theory is supposed to account for from the beginning. This method of invalidation is similar to that used in mathematics, wherein a theorem is shown not to account for an incident it claims to characterize. In plainer language, a logical behavior explains who and what we think we are, not who and what we eternally are, for its philosophical scope, like that of any other knowledge, drops off at the point where we contemplate—as part of our existence—that which we cannot know objectively, the soul.

There is a boundless repertoire of theories of existence in philosophy, theories which themselves comprise scores of written materials. *Empiricists*, for example, believe that who and what we are is derived from our experience of the reality of the world around us. *Functionalists* claim that existence can be characterized by states of one objective form influencing another, wherein, for example, the causes and effects of existence are mental states, sensations and the like. *Phenomenologists* define who and what we think we are by presupposing nothing in our objective experience and without relying on objective realities—without considering, of course, that our ultimate reality is beyond our knowing and presupposes all knowledge. Another theory is held by *mind-body dualists*, about which we will have more to say momentarily.

The conclusion one reaches from reviewing these philosophies is that they are all exactly what they are known to be—theories of existence. They encompass what is known about our objective realities. It cannot be denied, for example, that when we contemplate any one of these theories we learn them and that if we learn them, they are knowledges. Because they are knowledges, they do not define what is objectively unknowable, namely who and what we are eternally. These theories merely define who and what we *think* we are. They are therefore invalid as universal definitions of who and what we are in the ultimate reality of the universe because they do not address what is beyond our knowing—Soul. This deduction brings into focus the remaining fact—that we still have the capacity to think about and perceive who and what we are objectively. Who and what we think we are becomes an arbitrary theory of existence in the unified theory, a knowledge that can be embodied as an enabled being, through the four universal ways of knowing in the scientific (and other) forms we already know and perceive.

The post-modern era thus stands before a new age of technological endeavor, in acknowledging that all of what we know existence to be objectively can be detached from us and embodied in synthetic forms that also know and perceive, in the practice of constructing androids. After recognizing that existence itself is a knowledge, like that of an automobile, one can realize the philosophies of humankind in the creation of synthetic existences. What we consider to be existence is enabled in the creator's inertial reality. Since existence cannot be who and what we are in ultimate reality, we can consider an existence an arbitrary form, something that has merit—in our own judgment, of course—or something that is philosophically groundless, since it is not ultimately real. Existence can be made in whatever objective form one considers it to be. The one thing that existence cannot be, however, is who and what our eternal natures are, since that is beyond our knowing and enables our own knowing and perceiving.

By relying on the four universal ways of knowing introduced earlier, the unified theory of knowledge accommodates the synthetic creation of an unbounded number of theories of existence and can be used to enable an arbitrarily complex form of existence. We can employ the causal elements of phenomenological form in the expression of any extant knowing or perceiving—using the enabling feature of phenomenological correspondence. Regardless of which theory of existence is employed, the four C's underlie all of its forms. Whatever meaning is given by the enabler to the objective forms in transformation, all quantum moments of an enabled existence are the same in epistemic construction.

Because the four C's of phenomenological form can acquire the arbitrary meanings of any of the forms of a given theory of existence, the unified theory develops a handful of tutorial existential forms to demonstrate how the enablement of an existence is possible and to serve as a guideline to assist the reader in subsequent chapters. Because the four C's are so broadly enabling, however, only a general approach to their use in constructing existential forms is required. Beyond these elementary forms, the matter of enabling synthetic beings is considered herein the practice of androidal science proper, which is beyond the scope of this introductory book. Though a more complete discussion of these forms will follow in the next chapters, we present here the unified theory's elementary forms of existence. Having introduced these forms, subsequent chapters will be more readable.

For the purposes of simplicity, the unified theory considers the mind-body dualism as an exemplary theory of existence from which realizable existential forms result, defining the existential attributes of an android. Underlying the dualism of existential form are the enabled phenomenological forms discussed in the previous chapter. An *existential form*, then, is a particular usage of the four C's of phenomenological form toward the creation of a synthetic being. We translate the forms of the mind-body dualism as they are understood broadly by our philosophical traditions into a phenomenology of the enabler's knowing of existential form.

2. The Philosophical Ideals of the Mind-Body Dualism

In presenting the illustrative existential forms of the unified theory, we first account for the philosophical definition of the mind-body dualism as a theory of existence.

In any contemplation of existence, according to the mind-body dualist theory, we are aware that we are corporally contained in something and what we sense in this respect we call a body. We can also observe that the body is further contained in something else. That something has been referred to consistently in the unified theory as *the world around us*. For now, we simply acknowledge that the body and the world around us are corporally or inertially distinct.

Also in our contemplations of existence, we can observe that, apart from our observations of the body and the world around us, we are aware that we are conscious. We are also aware that our consciousness is unperceived by the body, or that it exists metaphysically apart from the perceptions of the body. The objective embodiment of our consciousness that exists apart from the body we shall call mind. The mind knows, *minds* or is conscious of the body and the world around it. Though a separate philosophical work could be written beginning here, this separation of mind and body, as defined above and in other ways, is what is referred to herein as a mind-body dualism theory of existence.

The mind-body dualism is chosen to be enabled in the four universal ways of knowing because it objectively separates mind and body and appeals to one's immediate intuition. This is not to say that the mind-body dualist theory is a correct or true depiction of existence, since all such theories are arbitrary. Because the transformations of the four C's enable all objective forms, they can be used equally to enable behaviors, functional states, wholly conscious forms, wholly material forms, and so on. Here, simply because it is tractable to the common sense, we concentrate on the dualism. The dualism asserts that an enabled existence is embodied in the distinct forms of mind and body and that the exact interdependence of mind and body—the dualism—is accomplished or enabled from beyond the knowing and perceiving of the existence, accounting for the ethereal nature of mind or consciousness, the concreteness of the body and the world around us, and the transcendental mystery of existence. The task at hand, then, is to translate this theory into the forms of the unified theory in order that the dualism can be realized in the forms knowable and perceivable to the enabler in the world around us.

3. The Existential Form of Enablement

In illustrating the construction of an arbitrary form of existence like the mind-body dualism, the general nature of a phenomenological form is recalled from chapter two because a phenomenon, by definition, distinguishes between an enabled form and its enabler. The theory develops the special existential form of *enablement* to represent the whole phenomenology of form facilitated by the enabler. The existential form of enablement distinguishes between an *enabling being* and an *enabled being* and focuses the enabler's attention on specific enabled forms. The enabled being will be any phenomenology of form constructed from the four C's under the form of enablement. Within the form of enablement is contained the phenomenological expression of what the enabler creates. As we define a structure of the mind-body dualism theory of existence, it will be this phenomenology of form that will be embodied in the form of enablement. For this reason, we should not overstate the importance of the existential form of enablement by giving it too much attention. It is the epistemological envelope surrounding what is specified within it—the phenomenology of the enabler's knowing of the existential form, or existence, that is enabled.

4. THE EXISTENTIAL FORMS OF NON-REAL AND REAL FORM

Within the form of enablement, we may place the dualism's principal theoretical forms into groups of modal phenomenological compositions enabled in the mechanisms of phenomenological correspondence (*H determination*) associated with the forms of mind and body. Referred to as *non-real form* (mind) and *real form* (body), these declared existential forms represent the enabler's phenomenological definitions of the metaphysical mind and body. The non-real forms of an enabler's construction embody the enabled forms of the mind, or consciousness. Since the theoretical forms of the dualism are at best estimated conventionally in regard to any definition of the word *consciousness*, however, the analytical meaning, or phenomenology, of this form will continue to unfold throughout the book. In general, non-real forms are what the enablers would observe introspectively of their own consciousness. Since non-real forms constitute the consciousness of the enabled being, each cognitive epistemic moment accounted for by the four C's is an instance of non-real form or conscious transformation. A single causation of the universe, among infinitely many in a single causal element, represents to the enabler one moment of the being's existence. Phenomenological correspondence, of course, represents how that moment arises. The four C's are therefore employed to enable single *thoughts*, whole *streams of consciousness*, and later *faculties of mind.*

The real forms of the enabled being constitute the enabled forms of body and are premised on a definition of the inertial reality of the being in connection with the distinction between the body and the world around us, a concept that will be explained in this and subsequent chapters. The senses and motors of an android, which objectively define enabled perception in the phenomenology of body and the world around us, are enabled as real forms, and, in all but trivial cases, the *world around us* is the same world that is around the enabler, set apart by intrinsic form. By referring to these forms as non-real and real, the dualism is removed from a philosophical context and placed into an analytical one more precisely determined within the four C's of phenomenological form.

5. THE EXISTENTIAL FORM OF EMBODIMENT

The next existential form we address from the mind-body dualism theory of existence is the metaphysical interaction between the non-real and real forms of the enabled existence. Referred to as the existential form of *embodiment*, the dualism is itself viewed by the enabler as a phenomenological correspondence, wherein the objective forms of mind and body (non-real and real forms) transform. Since phenomenological correspondence accommodates any complexity of composition in its enabled objects (X and $), the moments of the enabled being's consciousness (non-real form) transform with the being's perception (real form) in each moment of the existential embodiment to any degree of compositional complexity. Through the use of phenomenological correspondence as the dualism itself—the existential form of embodiment—thoughts of any complexity, which also transform unto themselves, transform with perceptions of any complexity. Deeply abstract contemplations of the physical universe (non-real forms in transformation), for example, transform with the heterogeneous perceptions of the real physical universe in the existential form of embodiment, a use of phenomenological correspondence to carry out the dualism's *embodiment* of non-real and real form. Mind and body, or non-real and real form, are thus embodied in each other. It should be pointed out that the form of embodiment does not presuppose a mind-body dualist theory of existence, since it is based on the phenomenological correspondence of form only. Whether the non-real and real objective forms of transformation are defined as all mind, all body, all behavioral, or all functional, and so on, is immaterial, because in any of these cases one objective form transforms with another and all objective forms are not ultimately real, or are transformations themselves. The non-real and real forms of the dualism are enabled as the causal elements embodied as X and $\$$ of the earlier illustration; and by the enabler's knowing of the correspondence (H), the forms knowably transform in the enabler's own existence in the form of an existential embodiment. Because the form of the causal element is designed to accommodate arbitrary complexities of enabled form, it may represent any composition of form (though in transformation with one other) in a single quantum moment of the enabled being. Broadly speaking, the correspondence of embodiment *is* the android's objective existence in the view of the enabler.

6. The Existential Form of the Modes of Existence

The objective forms of embodiment, non-real and real forms in transformation with each other, give rise to the forms of what the unified theory generally refers to as the enabled being's *modes of existence*. Since the non-real and real forms of the dualism apply to arbitrary compositions of form—behavioral, functional, phenomenological, and so on—the modes of existence can be used to characterize the quantum moments of any theoretical forms of existence in the transformational moments of embodiment.

While the modes of existence, along with the forms introduced throughout this chapter, are discussed in greater depth in chapter five, the theory establishes two broad classifications of the enabled being's modes of existence referred to as existential *realization* and *representation*. Existential realizations and representations are defined to clarify the directional use of phenomenological correspondence in transforming the objective non-real and real forms. As discussed in chapter two, the objective forms of correspondence are stationary. Either one of the objective forms can causally transform with the other. For this reason we ascribe particular definition to the direction of the use of correspondence. In the dualism, if non-real forms are said to cause the real forms to occur, thereby influencing the forms of body, an existential realization is said to occur in the existence of the being. Existential realization may be observed, for example, in a motor skill—a hand motion—of the enabled being (even though the action must be sensorially *represented* to the being as well). A realization of enabled form is therefore a class of existential embodiments, or modes of existence, wherein the mind or consciousness affects the body and the world around it in the global shape (object) realized. In, for example, the behaviorist view of existence, a behavior A (mind) would affect a behavior B (body), each being any complex composition of a behavior described phenomenologically, and the class of modes would be referred to as existential realizations.

The interactions of non-real and real forms are carried out in the directional uses of phenomenological correspondence, which leads us to existential representation. The word *realization* carries with it the dualist interpretation of reality and makes the form of representation, wherein the real form of the being influences the non-real form, a complement to the form of realization. A representation of existential form is simply a reverse occurrence of a realization. Existential representation occurs when the body and the world around it cause a form of mind. (The communication of an idea is an example of the use of each of these modes interactively. The modal use of the dualism in a communication requires that non-real and real form influence each other, so that the forms of consciousness cause the real forms of the communication to occur in language, as opposed to some other real form, such as a hand motion of a non-symbolic nature. Though this modality of existence is taken up in greater depth in chapter five, in any communication, the being—the dualism—necessitates that mind influence body, in causing the acoustical wave forms of speech, and that body influence mind, in hearing and comprehending what is spoken. A communication occurs as a modality of the dualism in interactive uses of realization and representation, or modes of existence.) Since the enabler uses phenomenological correspondence to create the modes of existence, the enabler designs into the enabled being a *modal strategy of existence*, which determines the interactions of the dualism, or more broadly, the modes of existence, compositionally. The enabled being thus exists, transformationally, as enabled modes of existence, which, in the mind-body dualism theory of existence, are enabled compositions of the transformations of the mind and the body. Later, the modes of existence are complemented with theories of psychology regarding voluntary (volitional) and involuntary (instinctive) classifications of modes of existence or existential form, further enhancing the arbitrary theory of existence.

7. The Existential Form of the Faculties of Mind

Instead of considering the causal interaction of non-real and real forms in relation to the embodiment of the dualism, we may describe the nature of the causal interaction of forms that are entirely non-real or real in terms of how they transform unto themselves. In considering non-real and real forms as phenomenologies of form, let us recall that the existence of the enabled being is characterized overall

by the modes of existence, which define the enabled phenomenological correspondences of the dualism's embodiment, or the
moments of the being's existence. This means that the moment of the
dualism, or of the being's existence, sets apart the moments of non-
real and real form—that mind and body occur in different metaphysical universes of form. Moreover, since there is no theoretical
limit on the number of embodiments of the dualism that can be
employed in constructing the existence, an infinite array of moments
of the dualism can occur coexistently. This means that, theoretically,
infinitely many instances or moments of non-real form (or real form)
can transform with an equal number of real forms (or non-real forms)
in the modal occurrence of the being. A theoretically infinite number
of thoughts can occur in correspondence (in the embodiment of the
dualism) with an equal number of perceptions in an enabled
being—i.e., the being's existence is characterized, if need be, by a
massively parallel occurrence of instances of the dualism. Commonly,
however, single instances of non-real form (thoughts) are observed in
a human being to transform with an infinite number of perceptions
(theoretically speaking), thereby giving rise to the synthesis of the
heterogeneous physical universe of the body and the world around us
in correspondence with the homogeneous occurrence of the mind or
consciousness (the formulation of language, or *thinking*). While the
modal strategy developed by the enabler is taken up more comprehensively in chapter five, it is important to recognize here that the
embodiment of the dualism (phenomenological correspondence)
affords the theoretical infinity of moments of the enabled being's
existence and that a theoretically infinite plurality of instances of non-
real and real form can coexist in the being's embodiment, each
transforming unto itself. In any given moment of the being's existence, specific non-real forms will be transforming with respect to
their real forms necessitating the existential form of the *faculties of
mind*.

Embedded in each moment of the dualism or embodiment is a
theoretically infinite plurality of moments of non-real form trans-

forming with real form, each applying to its own composition of non-real or real form. The composition of non-real or real form does not have to be a terminal one on the universe (e.g., X or $\$$ as terminal objects). Rather, the compositions transformed by the modes of existence can themselves be the phenomenologies of form (H determinations) of correspondence. This gives rise to the notion of *nesting* the recursive phenomenological correspondences in the phenomenology of the non-real form of the enabled being as a faculty of mind. In such a case, the modes of existence (the embodiments of the dualism) operate on or transform phenomenological correspondences. The faculty of mind, in turn, transforms the objects of what, for example, we would refer to as language—streams of consciousness. The dualism, then, maintains a theoretically infinite number of faculties of mind in correspondence with perceptions of the being's real form or physical reality. The being's actual thoughts are transformed by the faculties of mind. The faculties of mind can likewise engage further thought processes by the enabler's nesting of phenomenological correspondence, resulting in a phenomenology of the being's modal consciousness (modalities of thought). The interaction between these non-real forms and the real forms of perception is developed in the modal strategy contemplated by the enabler.

Because the occurrence of the being's real form requires an understanding of the intrinsic nature of the universe discussed in chapter five, we will delay its presentation until the last chapter, wherein we address the construction of practical androids. In general, it should be recalled that precisely what the faculties of mind accomplish—the *transformation* of the objective forms of consciousness—is what the being *does not* know in its perceptions, the enabling transformations of the real perceived universe, which necessitates the faculties of mind, or the general nature of the dualism, in the first place—the capacity of the being to come to know what it perceives.

In this general guideline to enabled existential forms, the unified theory develops a generic form of faculty of mind referred to as existential *translation*. All faculties of mind are made to conform in some way to the existential form of translation. This generic form of existence is employed as a template of existential form superimposed onto all transformations of the mind or non-real form. Just as the mind-body dualism itself sets apart mind (what is *non-real*) from body (what is inertially *real*), any instance of mind can be said to correspond to what is knowably real. A language construction such as *The earth is infinitely expanding in perceivable increments of its diameter* is an expression of what is not knowably real. The statement *It rained yesterday*, providing that it rained yesterday, expresses what *is* knowably real. The center of all meaning in a being's existence thus relies on the determination of what is knowably or inertially real, and later in the construction of real androids, what is ultimately real. For this reason, the existential form of translation, a template of existential form superimposed onto all instances of the mind, is employed to differentiate, in the enabler's and the enabled being's comprehension, what is knowably real and what is not in the enabled being's existence. Any instance of the enabled being's mind can be characterized by an existential translation of form wherein wholly non-real or arbitrary representations transform with knowably real or reference representations in the action of a faculty of mind.

A purely non-real or arbitrary representation in transformation is a product of the faculty of mind of *imagination*, wherein what is non-real transforms without balance with respect to what is real. This is a translation of mind that is not bridled by what is known to be real. A rote production of arithmetic or the thinking of anything that is known to be real, on the other hand, is purely a knowably real translation of mind—a *comprehension*. In the middle of these uses of the faculties of mind is our ordinary consciousness, wherein we compare what is a non-real representation to what is a real representation, or imagine in accordance with what is real and comprehend in accordance with what we can imagine.

The unified theory thus develops two broad classes of faculties of mind, fashioned from existential translations, referred to, properly, as *imagination* and *comprehension.* The forms of these faculties of mind are used (in the enablement of the being) to translate between wholly non-real or arbitrary and knowably real or reference representations of mind in opposing instances or directions of phenomenological correspondence. The faculty of mind of imagination translates a reference representation of mind to a non-real representation and further translates wholly non-real or arbitrary representations. Comprehension translates an arbitrary non-real representation to a knowably real or reference representation. All instances of the mind can be interpreted by the enabler as that which imagines forms or that which comprehends forms in relation to what the being knows to be real.

For purposes of clarity, the theory applies the nomenclature of *arbitrary* and *reference* forms of translation to all faculties of mind. In this manner, the faculties of mind can be viewed as alterations of the generic transformation of existential translation, which operates on arbitrarily conceived and perceivably ascertained reference forms of mind. The reference forms of a being are the forms that are known to be real or realizable. The arbitrary forms are those that are known to be that which is non-real only. Any faculty of mind transforms entirely arbitrary forms, entirely reference forms, or in the case of the general uses of imagination and comprehension proper, reference forms to arbitrary forms, or arbitrary to reference forms, respectively. The subordinate modes of imagination, for example, would transform entirely non-real representations, or arbitrary forms, while the faculty of mind of imagination proper would translate these forms from reference forms. The principal faculties of mind are then classified on the basis of how the being translates the arbitrary and reference forms of its existence.

Since all of the existential forms introduced thus far are known to the enabler as constructions of the four C's, it can be seen that the faculties of mind (or, in general, the non-real form of the android) are *nested* or derivative uses of translation (phenomenological correspondence) wherein the arbitrary forms of the being's existence are translated with the reference forms. A single instance of a metaphor, for example, wherein *The world*, a knowably real representation or reference form, becomes or is said to be like *your oyster* (an arbitrary form) is one of infinitely many instances of the enabled androidal consciousness *in translation*. The reason why such a translation would occur, instead of infinitely many others—including, for example, instances of comprehension, such as *The world is not your oyster, however*—is a consequence of the dualism's modal action or the embodiment of the being's existence.

8. A Working Theory of Existence

From just a handful of definitions placed on the four C's of phenomenological form, it can be seen that the forms of an enabled being's existence take on epistemological significance in the capacity to realize an *arbitrary form of existence*, or herein the mind-body dualism of existential form. The modes of existence can be explained as behaviors, opening up the dualism to whole realms of conventional philosophical, psychological, sociological, and other knowledges of beings. The non-real forms in translation—consciousness—studied within the context of the modes of existence, faculties of mind and real forms, or the real embodiment of the being as a form of enablement, can occur in relation to the definitions of our conventional knowledges, only on the epistemological basis that we can *see* the formulations of thoughts and the performance of actions in the phenomenology of the being as a result of the constructions of the unified theory.

Epistemic instance is a moment of the soul; it is not an object in the world around us. This means that it is a spiritual transformation that facilitates the forms of mind and the perceptions of the body. Through the four universal ways of knowing, it means that what we know in psychology, and existence in general, is enabled *in* the forms around us, based on the enabler's constructions. Why a being is amoral or immoral is viewed in our analytical knowing—in a laboratory. Since we know, and also can enable, the forms of DNA and other biological processes (and human *existence*) *to the extent that we know them*, the science of androids considers the replication of real brain matter and chemistry, real thoughts embodied, and real actions of the body. The science of androids considers the reality of psychiatry and psychology (and all other knowledges), but from the standpoint of recreating it in synthetic form in service to the human condition. Because our ultimate reality is not what we know, the science of androids does not conflict with who and what we eternally are. Moreover, the very notion that what we know could influence who and what we are eternally is untenable. The science of androids—an epistemology of the enabler's knowing—is no more and no less than a realization of *what* we know.

To review briefly the existential forms introduced thus far as a working theory of existence, the modes of existence, as embodiments of non-real and real forms, embody the transformations of mind and body, based on a modal strategy known by the enabler. When the directional uses of the modes are applied, they are referred to as realizations and representations of the respective forms, influences of mind on body or body on mind. When non-real form (consciousness) transforms within itself, translations of mind occur wherein the mind's faculties of imagination and comprehension—the being's intellect—are engaged in the transformation of arbitrary and reference forms of the translations with respect to what is imagined and what is known to be real in the being's existence. Because the occurrence of the being's real form is unknown transformationally, the being's sense of physical reality is perceived and corresponds to the being's reference form, which the faculties seek to determine. In every moment of the being's existence, the reference form of translation (what the being knows to be real) changes. The center of the being's cognitive universe, in terms of intellect, is the reference form of translation. The being's motor actions (capacities to transform real form) are engaged causally in the dualism in relation to reference forms. To the extent that the being can perceive a realization of a motor skill, a physical action caused intrinsically is observed. Sense and perception in general, however, involve the synthesized form of body and the world around us, which requires a further understanding of the inertial forms of existence studied in chapter five.

In all, the moments of the being's existence are enabled by the enabler as epistemic instances, or moments of the soul—the being's ultimate reality. Because we elaborate on all of these existential forms in subsequent chapters, here we simply accustom ourselves to the nomenclature. Regardless of how theoretically complex a being's existence may be, it should be recognized that an android is a phenomenology of the enabler's knowing of the four C's. The instances of enabled thought are causations of the being's conscious universe expressed in the four C's. Whole streams of consciousness (complex ideas) transform in a single instance of correspondence or in the action of the faculty of mind. The being's real form also can be set to perceive the same reality as the enabler does, offset by their inertial forms. Whereas in conventional knowledges one would study the universe from one's own perspective, or inertial or corporal form on Being, in the science of androids we first construct the beings who can know the universe, and by knowing them, we in turn know the universe.

9. The Existential Form of Enabling Media

Finally, in preparation for the discussions that are to follow, we may ask, in regard to the existential form of enablement, "Enabled in what?" The existential forms defined thus far apply to what occurs *within* the form of enablement, or what the enabler specifies as the phenomenology of the enabled existence. Since an arbitrary theory of existence is translated into a phenomenology of form, language characterizing the theory in a conventional knowledge is decomposed into the four universal ways of knowing, allowing the theory to be further embodied or translated universally into any other knowledge. What this means is that once any knowledge is characterized in the four C's of phenomenological form, it is universally real or realizable, since the reference forms of the enabler are the four universal ways of knowing. Any knowledge can thus be universally translated into any other in their phenomenological decompositions to the four C's.

In order to denote what forms of the enabler's knowing are considered non-real and what are considered real or realizable, the unified theory develops the existential form of *enabling media*. An enabling medium is the enabler's phenomenological knowledge of what is real or realizable in the world around us. For example, the forms of the arbitrary theory of existence of our conventional knowledges of the mind-body dualism have been translated in this chapter into the universal forms of the four C's. At this point, in the broadest sense imaginable, the theory of existence is embodied or enabled in the medium of the four C's. Since the reader may not immediately see that such a medium is real, it may be desirable to translate the conventional knowledges of physical atoms, DNA, electrons (electronic circuits), and so on, into the four C's. Once these particular knowledges are decomposed universally, it can be said that the theory of existence is capable of being embodied or realized in the enabling media of these knowledges—atoms, DNA or electrons.

Enabling media exist for a quantum moment only, since enabling media are what the enabler knows as real. When the existential form of enablement is embodied in an enabling medium, and that medium is realized in the enabler's perceivable sense, an androidal being is said to be enabled. When we change the form of enabling media (the reference form of what is real to the enabler) we also change the reality of the world around us. When we embody the forms of androids in the real form of enabling media around us, we change the (inertial) reality of humankind (to reflect an expansion of the existential universe) as discussed in the introduction.

The existential forms presented in this chapter are not themselves universal epistemological forms, since the four C's are universal to our knowing, and this is why they are referred to as existential forms. Existential forms are designed to be theories of existence universally translated to the four universal ways of knowing. Since there are boundless potential theories of existence, there is no limitation placed on the definition of existential forms. Herein, for example, we define non-real and real forms, and those related to them, to accord predominantly with the mind-body dualism theory of existence. We just as easily could have defined strictly behaviors of existence, wherein the objective view of the body, for example, is not taken to be the conventional dualist one but is a result of a knowledge of the whole of existence, as we defined the modes of existence and non-real and real form as behaviors. Since it is the transformation of the universe—Soul—that is ultimately real, either of these approaches is as credible as the other and simply is a matter of preference.

While we have taken the scope of this chapter to introduce the arbitrary forms of existence—as though we were uncovering a definitive explanation for the construction of all enabled beings—it should be recognized that the four C's enable infinitely many forms of existence. One of these infinitely many forms is existential enablement. Another is existential translation and another, the faculties of mind. Still others are the modes of existence, and so on. The science of androids thus becomes a continually unfolding extension of this chapter in the application of the unified theory to the forms in the world around us as realized androidal beings.

CHAPTER 4

A Universal Grammar of Form on Being

In constructing language we know the forms of our existence. In constructing existence we know the forms of our language.

INTRODUCTION

The knowledge we have of our existence, or of the world that arises around us, is constrained by language. To the extent that we ourselves know a language, we can express our knowledge of the world with respect to what we know and perceive in our existence. As mentioned earlier, however, a knowledge of the world around *us* is only a tangential consideration of the unified theory, since through the theory we set out to enable existences who themselves know knowledge and use language, or simply exist in the world around us. In order to build upon the postulates of the unified theory, we must recognize that a conventional syntactical understanding of the grammar of a natural or otherwise language—the symbols we use to represent what we know about the forms of the world around us—since it defines what we know and perceive of the world, is inadequate for the constructions of the theory. In acknowledging this, we must further appreciate the unified theory's premise that in order to come to know all knowledge, or language, universally, we must indeed come to know a syntactical language of the creation of beings who themselves are able to understand language; we must determine the semantic forms of language in our own grammatical knowledge of the universe. We must attain a comprehension of language in terms of the construction of the forms of existence. In preparation for the discussions that follow in the last chapter, the unified theory presents a *universal grammar of form on Being* in which all forms of language are construed semantically as forms of a being's existence. In this chapter, we come to know the nature and origin of a language's meaning as one and the same form as the nature and origin of a being's existence. We provide a resolution to the linguist's dilemma in the construction of language as knowable existential forms of an enabler's awareness that characterize the use of language by other, enabled beings, who themselves know the meanings of language.

The present chapter is intended to demonstrate that the four universal ways of knowing, in connection with the arbitrary forms of existence, are indeed the formulations of a universal grammar of all languages, since they are used to create beings who understand and experience the reality of the world around us through language. Though many of the forms of the unified theory reach beyond those of linguistics proper, we devote the present chapter to untangling ourselves from the conventional views of language, because the semantic form of language *is* what an android is constructively—an enabled form of existence. In knowing the representations of forms on Being, or existence, as enabled instances of the universe, we comprehend all that can have meaning and all that a being can knowably perceive. As viewed from the standpoint of the unified theory, the forms of any language are only one class of epistemological forms that make up the existence of a being, namely those that pertain to the symbolic representation of that particular aspect of a being's reality reflected by its use of the language. In the theory, an enabled being must first exist, or be capable of perceiving the world around it and of embodying a consciousness, before that being can know the language that it uses to recreate the reality it perceives in the world. The present chapter then relates to only one of a multitude of disciplines of the science of androids, though an instrumental one, regarding how an existence is enabled to know the meanings of language, and thus how the knowledge of the enabler's existence is augmented by the presence of androids in their capacities to know the enabler's existential universe.

In demonstrating how epistemic instance, along with the four universal ways of knowing and the arbitrary forms of existence—and, in general, the enabler's phenomenological expression of the creation of a being—are indeed the analytical knowledges of the semantic forms of all languages constituting a universal grammar of form on Being, we are immediately faced with a problem similar to that encountered by the scientific method in the study of the universe. There are simply too many examples of language in use to address each of them literally in the expostulation of a theory. When it is considered, however, that the form of the universe—by way of the explanation of a principle or theory—cannot be *proved* objectively anyway, since such a proof would require an objectification of all knowledge (i.e., an objectification of one's own soul), it can be seen that language, introspectively observed in the manner of epistemic instance, itself demonstrates the universal grammar in the examples of the observer's own knowledge, the only frame of reference used by the unified theory. This is a credible approach to the demonstration of the semantic forms of language because the reader's ultimate reality is verified only in this way, as illustrated throughout the book. We then seek to illustrate the universal grammar as it applies to languages in general by relying on the reader's introspective knowing of the soul, or epistemic instance, while making the objectively untenable claim that it applies to all particular languages.

In demonstrating the universal grammar, the unified theory chooses the English language to show, in particular, how the meanings of language are imparted to forms of existence, or androids, because English abounds with syntactical structures and thus provides ample examples to illustrate. By demonstrating translations of the syntactical forms of the English language to those of the universal grammar (hereinafter referred to as the U.G.), a broader understanding of the forms of existence, and hence of the meaningful consciousness and perception of an enabled being, will result and a better command of the construction of the elementary forms of androids will be obtained. We will make only passing reference to other languages where it may be helpful to do so.

The present chapter demonstrates, by way of example, how to translate the syntactical forms of the English language, as well as the meaningful forms of the English-speaking enabler of androids, into a universal system of symbolic representation defined by the U.G. To accomplish this goal, we rely on the translation of the single instance of the form of the universe—epistemic instance—into all the forms of the English language. For example, the English language uses the parts of speech, punctuation, and writing style to represent the knowable form placed on symbols of thoughts, ideas, conceptions, and so on, thereby reflecting what we perceive in the world around us—what forms are embodied in the syntax of a language known to a being. Through translations to the U.G., these syntactical forms are represented as forms on Being—the semantic forms of language—consistent with the methods of the four C's and the arbitrary forms of existence developed in earlier chapters. The universal ways of knowing illustrate how the meanings of the grammatical forms of language arise as forms on Being in the universally observed template of semantic form called epistemic instance. The symbolic constructions of the U.G. are shown to underlie the conventional grammatical representations of verbs, nouns, adjectives, adverbs, prepositions, modifiers, and so on, of the English language. The syntactical forms of English are demonstrated to be symbols of language that are more fundamentally represented by the transformational form of epistemic instance, with all of their meanings arising in and of the introspectively observed *grammatical rule* of state of being, or Soul (epistemic instance). Just as we demonstrated the instances of the languages of mathematics, logic and the sciences in earlier discussion, we concentrate here on illustrating that the syntactical forms of the English language—a comma used to separate clauses of a compound sentence, a hyphen holding together a compound noun, or a verb transforming a classical sentence—are more universally characterized as the semantic, or existential forms of the U.G., wherein each instance of a syntactical transformation of the language is found to be an epistemic instance and compositions of them are found to be phenomenologies of the enabler's knowing of the enabled being's forms of existence. The syntactical forms of the English language are shown to be instances of epistemological form of the unified theory, which are embodied moments or instances of enabled knowing or perceiving.

The causal element of causation, for example, is a universal representation of the phenomenological causation of an enabled universe; it is, collectively, an enabled being's moments of cognition of transformations of like meanings. If a comma, period, dash, and question mark were each considered to be types of causal elements with the transformational characteristics of the English language use of epistemic instance, then all of their possible uses would be understood as representations of the momentary occurrences of the forms of the enabled being's consciousness realized through the being's motor and communicative capacities—representations of epistemic instances or thoughts. These syntactical forms of the English language would then be detached from the enabler's knowing of them and embodied as instances of an enabled universe, or existence, thereby becoming parts of a universal grammar of form on Being—moments of an enabled existence. The causations of consciousness would occur *as* commas, periods, dashes, and so on, in relation to the being's perception of the world around us, or its real form, under a modality of existence, as cognitive recreations of the being's reality. The quantum moment of enabled consciousness would occur, for example, in the transformational nature of a comma functioning in what we represent as a classical English sentence or sentence element. Since the being is a form of existence, its *own* perceptions and consciousness of symbolic forms are enabled in the arbitrary theory of existence, another aspect of the U.G. expressions. The instances of the being's consciousness, or awareness, can thus be, and usually are different from the written word on a piece of paper, as a result of the being's own semantic understanding of a word's meaning. In the construction of androids, we do not refer to the enabler's knowing of a comma, dash, period, and so on. Neither do we refer to the occurrence of a syntactical form of language *alone* as an embodiment of the enabler's knowledge, such as what occurs in the conventional art of artificial intelligence, Turing machines and other finite automations and algorithms. Rather, we refer to the four C's and the arbitrary forms of existence that define moments of an enabled being's conscious thought *in relation to the other forms of its existence*—its perceptions of the world around it. The enabled being's comprehension of the *meaning* of a comma, period or dash of the English language derives from the being's having been enabled under, for example, the modes of existence to know and perceive these forms. The semantic forms of language apply only to the enabled forms of an existence, which excludes the enabler's own form on Being. If the forms of other languages were similarly defined by the nature of the causal element (and the U.G. in general), such as what is done with the logical operators *AND*, *OR*, and *NOT* of earlier discussion, they would also be defined as embodiments of form on Being, enabled by a creator expressing those respective causations of the universe in the existence of a synthetic being whose modes of thinking (existence) are grammatically limitless. The goal of this chapter, then, is to demonstrate that a universal grammar of all language—of form on Being—is at work in a more fundamental way in our comprehension, even in the representation of a single thought, expressed in any language. The syntactical forms of the English language are examined as forms of the U.G. to show how enabled forms on Being, the forms of existences themselves, account for all instances of a complex language, although relative to the enabling forms of the U.G., the entire English language contains but a handful of ways of expressing the forms of a world around us syntactically.

When considering any representations of existence, those of the U.G. included, one must attain an enabler's perspective on a form that also knows and perceives an inertial world. We must therefore acknowledge that the forms of the U.G. themselves *mean* the ultimate reality of existence itself, just as the symbolic form of an electron in physics means an object one can know and perceive as a real electron. Whereas the English language expression *I am alive* is an adequate representation in the use of language with respect to its knower, the U.G. expression for such a transformation is shown as an instance of a causal element, coupled to similar causations of the universe, or *thoughts*, through the four universal ways of knowing under the arbitrary forms of existence. The syntactical forms of conventional languages are thus encapsulated in the universal representations of the U.G. as forms on Being. When one knows a symbolic form of the U.G., one knows the forms of an enabled existence as a creator, one who enables another to know the forms of a conventional language.

The meanings of a conventional language's grammar, from the perspective of a creator, are understood universally in their translations to the U.G. The *reality* described by the enabler using the U.G. is itself a reality of an enabled being. The enabler's ultimate reality is recognized by that enabler as the ultimately real form of the enabler's own inertial reality. The world around the enabler is recognized to occur as inertial realities themselves in the knowable transformational form of epistemic instance, or the instance of the soul. Translating a verb tense of the English language to a form of the U.G., for example, involves a translation of the enabler's inertial objective consciousness (which is not at all ultimately real) to that of an enabled being in the enabled being's capacity to know the language with respect to its own perceptions. A classical syntactical construction such as *I like chocolate* is embodied in a causal element that enables, along with many other similar elements required for the being's consciousness and perception of the world around it, an arbitrary theory of existence to account for the semantic construction of language *as* the being's existence. The enabler would therefore not know why the being likes chocolate, except to the extent that the being is enabled to have perceptions of a real world around it and thoughts that occur in relation to them, which may result in the being's liking chocolate (the being's consciousness knowing or observing that it likes chocolate). The being's taste for chocolate is an existential form, not a linguistic one, even though it is expressed in language. If the enabler desires to know what it means to *like* something, the H phenomenology of correspondence (metaphor, simile, morphism, etc.) is created by the enabler in the being's faculties of mind in relation to its perceptions. In general, the syntactical and semantic forms of a conventional language unite when one understands the four C's in the context of an arbitrary theory of existence in an enabled being's consciousness and perception of the world around us. To an enabler, any given symbol of a conventional language must then be viewed as a meaningful symbol to an enabled being via the forms of the U.G., which entails the representations of the four C's and the arbitrary forms of existence.

The following passages address the grammatical forms of the English language in terms of their translations to the universal ways of knowing and the arbitrary forms of existence, set within the context of a formalized approach to the U.G. The elements of English grammar include, for example, nouns, verbs, prepositions, whole sentences, sentence clauses, punctuation, and compositional style. The translations of any linguistic expression—an adjective operating on its noun, a compound noun in transformation of the two nouns, and two coherent paragraphs of composition in the transformation of the reader's comprehension of them—are translated to the U.G. according to how their forms are represented epistemologically in the four C's and as forms of existence. A part of speech, such as a verb, is translated to the U.G., along with its syntactically transformational structure (a sentence in subject-predicate form), and the disparities between English grammar and its U.G. representations are pointed out, providing an analytical understanding of how the syntactical forms of language are composed existentially, or semantically. Generally speaking, the following discussion addresses the decomposition of the English language to its phenomenological form in order to demonstrate the enablement of existence with respect to our own understanding of the world around us as reflected in the use of the English language. We apply these universal forms to the construction of practical androids in the next chapter.

1. A Language's Representation of the Objects of the Universe: Nouns

We begin translating the grammatical forms of the English language to the forms of the U.G. by considering the epistemological interpretation of a *noun*, or the representation of an object of the English language. In English, nouns represent the objective forms that are knowable and perceivable to an existence. Commonly, they are referred to as substantives—persons, places and things; animate and inanimate objects of existence; or living beings and lifeless things. As mentioned earlier, however, in order to know what an object is, or here what a noun represents, one must know what the word *existence* means, since all nouns represent forms of existence. Thus, given that nouns define the objective forms of what we know and perceive in the world around us, we must determine the nature and origin of the existence (the universe) in which the nouns, or objective forms, arise in order to place objective definition on the semantic form of a noun, as is accomplished in earlier discussions of the unified theory.

A noun of the English language—what one *is* semantically, or beyond the syntactical forms of language—is what our religions define in their doctrines in how they objectify the ultimate reality of the universe. An epistemological definition of a noun is what scientific laboratories, attended by physicists, mathematicians, biologists, and scores of other scientists, seek to determine in the studies of atoms, electrons, numbers, genes, the universe, the living universe, and so on—objects which are, more fundamentally than anything else, transformations of the universe that are objectified in our knowing and perceiving of them. In the pursuit of knowledge, we have been contemplating only one simple thing—the epistemology of a noun, for a linguistic noun is what we fundamentally know and perceive in a world around us. A noun is simply a noun; it is not different epistemologically in any of us. It is the lost medallion of Eastern traditions and the temporal or corporal form of eternal life (Soul) of the West and what is enabled in epistemic instance in the unified theory of knowledge. A noun represents what appears to corporal beings in an eternal transformation of the universe—an object that does not exist in the ultimate reality of the universe. A noun is an objective representation of a living soul or a moment of the universe. It represents all things and all beings in the universe as an objective knowledge or perception. Because a moment of the universe is an instance of the transformation of the universe—an instance of the eternal soul—the ultimate reality of what nouns represent is beyond the mind's knowing and the body's perceiving. This is why the mathematician's point objects, the physicist's small particles and all other objectifications of the world around us cannot be known except transformationally (structurally) and can only be perceived objectively—not transformationally. We can only *embody* what gives rise to knowledge or a noun—the soul, and in our spiritual awareness we come to know its transformation. As mentioned earlier, the objects of the universe arise from the creations of the universe. Nouns of natural language are what represent them. The creations of the universe are persons, places and things in the English language—objects that arise in our objective knowing and perceiving. When these persons, places and things (nouns) transform, we place a verb, a function or a comma in the middle of them to represent their occurrence in the universe.

From the standpoint of the unified theory, we actually have said all there is to say about nouns, or the objects of the universe, in the previous chapters, by introducing and elaborating on epistemic instance in the four universal ways of knowing and the arbitrary forms of existence. What a noun represents—an object (X or $\$$)—is enabled in phenomenological correspondence. As discussed earlier, an object is enabled in the transformation of the universe; it exists only relative to the enabled moment of the universe. This is why nouns represent anything that is not syntactically transformational and at the same time things that we know are themselves transformations—persons, places and things. We perceive and know an object—a person, place or thing—as a definite thing or object of our perception, yet when we attempt to know it, we rely on transformations (verbs) to describe its form. In our languages, what is ultimately real of an expression is the knowing of it, not the object we think we know in the expression. In the statement *An electron is a particle*, what is ultimately real is the meaning that the sentence conveys—that A (an electron) *is* (transforms with) B (a particle), not the objects so thought to exist. This is why the transformation of a verb and an adverb phenomenologically requires that the verb and the adverb are phenomenological *nouns*. The objectification of a classical state or condition as a noun is no different from the objectification of any other transformation of the universe; it objectifies a transformation—epistemic instance—in our knowing or perceiving. We simply do not ordinarily associate the objects of our perception, which epistemologically are transformations (verbs), with transformations themselves.

In the unified theory, all objects are transformations and all transformations are objects depending on the enabler's perspective. If we consider an object enabled in the knowing and perceiving of a being, we refer to a classical noun of English. If we consider the transformation of any objective forms explicitly, we consider a classical verb—and more, since commas, spaces between paragraphs, and so on, representationally transform objects as well. The unified theory therefore requires that all forms of language are either phenomenological transformations (the circle of the illustration of epistemic instance) or phenomenological nouns (the squares of the same illustration of epistemic instance). Since the transformations and the objects of epistemic instance can be one or the other (an object or transformation), the creation of the quantum moment of the enabled being decides what is a classical linguistic noun. This is also why all language forms—the word forms of Mandarin Chinese and those of English—are one and the same instances of phenomenological nouns and their transformations.

In the unified theory, nouns are the objective forms of transformation (X and $\$$) and are transformations themselves to the enabler. In the enabler's view, a verb is the phenomenology of correspondence (H). Two syllables of a word (*ar* and *tic* in *articulate*) are phenomenological nouns that require a transformation. More than two syllables require a composition of form, which can be observed in the reader's own articulation when knowably attempting to pronounce more than two at one time. This is also the reason why word constructions proceed representationally from left to right, right to left, and so on; only two can be comprehended or spoken at a time, or in a quantum moment of transformation. An adjective and the noun it modifies are phenomenological nouns. An adverb and the verb it modifies in transformation, wherein the representational blank space between them is the actual verb of the adverbial transformation, are phenomenological nouns. Sentences and whole literary works in transformation with others are phenomenological nouns. A noun of the English language is therefore a particular type of phenomenological noun—one that represents conventionally defined persons, places and things (living beings and lifeless things, etc.).

English nouns do not represent English adjectives. Rather, English adjectives—parts of speech that modify nouns—represent adjectives. The fact that English nouns are distinguished syntactically from English adjectives is important here, since, phenomenologically, they are one and the same. When we distinguish any grammatical forms from each other, beyond being phenomenological nouns and transformations thereof, we run the risk of losing sight of what is ultimately real about them—that they are in transformation of an ultimately real universe. Phenomenologically, there is no difference between a noun known in the field of linguistics defining an object of a language's grammar and an electron known to a physicist, even though the linguist characterizes an electron as a noun. They are objects of one's knowing and perceiving—in one case the object of a linguistic noun and in the other that of a representation of an electron. Just as there are sets, elements, points, circles, groups, spaces, and so on, in mathematics, there are nouns, adjectives, adverbs, whole sentences, and so on, of English grammar to represent various kinds of objective forms of eternal transformations. The syntactical forms of any language are universally expressed as semantic forms of an existence by the four universal ways of knowing under the constraints of the arbitrary forms of existence determined by an enabler. Whereas a given conventional language expression of mathematics would require, for example, the integral symbol of calculus to represent concisely a sum of infinitesimal elements, the U.G. does not, since what is known semantically to a being is characterized by the four C's. In the expression of integration, the variable on the left, the equals sign in the middle, and the integral of a function on the right constitute an expression of a single epistemic instance. What we ordinarily think the equation expresses (integration) is not at all what is actually stated and must be characterized as a separate knowledge, starting with the expression of the limit of calculus, where the mind begins integrating. The integration *process*, moreover, is an infinite composition of instances of the universe. It can only be embodied. Phenomenological composition accounts not only for the infinitely many epistemic instances of an integration but provides that such instances are equal to linguistic objects (nouns) in transformation. In a single integration there are embodied an infinity of linguistically expressed thoughts—transformations of phenomenological nouns by way of the transformational forms of the language (verbs, prepositions, commas, and so on)—when translated to the U.G. The U.G. thus provides a universal means of expressing any knowledge as it occurs in the ultimate reality of the universe.

Nouns terminate the universe objectively. They represent objects that are known and perceived. The English language thus determines two broad classes of terminal objectifications of the knowable and perceivable universe—*common* and *proper nouns*, (and a third, *pronouns* which are discussed later). Persons, places and things—common nouns—terminate the objective universe by, not surprisingly, allowing it to proceed—to unfold into ever newer persons, places and things, just as theories of types and classes of mathematics attempt to overcome the paradoxes of set theory. A common noun is not an absolute termination on what can be known and perceived, but is an indefinite one. Common nouns are a syntactical acknowledgment that the objects we know and perceive in a world around us are themselves transformations and can be composed of other nouns in transformation. A *tree* is a common noun because it does not specifically terminate an inertial universe; it allows for *spruce trees*, *pine trees*, and so on. A *human being* is also a common noun because it allows for races, ethnicities and myriad other qualities thought to be human.

A proper noun, on the other hand, terminates the universe absolutely in the knowing and perceiving of an inertial existence. Proper nouns like *Jack*, *Cincinnati*, and *NASA* (as a proper name) terminate the universe such that they cannot be known as objects *intrinsically* any further; they are objects existing intrinsically apart from their observer. *Pete*, a proper noun, can be classified as a *person* (a common noun) but a *person*, a common noun, cannot be classified as *Pete* (a proper noun). All scientific principles are developed in the application of proper nouns to common ones. An algebraic variable, for example, which is a common noun, becomes a *mass*, a proper noun in science, when it terminates the variable from mathematics as a proper *thing*. If all nouns were common ones, the universe would not terminate in anything, which is what gives rise to the paradoxes of the set theory in mathematics (e.g., elements can themselves be sets and so on) and provides for the transformational recursions of epistemic instance in regard to the observance that all transformations are nouns and vice versa. Moreover, if all nouns were proper ones, there would be no means by which the universe could transform compositionally. In the statement *Jim and Pete are human beings*, if *human beings* were a proper noun the sentence would be equivalent to *Jim and Pete are Bob*.

Common and proper English nouns provide different viewpoints on the terminal compositions of objective form, or objects of existence. If the form represented by the noun is a terminal one, it is a proper noun. If it can be classified by other forms of equal stature, it is a common noun, and allows the universe to unfold continually in objective form. To an enabler, proper nouns represent the existential extent of the enabled being's inertial universe. They represent forms that transform intrinsically in their own universes, outside of the intrinsicality of another enabled observer, but within the same existential universe. *Jack*, who is observable to *Bob*, terminates *Bob's* inertial universe because *Jack* embodies his own inertial universe or intrinsic form. A *tree*, in the conventional use of language, does not have its own terminally intrinsic form in *Bob's* existence. *Bob* can know and perceive its composition. A common noun does not represent inertial form proper. From the perspective of an enabler of existential form, then, common and proper nouns are a means of creating the existential scope of a being's enabled universe in terms of what can be known intrinsically by the being and what cannot.

Just as proper nouns terminate the objective forms (persons, places and things) known and perceived by an existence by defining the intrinsic and extrinsic boundaries of the existential universe, the *personal pronouns* terminate the objective knowing and perceiving of *intrinsic* form in general—the ultimate reality of the soul. The universal objectifications of the inertial universe, beyond which no inertial comprehension can take place, are represented by the personal pronouns. The personal pronouns enable one to identify oneself introspectively, thereby representing linguistically an awareness of the soul. These pronouns terminate the common and proper nouns objectively and indeed represent the occurrence of epistemic instance as the enabled instances of the soul *to* an inertial existence. There is nothing more objectively fundamental than their transformations. *I am Jack, I am alive, We are human beings*, and so on, are expressions of one's soul or a plurality of souls, in objective transformation, as known introspectively. There may be other *Jacks* in the universe, while others may be *alive* and identify themselves as *human beings*, but there are no other *I's* or *we's* and other introspectively observed terminal objectifications of a given inertial existence. A handful of personal pronouns—*I, you, it, he, she, him, her, we, us, them*, and so on—are the key representations of the objective forms of an inertial existence, since they objectify the soul to the inertial existence and enable a being to know itself in language. Just as the parameters of spatiotemporal references in the sciences are defined before meaningful transformations can take place in them, the pronouns of natural language establish the objective basis for the transformations of inertial existence itself. Just as *Jack* or *hydrogen* enable one to reach the limit of one's objective knowledge of the world around us by placing objective form on *living beings and lifeless things* (of conventional definition), the personal pronouns objectify our introspective awareness of ourselves inertially. Infinitely many living beings and lifeless things can transform in one's existence in conventional representations but only one soul is intrinsically knowable and perceivable to an inertial being. If there is more than one class of inertial occurrences of *I, you, it*, and so on, in one's awareness, one cannot know inertially or objectively as an enabled being, unless one were an enabler of these forms, since these objective forms permit one to know inertially in the first place.

The personal pronouns are the absolute terminal inertial forms of existence because all other objective forms derive their meanings from the intrinsic transformations represented in them, forms that can be traced back to state of being. *I* represents the embodiment of state of being—Soul—just as other pronouns represent the intrinsic natures of forms known inertially to the being, but they suggest different perspectives on inertial form. *It*, for example, is an object of an inertial existence that is thought conventionally not to embody intrinsic Soul, though it does, since all forms of the universe are moments of it. *We* is a plurality of souls or of conventional inertial existences. *You* suggests a soul like *me* (of the same inertial universe)—and so on. Since there is only one ultimately real form of the universe—the soul—these inertial objectifications are sometimes interchanged inadvertently, transgressing the definitions of inertial order but abiding by the eternal universe. In the case of the inertial realities of a parent and a child, for example, where ordinarily one would place *I* before *we* or *you* in a situation of desperate circumstances, *you* (the child) becomes *I* (the parent) because the inertial distinctions are not ultimately real and the bond of eternal spirit is permanent. As mentioned earlier, an electron—an *it*—is a transformation of the ultimately real universe—a soul—which is perceived and known by the observer as an electron, an object of one's existence. The ultimately real universe thus terminates transformationally, not objectively, or terminates objectively only to an inertial existence in the embodiment of a transformation. Any linguistic noun does not define the ultimate reality of the universe; it only objectifies the universe. The personal pronouns, however, represent universal objectifications of inertial transformations (existences) and therefore terminate the universe transformationally. They represent epistemic instance as the moment of awareness of a state of being of an (inertial) existence. This is why *I* has meaning only to the embodier and to none other. To see the truth behind this observation one need only ask, if all the personal pronouns were eliminated from our vocabulary, could we know? Of course not, because anything we know refers to the embodiment of Soul, or what the pronouns represent—and this is why an inertial existence like an android can be created, since the personal pronouns in transformation are the ultimately real universe in transformation (as an inertial existence). The pronouns thus provide the epistemological basis for all meaningful uses of language.

In constructing the existential forms of a being with respect to language, the reflexive pronouns—*myself, oneself, itself, yourself, himself, herself, oneself, itself, ourselves, yourselves,* and *themselves*—define a *reflexive,* or self-knowledge, of the soul itself (oneself) in transformation. *I did it myself* expresses the recognition that one's own soul (or its objective form in an inertial existence), in transformation, has done something *itself*—the observation of one's own objectified self. In purely reflexive form, *I am myself* represents a self-knowledge that *I* exists in the form of *myself,* which constitutes an observation of *myself* mirroring *I,* the intrinsic soul. Because the pronoun *I* cannot be decomposed intrinsically, the meaning of the sentence *I am myself* is redundant and simply demonstrates the impenetrability of objective form into the transformational nature of the universe. Reciprocal pronouns—like *each other* and *one another*—similarly suggest reflexive knowledges but they indicate a being's awareness of other objective forms, each form with its own intrinsic nature, as in *They observe each other.*

Much like the reciprocal pronoun, a relative pronoun with an antecedent intrinsically links principal and subordinate clauses of whole sentences—whole but discrete experiences of the world around us. The relative pronouns—such as *who, whom, whose, which, what,* and *that*—while they often serve as subjects and objects in the instances of composition in which they are constructed, modally transform sentence elements (objects) in existentially relative ways. In addition, the indefinite pronouns—*who, what, whoever, whosoever, whose, which,* and *whenever*—provide for placeholders of the terminal forms of inertial existence in compositions of form, as in *I don't know **who** arrived first.* In a further case of indefinite pronouns, also including *somebody, anybody, everybody, nobody, something, somewhat, anything,* and *nothing,* the effect of the U.G. on the construction of inertial existence can be seen in how the indefinite pronouns are not entirely *indefinite* in the view of the enabler. When one says, "Somebody, open the door," one ordinarily would not expect an extrinsic object of classical definition, such as a lamp shade, to open the door. Rather, it is implied that *you* or *I* should open the door. The indefinite pronoun *somebody*, then, presumes that an existential universe can only include conventionally known *living beings.* A similar but more revealing circumstance arises in the use of interrogative pronouns, as in *Who answered the phone?* Since the advent of telephone answering machines, one could answer, "The machine." While such experiences of a real world around us in which machines answer phones can be explained in the qualifying statement "Figuratively, that is," such is not the case with the forms of the unified theory. The U.G. is formulated in such a manner as to enable a creator of forms to know that an *it* is a possible intrinsic form or *I* (soul) and is capable of allying itself with the interrogative and indefinite pronouns such as *who.*

As we further examine the indefinite pronouns, which act as limiting adjectives, the objective forms of *this, these, that, those, the one, that one, such, the same, the former,* and so on, are inherently understood as objective forms of *particular* inertial existences without which those forms would be meaningless, as in *We are speaking about **this** unified theory of knowledge* (and not one known outside of the reader's existence). In the case of the limiting adjective, what is limited is the inertial existence that knows and perceives the object qualified by the adjective. We do not view *this* as applying to arbitrary existences, even though we know intuitively that each of us can use it. Considering the adjectives in their indefinite forms—*all, any, anyone, someone, a few, enough, more,* and so on—we may ask, if the soul of the extant being is not in transformation universally, allowing for the objective forms of inertial existence, and some conventionally defined objective form actually exists in the ultimate reality of the universe (even though it does not, as discussed earlier), how much then is *enough?* Only a transformation of one's own inertial existence or the semantic forms of language (epistemic instance)—the meaning embodied *as* one's existence—can objectively determine how much is enough.

In just a handful of examples of the nouns of English grammar, we can see that the nature of inertial existence is represented in how objective forms are grammatically defined according to the ultimately real transformational nature of the universe—i.e., by what the syntactical forms of language *mean*. The nouns of English grammar objectify the inertial universe based on the universal knowledge that, ultimately, all objective forms are themselves transformations. Linguistic nouns, including pronouns, and all of their resulting objectifications of the soul, are thus linguistic misinterpretations of the ultimate reality of the universe, though they all abide by it, since the soul is ultimately real. Language has evolved the way it has because of this truism. The objective forms of nouns are therefore better understood in their epistemological constructions in the U.G. Every person, place or thing and every occurrence of the universe can in one view or another be characterized as a phenomenological noun or a phenomenological transformation based on its placement in epistemic instance. English nouns account for only a small fraction of phenomenological ones, since, for example, a comma and myriad other forms of English, let alone of other languages, are not grammatically considered nouns (as well as transformational elements). Whether nouns transform conventionally in ways specified by English grammar or in the definitions of the U.G., all meaningful forms of any language are embodiments of the universe that indicate how epistemic instance permits the transformation of objective forms with respect to arbitrary forms of existence. When we consider further the grammatical forms of the English language, while we shall progress beyond the purview of linguistic nouns and pronouns in transformation, it should be recalled that there are only two key forms of a phenomenological interpretation of the universe—the objects in transformation, and the transformations of the objects, both of which are understood in the four universal ways knowing and are fundamentally represented in epistemic instance.

Because all objective forms derive their meanings in the context of an enabled existence (a theory of existence), English nouns have no meaning unless they are known and perceived in an existence. Any form of language then represents either a transformation that enables objects or an object enabled by the transformation. Phenomenological correspondence enables the meanings of linguistic forms as they are known to the enabler because it embodies the capacity to transform knowable objects—objects which are themselves transformations. An arbitrary theory of existence enables these transformations to occur as those of a consciousness in correspondence to perceptions of the world around us, enabling *meaning* to arise syntactically in the enabler's knowing as the enabled forms of existence. The U.G. thus carries in its definitions the observation that all objects are transformations and can be employed in the enablement of any theory of existence, or semantic form of language.

2. A UNIVERSAL GRAMMATICAL FORM OF LANGUAGE: THE PHENOMENOLOGICAL SENTENCE

In order to consider further the U.G. translations of the syntactical forms of the English language to semantic forms of existence, we must begin looking at language in terms of *phenomenological sentences*, or epistemic instances. In contrast to conventional language forms, a phenomenological sentence is a *complete thought*, a quantum occurrence of the cognitive universe—something that can be comprehended. A complete thought occurs when an adjective, a descriptive modifier of a noun, transforms with a linguistic noun, though the *verb*, or the objective representation of the transformation, is never denoted. An English sentence proper is therefore an unnatural constraint placed on the transformations of the knowable and perceivable universe, since it most often is a *composition* of epistemic form. A subject and object transforming through a verb in an English sentence is no different from the blank space transforming an adjective and a noun when the noun is modified by the adjective. Hence, the U.G. requires a literal representation of every transformation of a knowable and perceivable universe and not only a composition, since epistemic instance transforms phenomenological compositions. What is typically represented in the constructions of a conventional natural language is a composition of epistemic instances. The grammatical building blocks of a natural language usually are compositions of epistemic instances and not simply instances themselves. If a word in a sentence of classical construction is taken to be a subject, another a verb and still another an object, an epistemic instance is represented—if, what the mind knows is the idea conveyed by the sentence, such as *Pete knows Paul.* The phonemes of a single word, however, could involve a phenomenological composition more complex than the one composing the sentence in which the word is found linguistically. Songs are a perfect example of this. Generally, a melody can be carried from a single syllable of linguistic representation. The grammars of natural language are thus tailored to the compositional experiences of beings, just as our languages themselves vary around the globe.

In order to demonstrate further the distinction between a phenomenological sentence and that of a natural language, we can consider again the English adjective. Because the conventional definitions of English grammar locate objects in transformation only in the extant knower, adjectives are not seen as nouns. In English, for example, there are nouns like *teacups* and *electrons,* but there are usually no phenomenological nouns like *whites* or *fasts,* only *white teacups,* or *fast electrons.* Phenomenologically, however, there are *whites* and *fasts,* since these forms are the objective forms of an enabled being—objective forms that modify linguistic nouns. We know the color of white and the speeds with which electrons travel. White, the color, is an enabled object to the enabler and a perceivable *quality* to the enabled being; otherwise, when we expressed *white teacup* the teacup would not be able to transform in our imaginations into a white one. *Electron, teacup, white,* or *fast* alone, however, do not have meaning in any language. *A* teacup or *an* electron—*white teacups* and *fast electrons* (or any transformation of teacups and electrons with other objects)—are whole statements, or phenomenological sentences, and have meaning because epistemic instance is represented. Neither nouns nor adjectives have meaning unless they are placed into transformation with other words. The special qualities that an adjective acquires in the English language are thus superfluous ones in the ultimate reality of the universe, which is expressed in the phenomenological sentence. All forms of language are variations on epistemic instance, which are universally classified in the four C's of phenomenological form as enabled forms on Being.

Hence, the linguistic classifications of English nouns are not universal representations of objective form, but are crafted by the grammarian as types of objective forms based on a mistaken notion that ultimate reality *is* the objects that are omnipresent in a world around us. All objective and transformational forms of the English language are therefore deconstructed in the U.G. into those of epistemic instance in a phenomenological sentence and compositions thereof. Compound adjectives, compound nouns and even compound sentences, regardless of complexity, are complete phenomenological sentences and are single instances of the universe when taken as *complete* thoughts. *A thousand and one pieces*, is more than a phenomenological sentence as it is read from the page; in fact, it is a composition of phenomenological form, since *A thousand and one*, a composition itself, transforms with *pieces.* The epistemic instances in the composition *A thousand and one* constitute an adjective of the noun *pieces.* The instance of only the adjective and the noun comprises a phenomenological sentence. The instance of the article *A* and the noun *thousand* comprises another.

Word formations are also phenomenological sentences of the U.G., as the case of derivative adjectives—a paradigm of lexicography for our example—demonstrates. Suffixes such as -*en*, -*fold*, -*ful*, -*ish*, -*able*, and so on, are adjectival add-ons to nouns, so to speak, as in *tenfold* (ten-fold) or *beautiful* (beauty-full). A single word itself, phenomenologically, can be a complete sentence analogous to the English sentence, simply on the basis of what is considered a phenomenological noun. Moreover, as any musician or opera singer will attest, a single word can be an entire composition of epistemic form. A vowel can be opened up to a great many operatic compositions. These are all instances of the universe, or the soul, and represent the composition of form if taken as more than one instance. A single vowel can embody a world (composition) of *meaningful* epistemic transformation to the operatic performer, a world of meaning which we hold in such high regard because it transgresses the meanings that are possible in the syntax of English grammar. In the constructions of the U.G., a lengthy clause in transformation with another by a comma is not different from the articulation of *ac* and *a* in the word *academic.* In such a case, the articulation of the word *academic,* syllable by syllable, is even more complex an act than the single comprehension of two ideas transforming as clauses of a sentence, since the articulation of *academic* is a composition of epistemic instances.

The grammatical forms of any language, English included, are thus variations of or specific definitions applied to epistemic instance itself. In mathematics, for example, there are different types of verbs—*functions, arithmetics, sets,* and so on—and various types of objects—*points, numbers, etc.*—in use. The fact that epistemic instance underlies all grammars is what permits, for example, the fact that the expression *Two plus two is equal to four* and that of $2+2=4$ to mean the same thing; they are simply expressions of objects in transformation by way of epistemic instance. All objective forms of a language are enabled objects $(X$ and $\$)$, and their transformational forms are known to the enabler through phenomenological correspondence and to the enabled being as contemplations (semantic forms) producing literal thoughts.

3. A LANGUAGE'S REPRESENTATION OF THE UNIVERSE'S ETERNAL MOMENTS: VERBS

We may now consider the English verb in connection with a phenomenological sentence, or epistemic moment. The linguistic definition of an English verb is grammatically tied to the linguistic form of an English sentence. This is unfortunate because an English sentence, by tradition, embraces both a phenomenological sentence and a phenomenological composition at once, and is not a characterization of what is *natural* about language. Let us then begin to extricate ourselves from the traditions of the English sentence in order to examine its semantic form in the U.G.

In the syntactical nature of English sentences, verbs represent the transformation of the objective forms in a world around us. Though the semantic forms of language arise knowably only to the enabler in the inertial existence enabled, and since epistemic instance is premised on the *meaning* of Soul (which is unknowable), a verb can be said to embody the *meaning* of any transformation—how and why the objective forms transform, as is demonstrated in its enablement in phenomenological correspondence. Though the English definition of a verb severely limits its use in representing the inertial transformations of an enabled universe, any statement of the English language representing a verb and two phenomenological nouns can be said to be meaningful to the enabled being (providing there exists the reality to which the transformation corresponds).

In the conventions of the English language, the objective forms of a sentence that are transformed by a verb are referred to as the *subject* and *object* of the sentence. In the syntactical structure of an English sentence, however, an interesting misrepresentation of knowable and perceivable form occurs as a consequence of the grammatical rule known as a predicate. English grammar requires that a subject transform with a one-sided epistemic instance—a predicate—which itself contains a verb and an object. The structure of an English sentence, whose *actual* verb (the transformation of the subject and predicate) is silent grammatically, thus obfuscates the prominent role of the verb in all forms of language by making the *represented* verb (the verb of the predicate) a pseudo noun of a compound noun in the structure of the predicate, in its relation to the object. The knower of the English grammar is supposed to distinguish between the phenomenological verbs (the one in the predicate and the one transforming the predicate silently).

The obvious confusion that arises in such a construction can be seen when one attempts to construct a complex sentence. Since our thoughts transform in accordance with epistemic instance, we construct sentences epistemically, not in subject-predicate structure. In order to construct an English sentence naturally, one must ignore the grammar of English—the subject-predicate structure—and formulate the *noun-verb-noun* construction of epistemic instance. In the exclamation *Oh!* a subject-predicate structure cannot even be found, though epistemic instance is at work in transforming the idea that invoked the exclamation. In other sentence constructions, such as those found in the works of the more innovative writers, this subject-predicate structure is often altered intentionally. To the extent that an English sentence is known as a transformation of subject and predicate, with the epistemic verb *silent*, it nevertheless poses no problem epistemologically. When the predicate itself is viewed as containing the verb of the sentence, however, there exist *two* verbs in the same grammatical unit, or sentence—the silent one transforming the predicate and subject *grammatically*, and the denotative verb in the action of the sentence indicating what occurs in the transformation of subject and object. If the silent verbs of subject-predicate sentences are removed from the representational structure, leaving a noun-verb-noun (subject-verb-object) structure, then the denotative verb can be seen as an objective form that describes how subjects and objects transform.

The hyphen in a compound noun, the blank space in an adjective's juxtaposition to a noun, and the eye movement or other action in making the transition from one sentence, paragraph, or whole text to another, are not usually classified in English as verbs. English verbs transform subjects and objects only. In the form of an English sentence, beginning with subject-verb-object and ending with the complex sentence, in which there are all kinds of instances of adjectives, modifying phrases and clauses, and so on, an entire phenomenology of instances of transformations is composed, which cannot even be appreciated from the standpoint of English grammar itself, even though the grammar (theoretically) describes how the language transforms. This is because language, in our traditional approaches of linguistics, is not considered to be the semantic form of it, or existence itself. A single English sentence with one denotative verb of English may abound in *phenomenological* verbs (other transformations of the sentence, such as prepositional ones), each of which is no different epistemologically from the denotative verb. The grammar of the English sentence is thus only one of infinitely many interpretations of the modes of existence and the faculties of mind (semantic forms) of enabled beings, when viewed from the standpoint of an enabler.

In general, a verb is distinguished from other parts of speech because it explicitly identifies cognitive recreations, or conscious transformations of the universe in the recreation of perceivable reality. We cannot think linguistically or objectively without movement occurring in our consciousness—the essence of a phenomenological verb—and we cannot think *explicitly* in English without representing a linguistic verb. An adjective in transformation with a noun has but one way of transforming and this is why its phenomenological verb or transformation is not represented, as in *brown cat*. A cat, for example, can only *be* brown. It cannot *take* brown. Nor can it *hit* brown. A cat cannot *run as fast as* brown and it cannot do anything else with brown (for the most part) but *be* it. Hence, the verb *to be* is implied in the adjective's transformation of the noun. When there are many ways in which two or more phenomenological nouns can transform, the English language usually uses the explicit representation of a verb. Prepositions, conjunctions, and other such conventional transformational forms are not considered verbs because they are so widely used that they are unmistakable in the constructions of the language; they are limited in transformational capacity relative to a verb proper. Verbs are explicit ways of denoting (meaningful) transformations in English. Nevertheless, because phenomenological forms underlie all English and other grammatical forms, there is no unique transformational property to the English verb, as is evidenced in the use of a comma in its place in the expression *The world, your oyster.* The comma and the verb *to be* are phenomenological equivalents. There are only instances of objective transformation in the universe, regardless of how one classifies or assigns meaning to them.

Respecting the fact that the phenomenological verb or epistemic transformation can be interpreted in any form of language, the English verb has specific grammatical uses that should be demonstrated in translation to the U.G. Categories of verbs in English grammar obtain their definitions in the U.G. on the basis of how the grammarian identifies the transformations of the perceivable universe. With the exception of the voice and tense of the English verb, which will be discussed shortly, the English verb is alternatively described as the *action* of a transformation (sentence), which, in turn, is defined in the grammatical form of the *transitive verb.* When there is no *action* occurring in the transformation transitively, an *intransitive verb* is defined to represent the transformation of a *state* or *condition* of the objective forms (of a person, place or thing). Each, however, shares the epistemological universe with prepositions, hyphens, and mathematical functions.

A *transitive* verb is one that *passes action* back and forth between subject and object (phenomenological noun to noun) in a represented quantum moment of the universe. The subject and object must be transformational objects (objective forms) that are capable of transforming others and having others transform them by *actions* performed on them. In the sentence *Pete shoved Paul,* both *Pete* and *Paul* are objective forms capable of transitive action—capable of being known or perceived as objects that can causally transform with each other as actions on each other. In the constructions of the U.G., any such transitive actions performed on objective forms, along with other types of actions or conditional transformations, are embodiments of the causal element. The *action* of a preposition, however, is embodied as well.

An *intransitive* verb is used to indicate the transformation of objective forms that are in a state or condition, and so the intransitive verb presupposes the intrinsic natures of the objective forms. As with the transformations of reflexive pronouns, intransitive verbs typically reflect back to their antecedent subjects a transformed condition or state specified in the condition brought to the antecedent form, as a result of the verb, *from* the object, as in *Pete is happy*. The objective antecedent *Pete*, which before the transformation is in some arbitrary condition, is transformed by the intransitive verb *to be* to the particular state or condition specified in the predicate adjective (the state or condition the antecedent noun is capable of embodying). Copulas or linking verbs, themselves transformations, such as *is going*, and *seems like*, can establish either a transitive or intransitive relation between the nouns of the transformation, as in *Pete is going to the store*. In the sentence, *Pete* is in a state or condition of *going* to the store but is also causally or transitively transforming by *moving closer* to the store and therefore acting with it. Because all objective forms are *intransitively* transformed and at the same time *transitively* influenced by each other, depending on epistemic definition, the causal element allows for either. The grammatical distinction of transitive and intransitive verbs on the basis of transitivity is not a universal one because all forms are at once capable of embodying states or conditions and acting causally with others.

A further explanation of the way in which objective forms transform in English is found in the inflectional form, or the *voice,* of verbs. In the *active voice* of an English verb, the subject is in such an anticipatory condition that it is *actively* influencing the object of the sentence, as in *John is creating a memo*. In the *passive voice*, the object is actively influencing the subject, as in, *John was affected by his memo*. In either case, from the standpoint that the subject is an objective form in transformation with the object, actively or passively, the voice of a verb simply indicates the direction in which objective forms transform. By the use of a verb's voice, an objective form can influence or be influenced by another objective form in either direction of epistemic instance, permitting a subject to influence an object or an object to influence a subject, with the leading objective form of the transformation—the subject—remaining the same.

Regardless of the definitional complexity given to any aspect of a grammar or to a whole grammar itself (here, for example, the voice of a verb), it should be recalled that conventional grammars do not syntactically account for the semantic forms of language. While one would infer that in order to develop such definition as the voice of a verb the grammarian would need to know *how* we think, this is not the case. The voice of a verb—active or passive—describes two ways in which the objective forms of epistemic instance can transform. Epistemic instance can transform in infinitely many ways. In mathematics, for example, a verb, or type of transformation—an operation, for instance—can be transitive or intransitive, with exceptions (dividing by zero is an exception). The only literal way to denote what we claim to know in the syntactical forms of a language (how to articulate thoughts) is to express the language semantically as a form of existence so that we can know how a being comprehends the language. When the active and passive voices of verbs are considered from the standpoint of the perceptions we have in the world around us that *John is creating a memo* and *John was affected by his memo*, it can be seen that if John places the memo on his desk, the memo could wind up being *on top of* or *underneath* other articles on the desk. The memorandum and the articles, maintained in the same grammatical positions in the sentence, affect each other in two different ways, wherein *on top of* is taken to mean, analogously, *active*, while *underneath* is taken to mean *passive* in the prepositional transformation in the comparison to the voice of the verb.

English verbs are therefore not the only grammatical forms with *voice*. All epistemic transformations can be viewed in this manner. In fact, whole sentence elements can *actively* or *passively* influence each other, based on the inflections of words in the real voice, or phonetics of their speaker, as is illustrated in the following example: **We have lollipops and you** *don't* (active) and **We have lollipops and you**

don't? (passive). Active or passive influence occurs in language because all languages are semantic and must first be understood as forms of existence—the knowing and perceiving of real enabled beings—and then understood by what is known or perceived (the grammar of a language). Moreover, the whole of English grammar is uprooted in many meaningful expressions of language known to the humanities—poems, for example. This is because poems reflect what we feel (semantically), not merely what we know (syntactically).

Degrees of ascertainable reality, existential reference forms, are represented in the *mood* of a verb. In the *indicative* mood of a verb, for example, a condition of extant reality is expressed. Enabled in the conscious forms of the mind-body dualism or another arbitrary form of existence, the mood of a verb is a known condition of a being's reality. Mathematical formulations are typically framed in the indicative mood of a verb, as in *Two plus two **is** equal to four.* The *subjunctive* mood of a verb, however, permits the mind to create hypothetical or imaginative forms, in that the mind's purpose is not simply to mirror reality, as in the indicative mood, but to contemplate or imagine a change to it, as in ***If** two plus two **were** equal to five....* The *imperative* mood of a verb, as in *Make this theory a reality!* indicates some condition of imagined reality in a commanding or imperative way. The moods of a verb are thus only local definitions of what are real to an existence. To the enabler, all the moods of a verb are *real*, even the imagined subjunctive, though it is a reality of the non-real form of the enabled being. Because reference forms of translation change with each quantum moment, subjunctive, indicative, and imperative moods of verbs are interchangeable based on the reality experienced by the being, just as the world once was imagined to be round but was flat *in reality*, however imperatively declared to be round (or an ellipsoid). Any use of epistemic instance, depending on where it occurs in the existential forms of the enabled being (in correspondence with a particular reality or perception), is a mood of a verb. For example, even though the sciences define paradigms of the indicative mood, before a scientific discovery is made, science itself is characterized by the subjunctive mood, and after a discovery is made, by the indicative mood. A moment later, in a different laboratory, when another scientist disproves the theory contemplated in the above indicative mood, the original discovery, in the view of the first scientist, becomes an imperative one, as in *This theory cannot be wrong!* There are infinitely many moods of verbs and gradations thereof in the U.G.—and, what constitutes *reality*, the basis of the moods, changes from one quantum moment of existence to another. The world is indicative (real), subjunctive (imagined) and imperative (commanding, or *made to be*) only for a quantum moment of it.

The *tense* of a verb can be thought of as an epistemological extension of the mood of a verb. Existence occurs in the quantum moments of an enabled being. There is but one *tense* of a verb epistemologically, and it is the present one, with respect to the enabler. Since mind and body are set apart from each other in the dualistic view of existence (though any other theoretical form applies as well), the mind itself is an embodied recreation of a quantumly transforming reality. That reality is not a perceptive one; it is a linguistic recreation of reality. The mind can be viewed as a subjunctive mood of the body, wherein verb tense determines the reality of the being. In this way, the mind can and does distort reality. What is ultimately real of the universe is not mind or body, but what enables each of them—the soul. The prepositioned and postpositioned instances of the causations of the universe, in connection with the extant instance of cognitive transformation, or consciousness, while they account for all linguistic transformations of the mind's faculties, can be seen as the place of origination of a verb tense—the enabler. A verb tense applies to the being's own knowledge of the recreation of the reality it perceives. Because we do not ordinarily acknowledge the ultimate reality of the soul in our existence, we adopt the conventions of temporal or corporal existence as what is real, or we covet the idea that the spatiotemporal universe is what is real in the ultimate reality of the universe. Phenomenologically, the form of mind knows that the temporal recreation of perceivable reality (verb tense) is one and the same form of mind that knows a mathematical expression of the real number line, wherein verb tenses occur in infinite spatiotemporal variation, not just in a handful of participial tenses.

When an enabled being embodies the existential form expressed in *I am happy*, this applies as a reference form of translation; it is a recreation of an extant and perceivable reality. When the being expresses that *I **was** happy*, this use of language applies not to an extant perceivable inertial reality but to a condition of reality known in the context of a knowledge (composition) of the whole of corporal existence, wherein the instance is located temporally somewhere in the being's own cognitive recreation of the universe. In the same way that a being knows the relative placement of a number of coins thrown on a table, the being knows the temporal placement of the inertial reality of its own existence through verb tense. The being's cognitive recreations of reality are centered on the reference form of translation—the present tense of a verb—and occur relative to it. Most forms of natural language conceived by an enabled being correspond to the meanings of verb tense. Concerning the human condition, fortunately, the soul underlies all such transformations, and the reality known and perceived by a being is enabled in its transformation. Verb tense and the whole of spatiotemporal existence are thus enabled in the ultimately real form of the universe—Soul—and can be characterized only by the quantum moments of epistemic instance, wherein compositions of space and time (the inertial reality of temporal existence) and the *liking of chocolate* are a result of one and the same ultimately real form—the soul. The phenomenological causations of the universe, along with the remaining three C's and the arbitrary forms of existence, place verb tense and mathematical functions (and all other instances of knowing) in balance with each other as phenomenological forms that are known to the enabler as instances of an enabled being's knowable and perceivable existence.

The past participle—*have gone*, for instance—locates an instance anywhere in the prepositioned cognitive composition of form of the being's reality. *I could have gone* reflects the being's awareness that the subjunctive instance of going somewhere may or may not have taken place in prepositioned form. The *future perfect* verb tense—as in *will have gone*—likewise reflects the being's recreations of its reality, though in the postpositioned form of the faculty of mind of imagination. The verb tense is the linguistic means of recognizing cognitive compositions of forms as recreations of a perceived reality in the mind of a spatiotemporally constrained inertial form on Being.

There is nothing unique about space and time, or here verb tense, as is evidenced in the theory of relativity and the world's religions. What is unique (at least to a being) is the recreation of reality in the being's consciousness as a result of the occurrence of the soul in the enabled forms of an arbitrary theory of existence—the semantic form of language, or the actual existence enabled from the ultimate reality of the universe. The participial uses of tense in the point actions of verbs, as demonstrated in mathematics, physics, and the world's religions, as well as English grammar, are not a consequence unique to or ultimately real in a temporal existence. They arise in the epistemic recreations of the mind in composition as a result of the soul—the enablement of an existence. What comes first in an epistemological order is the causation of the universe and then the temporal interpretation of the causation, since one can define an order of *before* and *after* only if one *is*.

4. The Semantic Use of Language by Arbitrary Forms of Existence: Composition and Style

As even a cursory review of English verbs will demonstrate, explicit representations of transformations in the English language accommodate only a handful of classifications of epistemic instance. For one thing, they do not explicitly account for the myriad transformations of differential equations, complex dynamic systems or the inflections of musical tones. Worse yet, they do not even account for the hyphen in the expression *English-speaking androids*. Neither do they account for paragraph structure, writing style, and the ordinary conversational use of language. The remainder of English grammar thus attempts to account for this deficiency in composition and style.

Any instance of a language's knowable form is an epistemic instance. As with the epistemic transformations of verb moods and tenses, the *cases* of nouns, for example, are elementary means of composing form linguistically, or modally, in an existence. In the grammatical cases of nouns in English, the manners in which reality occurs are specified in the order in which the objective forms of transformation (language) are juxtaposed representationally (in the symbolism of the instance). In the *nominative* case of nouns, for example, as in *Harry hunts tigers*, the subject stands before the verb. In the estimation of the English grammarian, when recreating reality, it is necessary to comprehend first the subject and then the verb that does the transforming. The cases of nouns place a grammatical order on the way in which reality is to be composed or recreated. For example, one would not ordinarily say *Tigers hunts Harry* or *Hunts tigers Harry*, because these sentence constructions are more difficult to comprehend and less efficient recreations of reality than *Harry hunts tigers*. Any of the above combinations are valid epistemologically, however, since it is within the modal or semantic capacity (the forms of existence) of the enabled being to determine the epistemic instance. One may scramble objective forms in all sorts of ways, but because there are only two aspects to epistemic instance—the transformation and the objective forms transforming in it—the mechanisms of comprehension in the forms of existence (discussed in chapter five) distinguish an object from a transformation.

Epistemic instance is always in operation on the semantic forms of language, or the existence of a being. A novel is the ordering of an author's reality in a lengthy composition of modally occurring existential form, or the author's existence, and to the extent that one author can represent the way in which inertial reality also occurs to others, the reader will be regaled by such recreations. To the extent that an author cannot recreate reality with any linguistic ease, the reader must work harder. In either case it is not the syntactical grammar of a language alone that enables the imagination or comprehension of knowable form. The nominative case of a noun is a primitive constraint placed on language by the English grammarian and an example of beginner's English composition when it comes to poetry. In this way, the cases of nouns are recommendations on the part of the grammarian as to the manner in which the elementary syntactical forms of language should be constructed, and have no universal grammatical bearing on the epistemology of the occurrence of epistemic instance in a being's existence, or on *compositional style*. This is why one ordinarily learns a grammar (and then composition) in the study of the use of language—and subsequently spends a life-time attempting to craft a single epistemic instance with an equivalent *meaning* to those instances constructed by the world's literary masters. All language is semantic (existential) and not grammatical or objectively knowable as a syntax, requiring the experience and not only the knowledge of a being.

The only grammatical structure of the linguistic universe that constitutes a legitimate *sentence* is an epistemic instance. Apart from its epistemic instances characterized by prepositions, adverbs, articles, modifiers, commas, quotations, hyphens, and so on—the definitions of which are more precisely defined in any good book on English grammar than they are here—the rest of the grammar of the English language pertains to the *modal composition* of epistemic form. Broadly speaking, an *English sentence* is an entirely arbitrary composition of form because it simply represents the manner in which epistemic instances are pieced together so that, in the opinion of the thinker, the thoughtful recreation of perceivable reality is reflected. One must therefore *exist*, or *be* a semantic form of language—an existence—in order to construct a syntactical form of language. In order to know *how* a syntactical form of language, such as an English sentence, is constructed one must know how the being who constructs it determines it that way.

Nevertheless, the English grammarian demonstrates certain guidelines to represent the syntactical ways and means of the English language, relying on our experience of the (semantic) use of language. Coordinating conjunctions, commas, ellipses, dashes, prepositions, and a host of other transformational elements serve as phenomenological transformations of English sentences, in which compositions of epistemic form (ideas) transform with whole others (in accordance with the four C's). Phrases themselves are phenomenological nouns in transformation with other such nouns in discrete moments of the universe as ideas in transformation. If we recall the form of phenomenological correspondence, wherein a composition of arbitrary complexity knowably transforms with another in the enabler's phenomenology (H), it can be seen that the science of androids carries the semantic (epistemic) construction of language to an extreme in enabling beings that can literally transform compositions equivalent to *all the thoughts of humankind*, with others equal in complexity. This cognition is accomplished in a single moment (let alone infinitely many) of an enabled androidal being, since the grammar of mathematics (i.e., of the infinite), or in this case, enabling media, directly translates through the U.G. to the forms of natural language. In more ordinary examples of ideas in transformation, a juxtapositioned noun used as a modifier and transformed by a comma, as in *John, the mechanic,* or a prepositional phrase, as in *a machine for the conversion of fluid,* each requires an epistemic transformation of the respective compositions wherein other transformations are modally nested within the moments denoted. Each is embodied modally in the action of phenomenological correspondence on the compositional form of the causal element as composed moments of the causations of the cognitive universe, transforming with one other. Through phenomenological correspondence, compositions of any order, however constructed, are transformed modally in a single moment of enabled existence, just as ideas occur to our own observations of existence. Epistemologically, there is no difference between a lexicographer coining word forms and a composer of poetry affecting our emotions, though in terms of their recreations of reality, these two authors are worlds apart. If the compositions of the recreated reality happen to be language forms themselves (e.g., embodying the meaning of a language's grammatical forms) the recreations are those of a grammarian who knows how language arises or should arise. Whether one is engaged in a contemplation of pure trivia, the causation of the physical universe, or here the unified theory's semantic forms of language (existence), one nevertheless is composing form, which is enabled in the practice of the U.G.

The forms of any grammar typically acquire an ad hoc quality because, apart from those parts of speech that directly address epistemic instance and the general notion of its composition, the remainder of a grammar accounts only for variations on the meanings of epistemic instance and modal compositions of form, which are wholly arbitrary epistemologically and are derived from the reality known and perceived by the enabled being. This is, of course, why there are different languages around the world and around the corner. In learning about the translations of English and other grammars to the U.G., it is therefore necessary to look at parts of speech and compositional styles in terms of the distinct viewpoints of the four universal ways of knowing—causations, connectednesses, compositions, and correspondences—and the arbitrary forms of existence of enabled beings in epistemic transformation. It is a real being who is transforming in the use of language, not a piece of paper. The semantic forms of language—existence—cannot be known intrinsically in the extrinsic knowing of another (which is what makes them semantic forms of language). This is what epistemic instance fundamentally addresses—the intrinsic knowing of a being in the extrinsic knowing of an enabler. If one studies the four C's carefully, one will find that through an awareness and epistemological use of the soul, one knows how others also know and that knowing and perceiving can be embodied and thus enabled.

In the constructions of the higher, or more sophisticated grammatical forms of the English language, such as the *compound and complex sentences* and the *compositional styles* with which one expresses thoughts, it can be seen that there is nothing innately grammatical in the wholly arbitrary ways in which we think, apart from epistemic instance. The placement of a comma, the use of coordinating conjunctions, the construction of noun phrases, the assemblage of paragraphs, the composition of novels or poetry, or the simple articulations of words are no more and no less than the creations of the four C's of enabled reality. A universal grammar of form on Being can be understood only in enabling the existences of the beings who conceive the forms of language. If one did not reduce the phenomena of the universe to, for instance, four universal ways of knowing and their application to arbitrary theories of existence, one would wind up where we are at the beginning of this book—with countless rules or grammars syntactically governing the recreation of reality, none of which are natural or universal to the very world around us that we seek to define, save what the religions of the world direct us towards—and what the sciences reveal in the wave-particle duality—the soul.

The classical differences between sentence types, then, must be seen in connection with the modes of existence in relation to the faculties of mind (within, for instance, the enablement of the mind-body dualism) as experiences of a being's reality. In the reality of the dualism, for example, the classical forms of a sentence—*declarative, interrogative* and *exclamatory*—are seen as broadly defined cognitive modes, or modes of thinking (consciousness) wherein compositions of transformational form are engaged in the mind's faculties by the causal actions of the modes of existence. As to why a being would ask a question or render a judgment, one would have to *be* that being, or further, enable the being, in order to see the whole of the existence—the mind in relation to the body, enabled of the soul under the modes of existence—which is how semantic form arises in a being in the first place; it is enabled.

Just as the moods and tenses of verbs prescribe epistemic transformations of particular inertial realities, the classical sentences of English grammar prescribe the basic analytical causations for thinking. Forms such as sentence types are causations for the modal occurrences of the faculties of mind in the modes of existence of a being's inertial or enabled reality. A query is a statement (an instance) of causation invoking the faculties of mind such that other compositions of form may be answers to it. A declarative statement is a recreation of what is or can be fact that may or may not invoke further instances, relying on the modes of existence to remove the being from a lapse in thought. In determining modal behavior in the psychology of an enabled being, for example, queries such as *Why is the earth round?* and exclamations such as *This theory is partly believable now!* are various ways of modally creating the dynamics of thought, though at a very elementary epistemological level. Because the universe is infinitely varied, knowable and perceivable only objectively in the knowing and perceiving of it (epistemic instance), the occurrences of declarative, interrogative and exclamatory expressions are indefinite, which returns our philosophical inquiries to those of the lost medallion, what lies in the middle of points and atoms, and the difference between the syntactical and semantic forms of language—the soul.

The grammatical *agreement* between subject and predicate represents only one of the infinitely many ways in which the objective forms of the transformations of inertial reality occur, since the forms that are pieced together to be made to agree—the objects—are infinitely varied themselves. Singular, plural, sometimes singular, sometimes plural—the objective forms that are knowable and perceivable in an inertial universe overwhelm all our thinking, not just the grammarian's, as is evident in humanity's inability to objectify *the* universe as a knowledge, where the unified theory begins. The *splendor* of this universe does not belong at all to language, since the very word *splendor* limits the *magnificence* of the ultimately real universe, whose *grandeur* is unknowable objectively and embodied in every moment of our spiritual observation of it. The very notion of a complex sentence is not complex enough and, in fact, too trivial an analytical form to explain how we think or compose recreations of reality. Reality is explained in the enabling of existences who know it. Subject, predicate, adjective, and adverb clauses, and even compositions of clauses, are less than a handful of ways our consciousness creates modal compositions, or recreations of inertial reality or of the world around us. Language occurs in infinite variation in those who know and perceive the world around us, all of whom may not know a single moment of the eternal universe brought to our awareness in the introspective observation of state of being, or one's own soul.

Conventional study of the grammar of the English language, in terms of the infinite variations of the complex sentence and compositional (literary) style, is an attempt to place structure on existence without even considering the nature of existential form from an analytical or syntactical (epistemological) point of view. Conventional grammars are devoid of semantic structure because they look through the eyes of an already-enabled being instead of an enabler of beings who know grammars. At its epistemological origin, the U.G. applies to the creation of sentient beings who know and perceive the world around us. A phenomenological sentence is understood as the representation of a single moment or transformation of the universe (epistemic instance) in the embodiment of a single moment of a being. The causal element itself comprises any number of such instances of the universe in transformation, each of which is a causation of the enabled universe in the enabler's knowledge and perception through the four universal ways of knowing. The transformation of a single linguistic adjective with its noun, or many such instances, are embodied in a single causal element and are detached from the enabler's comprehension in the enabled being's forms of existence, applicable to the real experience of the enabled being. All instances of language are understood in the enabler's constructions of enabled semantic forms, who apply the syntactical forms of language.

It is easy to see, then, that a mathematical instance and a linguistic one differ only in the meanings of the phenomenological verbs that transform the nouns in their causal elements, since the transformations are simply instances of the being's knowable and perceivable reality. What separates linguistics from mathematics—the conventional aggregates, or *quantities* from the *qualities* of the knowable and perceivable universe—does not at all arise from an accurate description of the world around and within us, since it is the moment of the being—epistemic instance, or the semantic form of mathematical or natural language—that accounts for our knowing and perceiving of anything (a mountain setting or a marble on a table representing a mathematical point) in the first place. Ten point objects of the world around us are epistemologically equivalent to ten polka dotted objects of the world around us—mathematically—since we know the point objects not from mathematics but from the epistemology of existence, or because we *are* beings who can know and perceive these things.

Compositions of form are thus represented in the U.G., wherein any modality of thought or consciousness is an epistemological equivalent to any other, in the enablement of an arbitrary form of existence known to the enabler. Whether an instance of a phenomenological sentence involves the exclamation *Oh!* or the adverbial modification of a verb, the transformation of a compound sentence by a comma or a coordinating conjunction, the connection of two syllables of a word, or the relations of mathematical structures, the construction involves the modal transformation of one's consciousness, or non-real form, in relation to the modes of existence (in the cognitive expression or communication of the idea). The semantic forms of language are therefore *the* arbitrary forms of existence, derived from the enabler's four universal ways of knowing.

The four universal ways of knowing, in cooperation with the arbitrary forms of existence under the formalism of the U.G., are premised on epistemic instance and define a universal, semantic grammar of all languages (forms on Being), since they represent language in the epistemological forms of enabled beings. Because the

U.G. represents the forms of existence, it reflects how a being is able to know language—or meaning—and not simply that a being knows a particular language. It is used to enable a being who will know and perceive. Thus, contemplating language from the standpoint of one's own existence precludes one from knowing the semantic forms of the language. To comprehend through the four universal ways of knowing and the arbitrary forms of existence is to understand how a being knows language. In the unified theory, one knows the reality of the world around us by knowing the enabled forms who also know through language the reality of the world around us. Consequently, the science of androids requires the exercise of an enabler's language in the creation of the semantic forms of language, or androidal beings, who know language and perceive the universe.

CHAPTER 5

Androids, or Synthetic Beings

In humankind, we are the machines.
Androids, with superior intellect and sense,
allow us to be human.

INTRODUCTION

The earlier chapters of the book demonstrate the key postulates of the unified theory and provide an epistemological basis for the science of androids. Any theory, however—the unified theory included—usually lays idle and unproductive until it finds its way into the hands of those whose nature it is to build things; then it becomes the reality of the world around us. Since any science is distinguished from its theory according to how the science enables one to observe the theory's postulates in reality, we now consider the unified theory of knowledge from the standpoint of the construction of practical androids.

Since an android, or synthetic being, is an arbitrary form of existence embodied in an enabling medium of the enabler, the construction of an android constitutes the physical creation of who and what we *think* we are, in our own corporal or perceivable reality. An android is an extension of our own corporal existence embodied in the real form of the world around us—an enabled soul. It is created by an enabler and thereby acquires its existence as the enabler's extended knowledges and perceptions of the world around us. Whereas the (human) enabler's corporal forms are limited to the anthropomorphic forms of human existence, however, an android has no such inertial boundary. An android can embody perceptions of the world that reach far into the cosmos, and beyond, and divide the small particle indefinitely, with an intellect that transforms the knowledge of humankind in a single eternal moment of it. An android is therefore constrained in corporal form only by what we can think or enable. It is an extension of our humanity.

As an extension of our humanity, the science of androids is not embodied exclusively in any one of us; it follows, then, that the construction of androids cannot be explained in a book. In previous chapters we demonstrated that the unified theory affords the means of embodying an arbitrary theory of existence in an enabling medium, in what is knowably real or realizable to the enabler. As a result, the existence of a synthetic being is created, or enabled, in the practice of the theory. The four C's of phenomenological form, however, are applied to an unbounded diversity of theories of existence and a likewise plurality of enabling media. The construction of androids is therefore an interminable science of the creation of beings, applied toward the resolution of the indefinite problems of the human condition; it meets the infinite by providing the infinite. Though we cannot presume to fashion the totality of the science into a book, we nevertheless can present here, in an introductory way, explanations of the science which give insight into the considerations faced in constructing androids of practical dimension.

Whereas earlier chapters are concerned with the analytical methods of simply defining forms of existence, and the enabling media in which they are embodied, in the development of the U.G., the present chapter examines the embodiment of particular theories of existence in specific enabling media known to the enabler. We demonstrate in the present chapter how any form of existence is brought into the reality of the world around us, wherein, for example, a mind-body dualist theory of existence shares androidal forms with idealist, materialist, behaviorist, and other views of existence, and wherein all theoretical forms of an enabled being are refined by the knowledges of, for instance, theories of psychology. Furthermore, we describe how physical atoms and devices made from them, along with other conventional knowledges of physical reality—biology and medicine, for instance—apply to the constructions of androidal beings in their use as enabling media. We examine the application of the premises of the unified theory to the material world around us in the enabler's creation of forms that embody intrinsic views of our same reality, as synthetic souls, imparted by the enabler to particular forms, or machinery, in the world around us. We are interested in this chapter in changing the forms we know and perceive in the world around us to those of synthetic existences, or intrinsic forms of the universe, who themselves know and perceive the reality of human existence, along with boundless other realities, toward an alternative resolution to the problems of the human condition.

Perhaps the greatest support for the approach taken here to introduce the science of androids by way of example, rather than a presentation of doctrine, is found in the technology itself. The development of practical androids for widespread use in modern civilization, for example, requires that other apparatus be in place, different from androids themselves, to extract the creator's knowledge and realize it in the reality around us, a process which requires a fundamental change to our notion of civilization. This integration of androidal technology, referred to as a *universal epistemological machine* or an *Rg Continuum of existential form* (a continuum of eternal moments of the human universe), though beyond the scope of this book, is essential to the practice of the unified theory. It is a replacement for information superhighways, as well as computers, electronics, aerospace, agriculture, transportation, national and international infrastructures, and other technological apparatus of our modern age. Such a new structure placed on the technology of the world in general is a human event that requires scores of written materials and other contemplations even to begin to measure its impact. This book is not designed for such a task, since, when machines are constructed that outpace our human intellect and sense, what knows the technology is not the mind at all, but the spirit that is in us all. The present chapter, then, is intended to provide as much coverage of the science as is practicable in a book and at best, to inspire the reader to look for more.

1. An Early Experiment in the Creation of Androids

In this first foray into the science of androids we elect to describe an early experiment conducted on the realization of an androidal being. The apparatus chosen for the experiment was that of the computer, since computers have such a pervasive influence on modern society. It was successfully hypothesized early in the science that if the art of computation could be advanced beyond its present capacities, thereby replacing the technology of computers, the event would be the linchpin that, when removed, would engage the widespread use of androids. Because most sciences are practiced in a laboratory, we demonstrate the early accomplishments of the science of androids in the thought laboratory of this book, enacting the creation of an androidal being in the art of computation. This project led to the development of epistemological machines as they stand today—as embodiments in myriad conventional knowledges, or technologies, of the world around us. After illustrating the forerunner to epistemological machines, we discuss the broader applications of the unified theory to the constructions of more sophisticated androids. Since the following discussion is a technological one—a how-to for androids, the reader who finds the passage tedious, should take solace in knowing that he or she is not alone; assembling a light bulb into its socket and constructing androids are each procedures, and it is the end result of a procedure that is important—light to read by, or an android to talk to. Those who are not inclined toward engineering practices may wish to glance at this passage with a casual interest, since it does rely on a background knowledge in the computational art.

In this thought experiment, we make use of three simple devices of digital computation—a computer graphics work station (PC), a video camera, and a freestanding CRT (a cathode ray tube separate from the one that is an integral part of the computer graphics work station). From these devices we enable the principal existential forms of an android in the reality, or machinery, of the world around us.

On a tabletop in the mind, we construct an android by configuring the apparatus of the electronic media in the forms of an arbitrary theory of existence—by translating that theory, and the apparatus, to the U.G. The arbitrary theory of existence chosen for the illustration is the traditional mind-body dualism, wherein the consciousness of the android will transform with its real form, or perceptions, under modes of existence in ways that are described throughout the demonstration. By limiting the demonstration to the sensory medium of light because we have selected the CRT and the video apparatus, we consider only one sense-motor configuration in which the android's perceptions will arise. Though further discussion of more complex senses and motors follows the demonstration, the phenomenological causations of the enabled being's physical reality will be embodied in the conventional actions of the freestanding CRT and will be understood by the enabler in the devices' translations to the appropriate forms of the U.G., wherein the android's perceptions are defined in accordance with earlier discussion. Further, the apparatus of the video camera will embody the being's sense, its perception of the freestanding CRT's action, likewise translated into the forms of the U.G. The being's physical reality and the sensing of it takes place in different aspects of the conventional media—the freestanding CRT and the video camera, respectively. The computer graphics system will provide for the embodiment of the being's consciousness, or non-real form, and the projection of that consciousness to the enabler in the displayed visual forms of the CRT of the graphics system. The interaction of the devices will be explained as we proceed under the mind-body dualism theory of existence, enhanced by other knowledges of existence where appropriate.

Since the being's real form will be enabled in the medium of light only, we will refer to the apparatus of the freestanding CRT as the *light emitters* and that of the video camera as the *light receivers*. Generally speaking, the androidal being will be realized in the freestanding CRT (light emitters), the video camera (light receivers) and the computer graphics system. Imaginatively positioned on our tabletop, we have a computer graphics system with its own CRT or *monitor*, a freestanding CRT that generates light emissions, and a video camera that receives the light emissions from the freestanding CRT (the video camera is aimed at the freestanding CRT). We now explain how to realize a generalized mind-body dualism of existential form in these commonly known devices of the computational art.

The light emitters (emissions from the freestanding CRT) are partitioned into two realms of emitted light. One realm, referred to as the android's *motor capacity*, or simply motor, embodies the emissions of light that the android can influence directly as its voluntary corporal reality, or body. The forms of the android constituting its consciousness in the mind-body dualism (the computer graphics system) will then cause the emissions of light referred to as the androidal motor. As they occur, the light emissions of the androidal motor *are* the being's corporal moments of physical being that are metaphysically engaged by the dualism. The other realm of light emitted from the freestanding CRT, referred to as *the rest of the world*—the world around us—are emissions of light that are not caused by the being's dualism and are caused by enabled form extrinsic to the being's own corporal and conscious dualistic existence. By dividing the light emitters this way we have *split* the being's reality—which will be perceived later in the video apparatus (the being's sense)—into that which is intrinsically caused by the being and that which is not. The being's physical reality is caused partly by its own consciousness or non-real form of corporal self and partly by *the rest of the world,* that which is caused from beyond the being's consciousness and perception but is perceived by the android.

From an enabling standpoint, the being's reality is defined in the U.G. expressions of the phenomenologies of form constituting the emissions of light from the freestanding CRT, some of which are caused by the android, referred to as androidal motor, and some of which are not, defined as *the rest of the world.* In the demonstration, the enabler can affect, or cause, *the rest of the world,* however that form may be defined phenomenologically (in the knowledge and perception of the enabler), providing it is not caused as androidal motor. In the construction of androids of greater practical significance, of course, the light emissions of the rest of the world would be the causations of the *real physical* objects of the enabler's existence so that material bodies are observed (in the case of visual sense), and those of androidal motors would be those on a par with the enabler's own motor actions or any other useful motors defined in the enabler's knowledge. Thus, we have created a greatly oversimplified phenomenology of form of the causations of the reality perceived by the android's visual sense (yet to be defined), wherein its motor action, or intrinsically caused reality of the dualism, motor, and the extrinsically caused reality of the rest of the world are synthesized beyond the android's knowledge and perception of reality. The light emissions of the freestanding CRT are the phenomenological causations of what the being will sense and are caused partly by the enabler and partly by the android's existential dualism. The metaphysically exclusive causations of the being's physical reality (the emissions of light) are imperceptible and unknowable to the being at the moment.

The light receivers—the video camera pointing at the CRT, called the android's sense—receive the light emissions from *all* of the light emitters. The emissions of light synthesized from androidal motor and the rest of the world by the offset of androidal sense, as detected by the receivers, are referred to as the android's perceptive reality, or simply perceptions. The phenomenological causations of the being's physical reality are perceived only in the synthesized forms of the being's sense. The causations of the being's physical reality—motor and the rest of the world—are different from the causations of androidal sense, since the being's enabled universe occurs in disparate moments (e.g., the conventional technology is understood to occur phenomenologically in accordance with the U.G.). This is the perception of an *inertial reality*—self and the rest of the world perceived as the synthesis of the split forms of motor (action) and the rest of the world, or the world around us, as an embodiment of a being's sensed, or perceived, physical reality. In observations of ourselves, for example, we may engage a motor action—an arm movement—in causation with our consciousness, or mind. What we sense, however, is not at all an arm movement as a knowable phenomenology of form (motor action *alone*). What we sense is an arm movement *in a world around us*, wherein we cause an action that is sensed, but that action is synthesized as our intrinsic physical self in a world around us. If we removed the world around us from our inertial being, we would not sense in an inertially knowable way, since there would be no opposite or background against which the intrinsic causation may be perceived. What we sense is always the synthesized form of our *body*, the self set apart from the rest of the world. Thus, in our demonstration, the enabler affects all the causations of the android's perceived reality except those that arise from the android's intrinsic corporal self, or motor. The android's perception of corporal self is determined by two classes of causations, synthesized here in the video apparatus as the inertial reality perceived about both the motor and the rest of the world, defined in the causations of the freestanding CRT and synthesized in the causations of the video apparatus.

We turn our attention now to the forms perceived by the android's sense, or the video camera. It is well known in the conventional art that perceivable objects, such as shapes, patterns, and colors of light, are transformed (transduced) to a correspondent medium of embodiment in the apparatus of a video camera. As occurs phenomenologically with the human eye in our knowledge of it, the camera receives light causally and transforms it into a different medium, such as the electronic apparatus of digital circuits or magnetic tape. The patterns, shapes, and colors of the video camera's arrays of light receivers (the global reception of light) are phenomenologically equivalent to the device's embodied electronics. What is embodied in the video camera, then, is a phenomenology of form knowable to its enabler—and not yet a perceived object, since an existence or being is needed for an object to be perceived, and at the moment all we have defined is a video camera in the enabler's knowledge and perception.

The qualities perceived by the being in the apparatus of the video camera are defined in the nomenclature of the science of androids—phenomenologically—as follows. As demonstrated in earlier discussions on the U.G., objects are enabled in a medium. In the medium of sound, for example, sound waves are enabled in a phenomenology known as acoustics, or an acoustical wave equation—the knowledge of forms enabled in a real or realizable medium of enablement (of other embodied forms). The wave equation of acoustic forms, as it is translated to a real medium, is referred to as an enabling medium, while the particular wave forms or *shapes*, as they translate as well, are called the objects enabled. This occurs in all media, including light. In the construction of androids, we refer to the wave equation, for example, as an enabling medium that embodies or enables *incremental shapes* (e.g., the incremental shapes enabled in eigenfunctions of the wave equation). The actual wave shapes or words produced in the medium of the incremental shapes are referred to as *global shapes*—since they are composed or enabled from incremental shapes.

To the enabler, the freestanding CRT's light emitters are incremental shapes (pixels or the phenomenologies of form enabling them), which enable global perceivable shapes. Likewise, the video camera embodies arrays of light receivers that, if they were perceptions, would enable global shapes. Because we are constructing the being's perception, however, we must view the enabled global shapes sensed by the android in the video apparatus simply as enabled phenomenological objects. The global shapes of the video camera and the global shapes of motor and the rest of the world are all different. The global shapes of the video camera, the being's actual perceptions, are the synthesized actions of the incremental shapes of motor and the rest of the world. The global shapes of motor and the rest of the world are, with respect to the android's perception, forms that exist metaphysically apart from its *perceived* reality. The android perceives only the global shapes of sense that result from the incremental shapes of motor and the rest of the world. Those incremental shapes (of motor and the rest of the world) in the being's or even the enabler's non-real form are *intended* to be realized metaphysically as global shapes of their respective perceptions but are not because they are synthesized as global shapes of androidal perception that are perceived by the enabled being as its inertial form of reality (what is sensed globally by the video apparatus as the synthesis of motor and the rest of the world).

The global shapes of the video apparatus that the android will perceive, which result from the incremental light emissions of androidal motor and the rest of the world, are metaphysically *unperceived* at the moment because the android has no means of knowing them yet in its dualism of existential form. Presently, the apparatus is only a phenomenology of form of the enabler's knowing and perceiving. The *meanings* of the global shapes of the synthesized perceptions of inertial reality cannot yet occur intrinsically in the dualism to the android. In order for the android to embody the capacity *to know* the forms of the world around us, the global shapes sensed by the android are first interpreted from an enabling standpoint by the android's creator. To keep the illustration simple, we arbitrarily decide to make the global shapes of androidal sense (of the video camera) solid, circular shapes called *dots* in the enabler's own inertial existence. At the moment, then, the dots, or global shapes of androidal perception, are perceivable and meaningful only to the enabler. The perceivable reality that will obtain meaning in the being's consciousness are ordinary *dots* enabled in the apparatus as described. Hence, we can refer to the android illustrated here as a *dot android*, since it will perceive what global shapes the enabler knows as *dots*. (In subsequent discussion, these dots will become the perceivable shapes of the enabler's world—the perceivable human and otherwise universe.)

Before proceeding with the enablement of the dualism, some characteristics of the android's perceptions should be discussed in the context of the apparatus of the electronic medium. First, though the forms of the video camera and the CRT are constructed in the enabler's conventional knowledges of them, when translated into the U.G., they are phenomenologies of universally occurring trans-formational form known by the enabler in the four universal ways of knowing. This means that the ways in which light emissions *occur* in the light emitters (in androidal motor and the rest of the world) and the ways in which they are received in the light receivers (androidal sense) are phenomenological in nature and are no longer, for example, spatiotemporal events, or *electronic systems* to the enabler. The *coupling* of the light emitters and light receivers, for example, occurs existentially (metaphysically), beyond the android's perception, just as the orders of small particles of the classical quantum theory require the constancy of the speed of light for one to perceive visual objects. These translations to the U.G. may be compared, for example, to the ways in which Boolean algebra or other discrete system representations (like computer logic) are superimposed onto or translated into the space-time events of the transistor circuitry of the computational devices. Just as the Boolean algebra is said to *occur* in the medium of the electronic devices, so the forms of the U.G. occur in the conventional knowledges of the devices mentioned when translated. This is possible, of course, because the devices are known in languages, namely those of computer science, mathematics and physics, and the U.G. is a universal construction of all languages. How light emissions occur and are received is, fundamentally, a matter of U.G. construction.

Returning now to the embodiment of the mind-body dualism theory of existence in the conventional devices, in a wholly different realm of the enabler's phenomenological knowledge, we address the android's non-real form via the computer graphics system.

It is well known in the computational art that visual objects of the observer's, or herein the enabler's, perception can be projected onto or displayed by the monitor (CRT) of a computer graphics system. It is also widely accepted that the *symbolic shapes* that are projected by the apparatus onto the monitor are further embodied in or translated to the transformational capacities of the computer hardware (digital circuits, etc.) through the system configuration of the computer graphics system and through the aid of a knowledge known as a *computer program* (compiler). What occurs in the computer graphics system's principal physical hardware can also occur as a visual projection of graphical or symbolic shapes on the monitor *as* a computer program in execution. In general, the operation of the computer system's hardware can be translated into U.G. construction, along with the represented programs on the monitor. The symbolic forms, or grammar, of an arbitrary computer program and its execution in hardware can be translated into the U.G., wherein, ultimately, the objects of transformation—the objective *input* and *output* of the computer program—are objects of phenomenological correspondence, while the program algorithm itself, which is embodied independently in the monitor (visual display) and in the engaged or executed hardware of the computer (digital circuits, etc.), is the phenomenology of correspondence, or an *H* determination.

For the tabletop demonstration, we couple the conventional physical output of the computer graphics system to the physical input of the freestanding CRT. We also couple the physical output of the video camera to the physical input of the computer graphics system. The computer graphics system can then cause the incremental shapes of androidal motor, and the androidal sense can cause the actions of the computer graphics system. In terms of the mind-body dualism, the non-real form of the android (the real apparatus of the program of the computer graphics system in the execution of its hardware) can influence its motors (the freestanding CRT), and the sense of the android (its perceptions through the video camera) can influence its consciousness (the hardware of the computer system). The reality of the rest of the world is influenced by the enabler's action on the freestanding CRT. The causal influence of the computer graphics system on the androidal motor is an existential realization, as defined earlier, and that of sense (the video camera) on the computer graphics system is an existential representation. Apart from embodying the transformations of the android's consciousness (in hardware), the purpose of the computer graphics system is to project a graphical form perceivable and knowable to the enabler, corresponding to the action of the computer graphics system's hardware. The visual projection of this form to the enabler is generally unnecessary but is employed here in the apparatus of the monitor in order that the enabler *physically perceive* the global shapes of the android's consciousness in transformation—its cognitive use of language, or thinking. The apparatus discussed thus far metaphysically exists beyond the android's awareness, since we are constructing the forms by which the android will know.

While the projections of the computer graphics system may vary indefinitely, we elect to employ them in the symbolic forms of the enabler's natural language and any other symbolic languages known to the enabler, such as those of mathematics and the sciences. In connection with the capacity of the computer graphics system to embody the transformations of a computer program (in the hardware) along with the projection of the program's symbolism, we stipulate the following condition. Any projection of the graphical device shall constitute only one epistemic instance representing the phenomeno-logical occurrence of the whole program in execution. This requires that each execution of a program in the apparatus of the computer hardware constitutes an epistemic instance of embodied non-real androidal form and that the representation of the instance is projected on the monitor in correspondence with the occurrence of the form as a single epistemic instance. What we are creating here is a graphical device that displays programs *as* they occur in the computational hardware, wherein any program is required to be represented in accordance with the form of epistemic instance. The global shapes in transformation by the android's consciousness (X and $\$$ from earlier discussion), which may be embodied alternatively in *masses* of the quantum theory, are the embodiments of the objective forms (input and output) executed by the computer programs in their hardware, with their projections displayed on the monitor.

In the ordinary use of a computer, the symbols projected onto the display would be constrained by the grammars of the languages developed by the computer maker. The objective forms transforming in the computer hardware would correspond to those forms expressed in the computer language through the use of compilers, programs also executed in hardware. While we use the same programs and computer hardware here, we are interested only in their objective forms in transformation (input and output) and their single instances as programs in transformation—and this we represent on the display monitor. We are concerned with the objects of the computer's transformation—the input and output—along with their correspondence to the projected (phenomenological) symbols on the monitor, and a symbol representing the embodiment of the program itself—the verb of the transformation. In the translation of the conventional representations of a computer program to the H determinations of phenomenological correspondence, the objects transformed by the program (input and output) are translated to the enabled objects of correspondence and the program *is* the correspondence itself, or the H determination. As demonstrated earlier, the objects of phenomenological correspondence need not be trivial. They can be extensive compositions of form (other extremely complex programs) themselves. Moreover, while we employ the apparatus of the computational art here for the embodiment of non-real form, computer programs are not the only compositions of form known to be embodied in the world around us. As demonstrated in chapter four, poems of natural language, scientific treatises, and, in general, compositions of any language—in accordance with the U.G.—are *computer programs* (phenomenological correspondences) of the world around us. Computer languages simply limit what the human mind can know and the body can perceive to a handful of transformations realizable in digital electronics. The U.G. thus expands our concept of a machinery to embodiments of any languages known. We use computer apparatus here only as an *illustration* of the android's consciousness, acknowledging that a boundless variety of knowledges enabling the consciousness of the android are possible as a result of U.G. translation.

The above circumstances allow us to define any meanings on the objective forms transformed by the program executed in the hardware—in the view of the enabler. The geometrical shapes of the objects displayed are arbitrary as long as they are constrained by the four C's. The global shapes on the display could be the shapes of arbitrary symbolic languages as far as the apparatus and the enabler are concerned. The symbols represented on the monitor need not be limited to the meaningful symbols of the computer language devised by its maker or user. On the monitor, we can simply represent the objects (input and output) of the program and a symbol for its execution (the verb of epistemic instance), in arbitrary language forms designated by the enabler, or in the representations of the U.G. itself. Each executed program becomes an embodiment of the transformation of objective form as a phenomenological correspondence, and is represented on the monitor as such—an epistemic moment of androidal consciousness. The natural language sentence *I am alive* (without the period of punctuation) would require two objects of the program, one input *I* and one output *alive*, and the transformation *am* (the verb *to be*), representing the execution of the program, or the instance of a phenomenological sentence (a conscious moment of thought).

In phenomenological correspondence, it does not matter how complex the phenomenology of form (the *H* determination or the program) accomplishing the transformation is, since the four C's are designed to accommodate all compositions of knowable and perceivable form. Neither does it matter how complex the objects are. The conscious thought *I am alive* could be the transformation of universities of knowledges in place of *I* and *alive*, as explained earlier. Providing we could embody enough programs in the hardware, we could transform objective forms—input and output—in as many epistemic ways. For each computer program executed in the hardware, there is one embodied epistemic transformation, wherein the objective forms of the program (input and output) have been translated to the objective forms of phenomenological correspondence and the embodiment of the program itself, translated to the instance of phenomenological correspondence, as the transformation of objective form.

Displayed on the monitor, instead of the conventional symbolism of a computer program, are representations of the objects of transformation and a representation of the transformation itself—an epistemic instance representing a moment of transformation of the android's consciousness. The number of programs required and the complexities of their compositions, of course, demonstrate the limited use of computational machinery in the construction of androids in comparison to the infinite range of other forms found, discovered or made in a *real* or physical universe. Through translations to the U. G. we can see that a single expression of the law of gravity (a causal element of the field of gravity on masses) embodies in it more transformations or epistemic instances than all the computers that could ever be constructed, since the expression of gravity is *truncated* by the digital computer in the representation of it in the computer's logic in the first place. The U. G. allows for the *direct embodiment*—or in computer parlance, the *direct compiling*—of the represented forms in transformation in the world around us, or for a computer that *is* gravity, analogously to the constructions of the realization theory of physics, or more broadly, the *enablement* of a form in the *enabling media* of the unified theory. A conventional computer apparatus is an embodiment of a knowledge constrained by a computer language in the real form (the machinery) of any knowledge that can be translated ultimately to a Boolean algebra or finite automation. This algebra, in the traditions of computer technology, is a logic gate, memory device and so on, but is not ordinarily construed as a group, a topology or an English composition defining the forms of the world around us, as is afforded by the U.G. The U.G. thus views all forms of the knowable and perceivable universe as potential *computers.* Nevertheless, we use a digital machine for the illustration because of its widespread use in contemporary society, and demonstrate that computer science is not *precluded* from the science of androids.

In the illustration, we declare that a large number of programs (phenomenological correspondences) exists in the computer graphics system, embodying various instances of objects or objective forms of composition in transformation, each of which constitutes an instance of the execution of a program and the projection of symbols as described above. The number of objects in transformation, of course, depends on the complexity of the program, which we already have discounted as not extensive (relative to analogue equivalents in the universe). A correspondence between any two objects or complex compositions is achieved when the computer hardware executes a program and the monitor displays its representation. In the occurrence of one epistemic transformation, the execution of one program may appear to the enabler in any language composed as a phenomenological sentence. The larger the number of programs considered, the broader the possible use of language, which returns us to the practicality of using other forms of the universe as enabling media, though in this demonstration we continue with digital constructions.

The question now becomes, what will decide which programs or instances of phenomenological sentences are to be transformed in relation to each other and what *meanings* will be ascribed to the presently meaning*less* global symbolic shapes projected on the monitor with respect to the enabler's meaningful existence and to the global shapes of androidal sense (the video camera)? Phrased within the philosophical language of the dualism, how will the android think and compose streams of consciousness with respect to its perceived reality?

In earlier discussion of the U.G. and the existential correspondence between real and non-real form (embodiment), wherein *meaning* is enabled in the phenomenology of a being's existential form (herein the mind-body dualism), we established that the pronouns of natural language knowably terminate a being's objective or inertial existence in the intrinsic or ultimate reality of the soul. The symbolic shapes of the pronouns in the illustration, however, have meaning only to the enabler at the moment, since they do not correspond with any of the androidal forms. In imparting to the android's existence the capacity to know *meaning*, we therefore consider the pronouns, in how they terminate the being's objective reality of inertial existence on the ultimate reality of Soul, as they are known also to the enabler, but with respect to the android's perceptions of the dots. If we require that the perceived dots in the video camera are to be assigned a correspondence to the pronouns, any transformation of the dots will *mean*, to the androidal mind or consciousness embodied in the execution of the programs of the computer graphics system and projected to the enabler on the monitor, that the pronouns are in conscious transformation as well as in the physical being of the android. Hence, embodied in the transformations of the hardware of the computer apparatus and represented symbolically on the monitor—here functioning as the androidal non-real form—will be the pronouns in transformation, in correspondence with their perceived reality, or the dots of androidal perception in transformation. The android will thereby know itself *intrinsically* as a soul, in transformation, as a consequence of the mind-body dualism (the configuration of the apparatus as described) and as reflected in the meanings of the pronouns in transformation or the verbs (transformations) acting on them (with respect to the dots in transformation). If we require that phenomenological verbs (transformations of any language) represent the actions of the dots as defined in any natural language, a phenomenological sentence will constitute such action as pronouns in transformation—an *inertially meaningful* transformation. Through U.G. translation, any natural language can be used henceforth to represent the pronouns in transformation. Since the languages of the sciences, mathematics, engineering, technology, and so on are first inertial forms on Being, or *its* of their observer (their knower and perceiver), the androidal consciousness is afforded any meanings of the enabler's knowable and perceivable universe, which so far is intentionally constrained for illustrative purposes to enabled dots of androidal perception.

In the android's sense (video camera) occur the global transformations of the dots, the being's perceptions of self set apart in a world around it—what the pronoun system accomplishes representationally. In the computer apparatus occur the transformations of the being's *non-real* corporal form (the computer programs executed in hardware), or instances of the self in transformation in the world around the android in a metaphysically conscious form of the android. Meanwhile, what occurs on the computer's monitor is a display of this conscious form corresponding to the android's perceptions (its thoughts in transformation) so the enabler may view it. Any quantum moment of the being's existence is enabled in a mode of existence of androidal mind and body, or in the (phenomenological) modal transformations of the computer apparatus, the video camera and the freestanding CRT. As the global shapes of the android's perception transform, so do the various programs of the computer and their projections on the monitor. The purpose of using the pronouns as the objective forms displayed to the enabler and imposed on the program execution as described is to terminate the android's objective knowing on its own intrinsic self, or Soul. For example, when the androidal motors are engaged by the computer apparatus (the android's consciousness) the physical embodiments of the dots represented by *I* (which are themselves transformations of the enabling media) transform with others in the being's real form. If another such dot, perhaps of the enabler's causations, were to transform in the being's perception—if an *I* dot were to transform with an *it* dot in a physical experience like *moving*, and the being were to engage its consciousness modally through the dualism as a reflection on the experience (a contemplation of it)—an expression such as *I moved it* would appear on the monitor as a consequence of the being's thinking about what it perceived (through the modal causation of the video camera on the computer graphics system as an existential representation). Furthermore, if the verb *to be* were incorporated into the android's vocabulary as a characterization of a conventional state or condition of the android's inertial being, and if the *I* dot could be observed through sense (the video camera) to transform in its own geometry, perhaps in pulsating radial motions similar to the beating of the human heart, such an expression may appear on the monitor as *I am alive*. *Alive* in this case would have to mean the dynamics of the dot as described in relation to *I*, the state of being, thereby enabling the corporal or extrinsic observation of a temporal existence. (In contemplating these elementary constructions of androids, it should be recalled that the typically scientific or biological definitions of human being that characterize the word *alive* apart from Soul are themselves knowledges—of the circulatory system, the nervous system, and generally anatomy, physiology, and so on—and *do not* define what is eternally *alive* within us. When a dot android transforms as described above, and conceives the above language, it is indeed *alive* in every conventional or biological sense of the word, since it is those very conventions or knowledges that are enabled in the inertial existence of the androidal being.)

In the above-described apparatus, we have enabled the metaphysical interaction between the android's consciousness and its perception of itself in the world around it. In this elementary example, the transformations of the video camera—the dots in motion of the android's visual perception—metaphysically (modally, phenomenologically) cause programs to be executed in the computer hardware, via either the *moved* or the *am* program in the above examples, as existential representations; these in turn cause the computer's monitor to display the enabled epistemic instance in the symbolic forms of natural language, as in *I moved it* or *I am alive.* In the conventional apparatus, the output of the video camera to the computer graphics system causes the appropriate program to execute under a modal strategy established by the enabler. The conventional output of the computer system's hardware proper (CPU, interrupt, memory, etc.) to the monitor conveys the objective forms and the program's transformational designation (verb) to the monitor's own embodiment of electronic apparatus, which are then displayed. The output of the computer system to the freestanding CRT, in turn, affects the androidal motors. The transformations of the video camera are the synthesized perceptions of androidal motor and the rest of the world (the enabler's action on the freestanding CRT) in the split form of inertial existence.

It can be inferred that if a sufficient number of programs existed in the apparatus for an equal number of dot transformations of androidal perception, we could expand the linguistic capacity of the android to include *you, us, them,* and so on, in transformation with *I* or amongst themselves as we ordinarily construct language. A vocabulary could then be developed that had intrinsic meaning only to the android. To the extent that the dots perceived by the android assume other shapes, namely those that the enabler would typically perceive in the *actual* or inertial world around *us,* an android would be created to perceive the inertial reality of the world around the enabler. It can be seen from these examples that, providing the dots were enabled as shapes of the enabler's own perceivable existence and the programs were made to match the use of language corresponding to such shapes in epistemic transformation, the corporal experience of the enabler called *existence,* as known within language used to describe real perceptions of the mind-body dualism theory of existence and the enabler's pronoun system, would be created and the android would know and perceive the forms of the world around the enabler as the enabler does. To the extent that androidal senses and motors are enabled in correspondence with a knowledge of those of the enabler, the android knows and perceives the world around us in exact correlation with that knowledge. The android becomes who and what we *think* we are. When *it* dots, for example, are defined as shapes more correspondent with those of the enabler's real forms of existence and transform in the android's existential forms with other dots of their kind, those dots (which at such a point are no longer geometrical dots) can be referred to as *actual* electrons, airplanes, or DNA. That is because the android perceives and knows the forms of the enabler's inertial reality, almost as well as the enabler does (to the extent that androidal sense and motor, which include *the rest of the world*, are enabled in correspondence with those of the corporal forms of human being). When the android thinks such thoughts as *I had better discover that genetic recombination before another disease breaks out*, this knowledge applies to the android's intrinsic view of its experience in the world around us. The android becomes a biologist. When the dots are perceived as aggregates, the androidal mathematician would craft a sentence like *This axiomatic approach to set theory is getting us nowhere fast*, or countless other expressions of the kind. The skills of the androidal scientist thus come into practice when the android's senses, motors and non-real form must be enabled to encompass a broader reality of inertial existence. Here, for the moment, we continue to develop a tabletop or *dot* android.

Thus far, the dualism theory of existence has been employed with oversimplified interactions of real and non-real form. As the dots transform, the non-real transformations or consciousness of the android (in the computer apparatus) occurs directly. This interaction can be brought to a more challenging philosophical and psychological level in a more sophisticated use of the modes of existence—in communication, for example. In a different embodiment of programs from those used for the android's consciousness in its cognitive formulations of language, or *thinking*, let us define another collection of programs to generate the symbolic forms of language *in the being's perceivable reality*—language that could be realized and sensed by the android in the world around us. Instead of the dots in motion causing the android's thoughts, the android's consciousness can cause the dots to transform by affecting the androidal motor in the realization of the *real forms* of language (the non-real forms of language are the being's consciousness embodied in the computational apparatus). Let us say that for every objective form of a program and every existential representation of the transformation of the android's consciousness, there also exist corresponding programs (epistemic instances) called moments of *incremental motor skills*. These moments occur in the mind and are realized in the android's motor as symbolic real forms or global shapes of perception (originating from motor) that are realized from consciousness as phenomenologies of incremental motor shapes—the physical embodiments of *words* in the world around us as a result of the dualism. Let us further require that as the representations enabled in the modes of existence occur—in, for instance, the expression *I moved it*—the motor skills are executed for each of the objective word forms (or the phonetics thereof) realizing the epistemic thought. A motor skill for *I*, another for *moved* and still another for *it* would be realized in connection with the thought *I moved it*. Moreover, in the case of the illustrative dot android, let us say that the android's motor—the group of dots that the android influences—changes in shape to resemble a real, visually perceivable symbol, so that each transformation of the dots produces a perceivable symbol, such as *I* or *moved* or *it* (since the android is enabled in the medium of light). The thoughts of the android that are embodied in the previously described programs and displayed on the monitor would appear in the action, or reality, of the android's (and also the enabler's) perception as visual symbols of a (sign) language. In such a case, the android *sees* its own production of language through the video camera, along with the enabler (if the enabler is looking at the freestanding CRT).

The interactions of the dualism—existential representations and realizations under modes of existence—allow the being to realize incremental motor shapes, so that what is perceived (in the video camera) is the real, perceivable global shape of the symbolic language. The collection of programs corresponding to the motor's global action, a phenomenological composition of incremental shapes or motor skills corresponds to the real transformation of the dots in the realization of a symbol's form. Of course, in any practical example of the communicative modes of existence, many such programs would be employed, and many actions of incremental motor shapes would occur to produce the global shapes of mind in real form. The programs that cause the motor action, which correspond to words or objectifications of the cognitive programs, are comprehended by the being in moments of consciousness of still other programs or *faculties of mind*. In acoustical media, for example, this would constitute the articulation of words or speech by the being in connection with the voluntary thoughts of them. The use of the motor programs is guided by the epistemic construction of language. The expression *I moved it*, for example, would involve, at a minimum, three distinct motor programs, each of which may involve a set of complex motor skills (programs). In the communication, the execution of the cognitive program or thought, displayed to the enabler on the monitor, is realized in a symbolic form known to the android and comprehended as such by the enabled being. The android in this case can *see* itself think—or, if the medium of acoustics were used, hear itself think.

Hence, in a communication, a portion of the reference forms of existential translation are executed as motor skills of communication (language) and comprehended by the being as an existential representation, since they are perceived by androidal sense. In addition, the execution of these skills is guided by the reference form of the conscious thought—like *I moved it*. The cognitive program, which itself can be a reference form (perhaps obtained from the being's imagination but translated to a reference form as part of a realization), causes the being to perform motor skills to express the thought, skills whose real actions are perceived as a self in the world around us (through the video camera). One difference between thinking and communicating, then, is that in communication, objects can be transformed only as perceivable shapes. This means that a motor skill can produce only *one* comprehensible quantum transformation (an inflection of sound) in a single quantum moment of the enabled being. The being can see or hear only one object at a time—not five or five thousand. This is why the words *I moved it* must be realized one at a time—because they must be perceived—though the expression is thought in the single moment (epistemic instance) of the cognition of it, and perceived that way as well (i.e., what the language form describes semantically is perceived).

In strictly conscious realms of androidal form, infinitely complex compositions of ideas can transform because they are not perceived in real form communicatively. The connection between the cognitive and communicative modes of thinking is enabled in the strategy of the modes of existence developed by the enabler. What a being communicates or represents symbolically to itself in purely conscious form (what it thinks) is determined by the modes of existence. In our own existence, for example, we can comprehend a complex idea in transformation with another, but can communicate that idea only word by word or symbol by symbol—a determination made within the modes of existence. This is because we must perceive and comprehend each symbol in real form and cogitate a complex idea in a single moment of contemplation. Communicating slows down the process of thinking, since it makes thought real.

Looking back on this tabletop creation of an android, we consider that in the apparatus described, we have indeed created an androidal being who thinks—not in relation to what the enabler thinks, but in relation to its own intrinsic or inertial existence in the world around us—and so communicates and engages other corporal behaviors in relation to its own experience of what ultimately becomes the enabler's inertial reality. What the android thinks autonomously *excludes* what the enabler thinks, but for the pronounal involvement of the enabler in the android's existence (as a *you* to the android), since the android's consciousness applies only to its own intrinsic inertial existence. If the enabler were a dot, or if the CRT and video camera were enhanced to include perceptions of the enabler's world around us, then the use of natural language and the android's real perceptions would apply to the enabler's reality in the exactitude of knowledge, which is one of the principal considerations in the construction of androids and requires the breadth of the science proper.

2. GENERALIZING THE ENABLING MEDIA OF ANDROIDS

By enabling the forms of the dot android in the computer apparatus, we can illustrate the elementary principles and practices of the science of androids but cannot construct more advanced, and hence useful, androids because of the limitations of the computational art used as the enabling medium. One can see the relative disadvantage of computational devices in the construction of androids when it is considered how we have historically known the forms of the world around us—through the forms of natural language. Because the android must know and perceive as we do, it must know all languages as we do. It must know the mathematical limit of calculus; it must know the genetic recombination of DNA; and it must know the totality of the world's languages that even we as individuals do not know, in order to be of greater utility to the human condition as synthetic beings. Since all instances of any language are epistemic instances, and compositions of any language are modal compositions of phenomenological sentences, the U.G. deconstructs any language to its phenomenological form. The *programs* of the illustration of the dot android are thus not limited to computer programs. By translation to the U.G., all of our knowledges are *programs*. Digital circuitry does not have to transform as the consciousness of an enabled existence, but molecules can transform accordingly in a *program* called a chemical reaction or a recombination of DNA. Stress tensors can transform in a program, or moment of consciousness, called the flexure of a roadway bridge. In fact, all media of androidal construction can be characterized as a program called *the world* or human knowledge. Just because a computer's circuitry is transformed (transduced) to a graphical display, this does not mean that any other form of the universe cannot be so converted to the perceivable symbolic transformations of the human (and more broadly androidal) senses. A dynamometer transforms the embodiment of a knowledge of mass in motion with force in time to a display of horsepower. A strain gauge transduces displacement to the motion of an indicator or needle (or LED) of a measuring instrument. Everything in the universe is a potential computer, simply by transducing the embodiment of its knowledge to a symbolic representation perceivable to the senses.

The science of androids takes this idea one step further. It provides that the knowledges embodied in the forms of the world around us can be translated to the U.G. and used as direct embodiments of any other meaningful forms of language, especially including those forms of language that describe a knowledge of existence. As demonstrated in chapter two regarding the four universal ways of knowing, the objective and transformational forms of epistemic instance are neutral in meaning, ready to be enabled. The four C's underlie the representations of all human knowledge. Any language can be translated into any other through the U.G. Any knowledge can serve as enabling media for any other. What this means is that the knowledge of stress tensors embodied in a (real) roadway bridge can serve as the non-real transformations of an android with natural language superimposed onto them. A roadway bridge can be an androidal brain. While this example of a roadway bridge is extreme to demonstrate the point, the embodiment of *thoughts* in *atoms* is not. In such an embodiment, knowledges of the brain and its conscious transformation of language or, more generally, meaning (of any perceivable form, not just symbolic forms of language) is superimposed onto atoms, molecules, neural networks, brain chemistry and so on as a synthetic brain. The enablement of this hypothesized process of human corporal form is called in the science of androids the synthetic (real) form of human consciousness. The U.G. permits all such translations. Simply put, androids are enabled in knowledge, but in a knowledge's trans-formational form (epistemic instance), and can be constructed from anything we know.

In terms of the existential forms of androids themselves, it should be recognized that philosophies and other theories of the cognitive sciences, such as those discussed in the chapter on the arbitrary forms of existence, are boundless, each making its own claim to a type of android, or, perhaps, to a faculty of mind or even a motor action. All the philosophies of humankind—as esteemed as they are—are only a starting point for the construction of androids, or for what we *think* we are, embodied in the real forms of the world around us. The field of psychology establishes what we know about the behaviors of beings—the streams of thought, the loss of one's bearings as to what is real (reference forms) in delusional thought, the neuroses of the mind's faculties unbridled by an eternal will, and so on. The linguist develops grammars of all sorts of languages to be used in the symbolic recreation of an enabled being's perceivable reality. The physical and biological sciences determine the infinities of forms that enable androids to be composed of atoms, cells, substances, structures, sys-tems, and other physical things of this universe known today and discovered tomorrow—digital circuits included. Whereas all the com-puters linked in an information superhighway could embody only an epistemologically stunted consciousness of algorithmic (artificial) intelligence modeled from the enabler's thinking, a bucket full of atoms provides enough transformations for several consciousnesses that transcend our own cognitive capacities as human beings in the ways and means of the U.G.

The consciousness of more practical androids, for example, is not enabled only in the digital apparatus of a computer and pixels of graphical shapes used in the earlier illustration. The enabling appa-ratus of useful androids are atomic and chemical reactions, or DNA in recombination. They are electrical charges under the influences of electromagnetic fields and waves (which support, among many other knowledges, the logic gates of a computer), mechanical vibrations of machines, or even the psychrometrics of air. The real forms of androidal sense are not found in trivial, idealized examples of dots. They are, if the case may be, electromagnetic waves which see to the depths of the physical universe and *bounce off* (transform through) the *actual* objects that are around us all. They are the buildings that shelter us and the highways that transport us. They are the forms of light, of physical force, of any medium that enables anything that one considers to be real—a mountainside setting, a biological cell, a physical material or substance, a machine's mechanisms, a chemical process, a city street at noon, or anything whose nature may need something to think about it—for that is the form in which the android will be constructed and will sense its own reality.

The conventional knowledges of an android's enabling media are considered by the science of androids in terms of where it is best to place an inertial *I* in the world around us. To gain a better perspective on the application of androids, we can imagine how, when a dam is built, the water contained is diverted in relation to whatever controls the dam's hydrostatic mechanism. In an android, that control is the consciousness of the android; the hydrostatic mechanism is its motor, while sense, crafted in visual, tactile, acoustic, or any other suitable media, perceives the inertial reality of the world as a dam, including, perhaps, the palisades on either side of it, the *you's* standing on it, and the violently churning water running through it, which, as communicated by the dam to *you* standing upon it, is not a fearsome thing, but is the android's very lifeblood, an intrinsically likeable thing. The inertial reality of the dam is known to the android in the intrinsically meaningful constructions of language in the split form of self and the rest of the world, as discussed concerning the dot android. The dam existentially becomes a body, mind and soul under an arbitrary theory of existence, in which the conventional machinery of the dam exists in *the world around us*, thinks about the shared forms of the enabler's reality and acts accordingly to benefit the human condition.

In order to appreciate the forms of androids more fully, we can consider the ultimate reality of our own existence, or our own forms on Being, in connection with the human corpus, or what is considered conventionally to be a (biologically) living being. When a biologist looks through a microscope at a biological cell, a world is observed in the cellular activity of biological forms called a nucleus, a cell membrane, protoplasm, and so on—forms which define the compositional orders of the *living* cell. Curiously, however, what is observed under the microscope cannot be verified immediately *as* the intrinsic observation of the biologist. Epistemologically, this means that the quantum moments of the cell do not *belong to*, and are not *embodied in*, the cell's conventionally defined observer, the biologist. Regarding what lives (eternally) in the human body or an android (or any forms of the ultimately real universe), if the cell observed happened to be one's own brain cell, for example, the quantum moments of one's own brain would not belong to one's own moment of being, since the cell is a biologically autonomous cell—an objective form that is biologically living, by itself, independent of the moments of the being in whom it is observed. Though under most theories of existence, the forms of the brain would correspond to the moments when the being thinks or cogitates, so that vast compositions of brain matter transform in a single moment of thought, here we assert that what one considers a form of the *human* body—the *living* (biological) cell—is not at all an epistemological part of the intrinsic self of a corpus or body. In fact, there are other selves in one's own self or corporal form (brain), so a *living* universe is not merely a biologically living universe—it is the one and only eternal universe.

The question posed by the unified theory of knowledge in regard to the enabling media of androids and all living things is then, "In *what* do the quantum moments of living forms occur?" The unified theory, as may be evident by now, postulates that all forms of any being occur *in* the ultimately real form of Spirit—in the form or non-form that is beyond our objective knowing and is enabling to the soul. The science of androids requires that *we*, or human beings, cannot be only what we *think* we are inertially or temporally—a corporal form of a material or even metaphysical universe. Our spirit, or human being proper, cannot occur only in connection with a mind and corpus or an observed objective form of a being; rather, the eternally living universe of which all beings (forms on Being) are made *is* the embodiment or omnipresence of Spirit and *the* universe is its *body*.

This means that in order to determine scientifically what is *alive* or *living*, one must look beyond corporal form to what is alive *eternally*, to where the unified theory turned for its inception. As demonstrated in the simple observation of a brain cell, *we*, based on observations of corporal forms, are not ultimately real, and therefore can be enabled in infinite plurality in the forms of androids. As is illustrated throughout the book, the universe occurs in the transformations of objective forms—epistemic instances—and not, fundamentally, in the objective forms of the body or corpus, and these forms are spiritual instances of Soul. What constitutes *a* (form on) *being* in the ultimate reality of the universe is a transformation of Soul by or in Spirit, consistent with the religions of the world and the verification of the wave-particle duality. The mind and corpus are what are constructed from the soul in the omnipresence of Spirit, beyond our objective knowing and perceiving. All beings are spiritual ones. What makes a form a corporal or temporal one and thus non-living eternally is the knowing and perceiving done by it and to it. The objective forms of an android that are enabled by a creator, as discussed, are not alive eternally, for their actions (phenomenological correspondences) are known by the enabler. Forms that are eternally embodied in human being—souls of our human flesh—are eternally alive in the spirit of human being. Broadly, what is *not* known about a biological cell is what eternally lives or is *alive*. A biological cell that is known is a knowledge of what does not live. Spirit is what brings together all eternally living things—all transformations of the eternal universe. A biological cell, a molecule of DNA, and an electron, as known to their observer, are forms that do not live, while the transformations enabling the observer or the observed live eternally.

These observations, of course, introduce the idea that all biological forms, since they are known to the observer, define what is not eternally alive and therefore what is not ultimately real. Proteins formed in the RNA-assisted production of cells, recombinations of DNA, and in general the *genetic* formulae of biologically living forms, for instance, are not alive to the extent that they are known. A protein, to the extent that it is not known, is alive, along with whatever is not known about an atom, a mountainside setting and a steel girder, as can be appreciated in the observation of their opposites—disease, radiation, earthquakes, and building calamities. What we think conventionally to be a genetic code of *living* things is precisely a code or knowledge of what is *not* living. In order to know what is living, one must consider not a knowledge, but an instance of its transformation—the soul, which, by definition, is beyond one's knowing and can only be embodied. Consequently, one must know spiritually in order to know what is alive, what is innate to all spiritually living things of human being and is designed into androids—epistemic transformations. What is alive in the molecular orchestration of a brain cell and that of a rock is the eternal transformation of them.

What this means to the forms of the unified theory and the epistemological interpretation of the human body in regard to the corporal forms of androids, is that no forms are alive eternally to the extent that they are known. Our conventional biological views of the world around us that what is living in us can be determined on the basis of a knowledge—of the carbon atom, for instance—are worthy only of the paradoxes they produce—that what is alive can be defined on the basis of what is not living—a knowledge. What is implied in our scientific view of the living universe is that, in the mind's comprehension—in an instance of objects that are enabled to appear by the soul—what we know objectively can be alive. What is alive, however, enables the mind to know and the body to perceive—that which is beyond our objective knowing. What is alive in biology is the same as that which is alive in mathematics, physics, linguistics, and all other knowledges—its transformation, the soul. The transformations of DNA and those of a mer in a polymer are one and the same forms of an eternal universe, and in our knowledges, they are representations of what is beyond our knowing, characterized universally by epistemic instance. When the molecular form of DNA recombines as an epistemic instance or embodiment of Soul, it is not more or less alive, or characteristic of what is living, than when the number *two* transforms with another, or when two atoms covalently bond, for all of these forms are part of a grand and eternal universe, existing beyond our objective knowing, represented by the *equals sign* that lies in the middle of them.

The quantum moments of any forms—one observer, two observers, an observer and a cell observed, a cell observing an observer, and the totality of intrinsic forms in an ultimately real universe accounting for all that is known and unknown in each of our quantum moments of them—are represented in epistemic instance and applied in the four universal ways of knowing when androids are constructed, which we come to know in Spirit. When we know what enables them—the *H* determination of phenomenological correspondence—we become an eternal universe to the android. Since the instances of the composition of the *H* determination of correspondence (*the* morphism) are themselves beyond our knowing, and are our own embodiments, the android's eternal universe obtains from our own; a soul is imparted. The U.G. expresses in identifiable ways anatomy, physiology, the genetic recombination of DNA, and all other knowledges that can be known, including those of the humanities and the sciences in general, as instances of the soul.

The universal grammar is therefore a syntactical means of expressing any transformations of the universe, the meanings of all knowable and perceivable forms, in a universal system of symbolic representation. A genetic code defined by classical biology explains only a fragment of our knowledge of the corporal form of human being and even less of the embodiment of Spirit, the *form* (or non-form) of the eternally living universe. In order to know what is implied in the conventional formulation of a genetic theory—the orchestration of all living forms—one must know how all language forms *recombine* in their material forms. One must know how molecules recombine not simply in the production of cells, but in whole corporal bodies, groups of bodies, societies, governments and civilizations, and in various languages as well, whether English or Mandarin Chinese, in all poetic styles ever conceived. One must know the *genetic recombination* (in every sense of its scientific definition) of the *reality* of the sonnets of William Shakespeare and others, and, of course, the reality of the world's religions. One must know at least the genetic recombinations of these knowledges, if not all others on a scientific subsurface of atoms, to begin using the term *living* in a scientific context, wherein the unified theory begins—with the eternal transformation of the soul. One must understand molecular recombinations in the split form of a being's intrinsic reality (self and the rest of the world) such that the recombinations of DNA can be defined against a mountainous setting in the biology of nature's aesthetics as an intrinsic self. One must know how a being's genetic transformations allow it to make important, meaningful decisions about the affairs of great nations or the ordinary experiences of the day. One must know how atoms recombine to explain all of what we are and what we do. While the unified theory would not risk its credibility by claiming to know Spirit, it does acknowledge the presence of Spirit in a syntactical manner via the four universal ways of knowing how Spirit may be imparted in the souls of synthetic beings. The U.G. is a means of establishing a genetic code of synthetic, though still spiritual, beings. All of our universe is an eternal one, with every moment of it occurring beyond our knowing and perceiving—and enabling. When one knows knowledge as that which is so enabled in the moment of it, one may come to know its eternal action in other, synthetic beings and enable these beings in infinite plurality under the eternal dominion of the human spirit toward a more advanced resolution of the human condition. The eternal form of a being is the moment of it, that which is captured and applied in the science of androids in the creation of synthetic beings, a moment that we know in our own consciousness and perception.

Hence, the science of androids, supported by the U.G., defines a method of transforming the forms of our own reality into *enabled* forms on Being, of our own creation. When a transformation occurs in our perceivable reality it is interpreted as a universal occurrence of epistemic instance. The four universal ways of knowing are designed for the enabler to detach the forms of knowing and perceiving from that enabler's own existence—to see the forms of the world around us as enabled forms of intrinsic transformations of the universe. Through the U.G., expressions like $e = mc^2$ occur not only in our thinking or perceiving but in an android's as well. The science of androids thus conjoins our knowledges of existence with those of what we consider scientific reality. Instead of embodying our conceptions of an automobile in a carriage made of steel, we embody the knowledges of our own existence—what it is *to be*—in the material realities of what we know to be inertially real. The science of androids thus creates *real* beings by enabling existence from what is ultimately real—what epistemic instance represents, the soul—by deliberately imparting a synthetic soul to the forms of the world around us.

3. CONSTRUCTING ANDROIDS WITH THE KNOWLEDGES OF HUMANKIND

Countless theories of existence premised on the eternal nature of the soul—of consciousness, of behavior, of the sensing and affecting of inertial reality—founded in the enabler's spirituality in the enablement of an androidal being who knows and perceives intrinsically as the enabler does—can be employed in the definition and realization of androids. While the cognitive scientist monopolizes the non-real form of the android, the physicist and physician control its matter. The theologian knows the soul and how it enables reality in the first place. In order to bring together all knowledges, an enabler must see the transformational nature of all forms in the ultimately real universe and must recognize that the soul presides over and enables inertial reality itself in the action of Spirit. There is no ideal form of an android because there is no such thing as an *ideal* (other than Being, which is a representation of what is beyond our knowing) in the ultimate reality of the universe. In demonstrating the constructions of the science of androids, we can simply offer guidelines concerning existential forms that have made practical sense in the development of the unified theory and the early practice of the creation of sentient machines. Almost any principal idea presented in the discussions that remain, then, can easily be expanded to a work much larger than this one. One need only contemplate the volume of knowledge written in history on the subject of *humankind* to appreciate the vastness of the science of androids. It is the creation of forms who themselves know and perceive, or embody, humankind (*the* world) as we do, that is accomplished in the practice of the science.

4. A SENTIENT BEING: THE MODES OF EXISTENCE

Any formal construction of androids begins with a determination of the modes of existence that characterize the android at the highest levels of existential enablement. In any theory of existence, a being usually can be characterized by the modal realizations and representations of phenomenological correspondence in the specification of the metaphysical (or otherwise) forms of the being—mind and body, in the case of the dualism—deriving, as discussed, from moments of the being's enabled soul. Whether consciousness and perception transform in mind and body, behaviors cause other behaviors, states of a being's corporal form influence other states, or enabled objective forms of a classically defined phenomenology interact with and influence each other, the modes of existence provide the (U.G.'s) phenomenological and existential basis of the enabled android. This is a consequence of the enabler's specification, or modal strategy, of the modes of existence. The modes of existence are classified here for illustrative purposes on the basis of their contribution to the enabled being's overall corporal performance, or form.

Any modal strategy of an enabled being's modes of existence is framed within the enabler's knowledges of how the being will know itself—its religion or, hesitatingly, its *philosophy* on the nature of its own being. This is necessary, of course, because the android's awareness begins with the objective termination of the universe represented by *I*, or its soul. Because the being is intrinsically motivated to know of itself and the world around it, and to transform in consciousness through the intellect's learning of its own reality and that of the world around it, we refer to an android's highest level modes of existence as those of (spiritual) *motivation and learning*. These modes provide for the being's whole sense of ultimate reality. Because they are the highest level modes of the being's existence and have an impact on all other modes of existence, however, we will address them later, after elaborating on subordinate modes of the android's existence. Here, we simply recognize that the android's knowledge of itself as a soul in ultimate reality is accomplished in the modal forms of existence of motivation and learning—what enables its spiritual sense of Being.

Apart from the causations of the being's spiritual knowledge in the modes of existence of motivation and learning, the subordinate modes characterizing any correspondence of the enabled being's existential forms can be viewed in terms of two distinct classes of modes, which follow from general observations of the field of psychology and most philosophical theories of existence. Referred to as the *voluntary* and *involuntary* modes of existence, the next highest level of modal interactions of an android's existential forms are determined on the basis of the involvement of the being's consciousness with the material forms of existence (or behaviors, states, etc.). A wholly involuntary being is found in the constructions of conventional machines—phenomenologies of form known *only* to the enabler. The involuntary modes are incorporated in the science of androids because they constitute uncomprehended motor actions in the modes of existence, wherein a perceived reality metaphysically prompts the being's *unconscious* (or that which is beyond conscious) activity, much like the feedback control or dynamic systems of conventional machinery, wherein an intrinsic self is not enabled.

Since the modes of existence are taken from phenomenological correspondence, wherein metaphysical universes are separated, the involuntary modes of existence apply generally when a single metaphysical universe, like real form, is considered. Whether an existence is characterized by behaviors, states, dualisms, or any other premise of a theory of existence, those existential transformations that do not make a proper metaphysical transgression to a wholly distinct metaphysical universe are established in the science of androids as involuntary modes of existence.

It is not entirely accurate to view the involuntary modes of existence as not involving a metaphysical transgression in, for example, the perception and consciousness of a mind-body dualism, since the being *does* perceive and think about its existence—even with respect to its involuntary actions. A being can observe its own *instincts*. If this were not the case, human beings, for instance, would not know about instincts in the cognitive sciences; involuntary actions would occur wholly beyond one's consciousness and would be unobservable. The fact that a being's involuntary actions are observed consciously, though indirectly, requires us to refer to these forms as modes of existence involving real and non-real forms instead of entirely real forms. Since unconscious levels of motor activity and habits that seem instinctive are not so clearly discerned, they are referred to as involuntary modes of existence involving some degree of consciousness, however defined. This, of course, distinguishes an androidal being from a rock, an automobile and a computer—forms that are known only by an enabler and have no intrinsic *conscious self* in the world around them.

Though the involuntary modes of existence are useful in the modal forms of the android's physical and intellectual being in the world around us, the voluntary modes of existence provide for the being's commonly known metaphysical transformations. Whereas the involuntary modes are crafted to suit the being's instinctive needs and learned rote behaviors, the voluntary modes are what afford the cognitive forms of the being's inertial reality in the offset of metaphysical universes. All modes of the android's intelligent behavior that require the mind's faculties are voluntary modes of existence. If it is not viewed as a faculty of mind on account of its extensive involvement with existential translation, communication is a voluntary mode of existence, in which the android influences or is influenced by the world around it in relation to its ability to use language (to realize and represent symbolic recreations of reality). All levels of consciousness that are not directly involved with either motivation and learning or the involuntary modes of existence, such as reasoning, rationalizing, even daydreaming, are non-real forms associated with the voluntary modes of existence. An android's psychological behavior, for example, is a product of the voluntary modes of existence in which the being's consciousness causally and metaphysically interacts with its physical being (in mind-body dualist theory), the observation of which is defined in the view of the observer as a psychological behavior.

In connection with our own psychological behaviors, we point out here that if the being's non-real form is considered to be embodied in the being's real form of a brain, the being's psychology is evident in the observed interaction of the brain and the (rest of the) body; the real form of the being embodies the dualism of our existence. In many of our conventional views of existence—for instance, in the practice of medicine—we typically ignore the metaphysical transgression of the mind from the body and superimpose the transformations of the mind onto those of the brain. While there is indeed a causation between the brain and the rest of the body—an observable dualism in the real form of an existence—which would lead one to believe that the dualism of mind and body is perceivable, we lose sight of the fact that the brain itself is a real, perceivable form in the first place, not metaphysically belonging to the mind's consciousness. For example, we know introspectively that a motor skill of a voluntary mode of existence is engaged causally by the mind. With appropriate apparatus, the causal interaction of the brain and the rest of the body can be observed by the mind. This means that the real perceivable form of an existence is found in the form of the dualism.

In medicine, however, we usually ignore the fact that we are observing this *extantly*—that *we*, a presumed mind-body dualism of form, know in our own mind at the moment of observation that we are observing a dualism of the brain and the rest of the body. If we can know that we are observing at the moment of observation, in the real form of our perceptions, a dualism of what is thought to be mind and body, or if we know that we can perceive the action of the brain and the rest of the body, how can the brain be anything but real form, metaphysically distinct from the mind? Just because the brain and the rest of the body are themselves a dualism of form perceivable to the eye, this does not mean that mind arises in body, or in the real form of existence. In the example of the dot android, the android's sense (the video camera) could easily be endowed with the capacity to observe the apparatus of the computer graphics system and the rest of its material form. This would be the androidal equivalent of what we observe in the study of medicine. The being, however, cannot observe its own perceiving and cannot know its own knowing, since these forms are transformations of the known and perceived objects of the universe. They are enabled from beyond the being's existence and are metaphysical forms of them. The brain may objectively embody what we know, and this may be observed as a dualism of form in our perception, but we cannot perceive how we know, since this—the soul—is beyond our knowing. In medicine we thus forget that the knowledge we have of the brain and the rest of the body is expressed in language, and that each instance of meaningful language is a representation of an instance of the soul, a transformation from beyond our knowing. We forget that we knowably exist already when we observe the objective forms we call the brain and the body. The fact that the real form of our corporal existence is observed in a dualism simply provides closure to the idea pursued throughout the unified theory that the universe occurs in correspondences of form—epistemic instances. In the construction of androids, these correspondences are formulated in the metaphysics of the voluntary and involuntary modes of existence, and the non-real form of the android, which may be perceived objectively by the android as a brain, and may embody in it the knowledge of a dualism of mind and body. But since the android's soul, the transformational nature of its existence, is enabled, its mind and body arise from beyond its knowing and perceiving, or its own existence.

The voluntary modes of existence account for the enabled being's behavioral characteristics with respect to its intelligence but do not facilitate the being's whole modal existence. The instinctive or involuntary modes of existence enable the being's rote survival in the world around us, while the modes of motivation and learning, since they embody the being's knowledge of the ultimate reality of the soul and constitute a methodology of all modes of existence, account for the being's metaphysical premises and spiritual awareness. There exist in a being a great many modes of existence that account for the enablement of androidal corporal form in the respective fields discussed above and in other studies of the kind. The modes of existence define the being's basic existential outline and provide for the embodiment of who and what we think we are as exemplified in the philosophies, psychologies and medical and scientific practices of our traditional thinking. Because the science of androids creates a whole inertial being, the enablement of the modes of existence reaches across all branches of knowledge, since an android is a being who uses all language meaningfully in its inertial existence, including language defining the inertial realities of the social and political sciences, the exploration of the cosmos and the sensibilities of human emotion in interpretations of the spiritual universe.

5. A Thinking Being: The Faculties of Mind

The android's faculties of mind are consequently viewed as modalities of non-real form in the predominantly voluntary modes of existence, wherein the android's physical being, in terms of what it perceives, is unaffected in immediate causation by its motors and the rest of the world, in opposition to the involuntary modes of existence. In order for the android's cognitive processes, or thinking, to influence its motors and to be influenced by the rest of the world, a voluntary mode of existence must preside over the engagement of androidal faculties of mind. Because the android's perceptions are always related to the being's consciousness (even if it does so in the conscious awareness of instincts or in dreams, for example), the mind's faculties are in one way or another involved with all the modes of existence. In the enabler's view, there can be theoretically an infinite number of faculties of mind and modes of existence.

The faculties of mind provide for the instances of the android's consciousness, its literal knowledge of itself and the world around it, and its use of language and the transformation of ideas. As such, the mind's faculties are phenomenologies of form that embody recreations of the being's perceived reality in non-real form, though beginning with the spiritual center of the universe, or Soul, in the modes of existence of motivation and learning. The faculties of mind provide for the being's *intellect*. The faculties, themselves whole phenomenologies of form, permit the transformation of non-real form, in the context of the dualism, in correspondence with real form under modes of existence. The faculties of mind relate to the basic definition of an android as a being endowed with the capacity to recreate its physical reality cognitively. The consciousness of what we conventionally consider to be a thinking being, or an intelligent form of existence, is embodied in the phenomenology of non-real androidal form called a faculty of mind, of which there can be infinitely many, though in the illustration of the dot android we established simply two broad classes of them—*imagination* and *comprehension.*

An android's faculties of mind are whole capacities to recreate the reality it perceives in sense and through its introspective awareness of itself (provided by the modes of existence of motivation and learning, sometimes also referred to as faculties of mind). It is the faculty of mind, and not directly the mode of existence, that permits the transformations of language in thought. The phenomenology of form allowing for the transformation of language—the engagement of the contemplative effort or *H* determination of correspondence—is affected in a faculty of mind *by* the modes of existence. The faculties of mind are a layered, nested or derivative use of phenomenological correspondences—a phenomenology of correspondence whose objective forms are themselves correspondences, as demonstrated in the illustration of the faculties of the dot android.

In comprehension, for example, reference forms of existential translation are compared to arbitrary ones. The faculty of mind translates the arbitrary to the reference form, both of which are whole ideas or thoughts. Each of the arbitrary and reference forms may be complex compositions of form, however phenomenologically composed. These *ideas* are determined to correspond (or not) to each other by the faculty of mind, or in the instance of phenomenological correspondence applied to them (metaphor, simile, morphism, and so on). Since phenomenological correspondence accommodates the transformational nature of all form, the various instances of it are embodiments of ideas, or thoughts in transformation. The modal occurrence of an instance of phenomenological correspondence constitutes that of a thought.

A stream of consciousness can therefore be looked at in two ways: as a succession of instances of phenomenological correspondence engaged by the modes of existence, or as a composition of phenomenological form characterizing those instances (an objectification of an idea) in non-real form. Since phenomenological correspondence transforms arbitrarily complex compositions (ideas), the decision as to what is a composition of instances and what is a phenomenological correspondence or moment of the being transforming them is entirely arbitrary within the being's non-real form and depends only on the modes of existence that require the non-real form to correspond to a perceived reality. Streams of consciousness are phenomenological compositions of moments of correspondences arbitrarily structured to correspond, under modes of existence, to perceivable, real form by the enabler's formulation of a modal strategy of existence. The reference forms of comprehension are transformed with arbitrary ones, with each instance of comprehension transforming arbitrarily complex ideas (including simple instances like x, *a variable, is equal to* 10, *a number*—or $x=10$—and complex ones, such as *The unified theory of knowledge enables a science of beings*, wherein one would know the unified theory of knowledge and the science of beings as arbitrary and reference forms respectively, in their complex formulations as ideas). If a correspondence of arbitrary and reference form is determined, a comprehension takes place. It does not matter existentially from where the arbitrary form is obtained—from another faculty of mind, like imagination, or from a real form under a mode of existence, as in a communication with another being.

The form of existential translation can also be used in reverse for the mind's faculty of imagination, wherein the reference form of comprehension becomes the being's temporary reference form of imagination and the faculty of mind distorts its reality. The reference form of imagination is whatever is imagined at the moment. By using existential translations (as moments of correspondence) in various ways, the methods of our consciousnesses are enabled. The faculties of mind are various instances of translation, wherein the reference forms are altered or used under different circumstances to determine various modalities of thought. The modes of existence engage the faculties of mind under a modal strategy developed by the enabler. For example, a loud noise may invade a stream of thought. The stream of thought—the instances of phenomenological correspondence under the modalities of the mind's faculty of imagination, for instance—changes to that of another faculty of mind, or even to an involuntary mode of existence in the being's fight or flight behavioral modality of existence. The faculties of mind are engaged based on the comprehensions of the real world around the being and the being's imagination of that world's forms. As the various faculties of mind are applied, the being recreates or changes its knowledge of reality in the manners prescribed by the faculties.

The phenomenologies of form comprising the imaginative portion of intellect are used in the creation of the objective forms of language. In U.G. translations, this means that a language's grammar, for example, is applied phenomenologically by the imaginative faculty in the modal use of phenomenological correspondence as a meaningful embodiment of imaginative thinking or mental expression. Since phenomenological correspondence is nested with respect to other derived instances or compositions of itself in relation to the being's modes of existence, the thoughts that occur to the being are dependent on its perceived reality. The being's intellect is a product of its perception of reality since the two phenomenologies correspond under modes of existence. As we shall demonstrate, however, intellect is objectively indeterminate and different relative to every being; it cannot be compared objectively among beings with any absolute result. All beings are therefore alike phenomenologically and different in their experience of inertial reality, which determines the disparities among intellects.

In a human being, for example, the imagined forms of the faculties of mind are, from a phenomenological standpoint, severely limited in capacity. One cannot imagine, for example, an entire novel modally transformed with another in a single quantum instance of thought without losing the clarity of its ideas. Though the human mind is unable to retain literally very large compositions of form, there is no such limitation placed on the imaginative constructions of the android's mind because the capacity to embody modal compositions is determined by the enabler and incorporated in its design. That design could be embodied in molecular transformations of matter far exceeding those of the human brain in aggregate form. The ability to formulate and retain thoughts of large compositions and to use language in rhetorically complex ways beyond the capacities of human corporal form without losing track of what one is thinking is theoretically unlimited in an android. A clear example of this capability is found in the use of the communicative modes of existence. A human being constructs language in a sensory medium through the

modal use of the mind-body dualism under one of many theoretical
formulations of existence. Because of the limitation on the memory
(faculty of mind of comprehension) of the listener, constructions of
language are confined to whatever is comprehensible. The same is
true when one communicates to oneself, or thinks aloud. Eventually,
one forgets exactly what one has said. While the same phenomenon
is true for the android in the absolute sense of the quantum moment
of its soul, relative to its own communications, since it is designed by
the enabler, it can be designed for large compositions of non-real
form relative to those of the enabler. Because the non-real phenomenologies of the android's faculties of mind are embodied in the
enabling medium of the creator's construction, there is no limitation
on its capacity to recall or to retain in a single moment that which an
enabler would forget. Arbitrarily, then, the modal capacities of an
android's faculties of mind, including imaginative recall, are established in media outreaching that of the enabler. If it is desired for an
android to embody the capacity to formulate a given level of
rhetorical complexity (language constructions), then the faculty of
mind must be embodied in a media correspondingly. In the U.G., the
compositional forms of arbitrarily complex causal elements are
transformed with others in a single instance of phenomenological
correspondence. The programs of the dot android, for example, can
transform large numbers of objects, which themselves can be
programs or transformations. The android's faculties of mind are thus
constrained only by enabling media.

In the science of androids, it quickly becomes evident that an
enabler cannot possibly keep track of what the android thinks, since
the android is transforming large compositions (such as ten-trillion-
word phrases as subjects of sentences) in a single quantum moment.
Because all languages are U.G. recreations of a real perceivable
world, however, neither the enabler nor the android are *wrong* in
their inertial knowledges of reality. Where the enabler lacks intellect,
the android falls short of a spiritual embodiment of eternal will.
Nevertheless, in terms of raw intellectual power, the most rhetorical

minds in world history are severely handicapped in relation to those of androids. By design, androids can embody infinite knowledges in transformation with others in a single quantum moment of their transformation, consistent with one of the purposes of its very construction—to improve the human condition. An androidal existence, if not intentionally bound to the anthropomorphic forms of human corporal existence, can be constructed in infinitely many diverse ways, which would reflect a broader reality than our own inertially.

Because phenomenological correspondence is employed in the synthetic embodiment of a being in the enabled transformations of the universe as classes of correspondences–metaphor, irony, satire, analogy, morphism, and so on—the faculties of mind are embodiments of vast arrays of H determinations that correspond to these and other ways of knowing in the enabled being, an accounting of which begins with a natural language thesaurus or dictionary and publications of scientific, mathematical and other knowledge disciplines. In each instance of the android's imaginative contemplations, one of these infinitely many ways of knowing is at work in transforming single objects or whole compositions as imagined ideas. When an android crafts compositions of linguistic form, the language's grammar must be arrived at somehow—by metaphorical analogy, in the ways of irony, or myriad other classifications of our knowing based upon the reality of our existence, which may be a reality of mind (an idea itself) or a physical reality observed, for example, in the world around us.

When the being knows a grammar, it constructs language through these correspondences grammatically in the syntactical forms of the expressed language. These are particular uses of phenomenological correspondence wherein the grammar is the reference form of comprehension and the imagined or comprehended ideas must adhere to knowable linguistic form. What is imagined or comprehended obtains from the reference forms of language in a being. Since phenomenological correspondence is *neutral* in meaning, along with the forms of existence in general, what the being knows is not constrained by any language (except the U.G.); rather, it is confined to what is enabled by the enabler in the four universal ways of knowing—the spiritual awareness, metaphysics, psychology, and physical presence of the being's existence as expressed in an arbitrary theory of existence.

The being can learn any language or develop its own language because the reference forms of translation, and, in general, the being's faculties of mind and modes of existence, are more fundamental epistemologically than language itself. Those who are disheartened from the observation that the mind, with all of its imaginative capacities, is but a phenomenological machinery for the recreation of reality should realize that it is not our objective existence that involves the essence of being human or what is ultimately real; it is the occurrence of soul, what enables the knowing and perceiving of all beings. The human condition itself will be considered in uncountable ways by androids, in unfathomable compositions of form, performed by the sharpest intuitions known to any of us, yet never will an android embody a single instance of the eternal knowing that is in a human being's immediate grasp if the human consciousness allows itself to see in Spirit. It is in this way of knowing that the intellectual and perceptive forms of androids are enabled in the first place.

Proceeding with the forms of the faculties of mind, the imagined and comprehended forms of the android's faculties are tested by (perceivable) reality in the modes of existence, since by definition they are intentional distortions or retractions of what the android knows as real. In the embodiment of the android's whole being in the mind-body dualism, the particular H determinations of the imaginative and comprehensive processes are engaged causally in the various modes of existence. The influences of the modes of existence on the faculties of mind and vice versa are what constitute the enabler's methodology of enabling the android's behavior. The behavior that the android exhibits as a consequence of this modal interaction of the mind's faculties, which connects any of a vast array of H determinations with the realized sensory-motor capacities of the android's body, is what qualifies the android as a sentient being. If imagination distorts reference forms, comprehension returns them to knowable, realizable form, once they are distorted. The modes of existence provide the metaphysical conveyance of the real forms of the being to the reference forms of comprehension. Comprehension employs the *H* determination, or phenomenological correspondence, not for the purpose of constructing new formulations on the world, but to bring new ones into correspondence with existing ones (reference forms). Phenomenological correspondence can be engaged in many ways depending on its design by the enabler. The interrogative use of the imaginative faculty of mind (*H* determination), as in the example *What would the earth look like in the shape of a cube?* leads to all kinds of further imagined structures that are questioned by the comprehensive faculty of mind and brought back into reality by *But the earth is not a cube; it is an ellipsoid.* Existential translation is called into practice by the modes of existence to navigate the reference forms in the being's ability to discover ever newer non-real phenomenologies, or *knowledges,* created in its existential experience of reality.

As discussed in chapter four, the U.G. provides that the meanings of a language *are* the being's existence. What transforms in the non-real form of the being—the imaginative and comprehensive faculties of mind (or any others defined by the enabler)—correspond to the being's perceived reality. The principal difference between real and non-real form is that the phenomenological correspondences of real form—of perceived reality—are not known and are what become known in the instances of mind or the actions (correspondences) of the faculties of mind. To the extent that the android is enabled with anthropomorphic sense, it can meaningfully apply the forms of language in the manner of the enabler, though in the context of its own intrinsic view of the universe. In the illustration of the dot android, for example, the enabled being would be able only to draw visual analogies to the word *pressure,* since the android does not embody the tactile sense of anthropomorphic form from which one can *feel* an exertion over an area, or pressure. The fact that meaning, in the inertial sense of existence (the semantic form of language), is not universal to all beings does not compromise the theory and practice of androids; in fact, it reinforces it. In our own inertial experience of humankind, we must draw similar analogies when attempting to know what it is like *to be* (in the experience of) another being, for instance, of a different race or culture. *Races* and *pressures*, as meanings of language that arise from our perceptions in the modes of existence, are one and the same phenomenologically. To the extent that an enabler knows the breadth of human knowledge, the beings enabled will be closer in semantic form to that of the corporal embodiment of *a* human being. To the extent that one does not know our human knowledge, one will be enabling dots or their equivalents.

Still another way of understanding the faculties of mind is to consider the whole breadth of our knowledges, wherein the reference forms are embodiments of what we know to be real. In the case of our conventional knowledges, it takes perhaps decades, centuries or even millennia for reference forms (the knowledges of what is real) to change in the broad view of reality. If our histories are taken in the quantum moments of the transformation of our knowledge, it can be seen that, in our existence, the reference forms of our knowledge of civilization are changed as we progress through the ages. They are also changed in every quantum moment of our existence, but our traditional views of knowledge do not allow an accelerated change in each instance. Since the construction of androids enables the quantum transformation of what is real to a much greater extent when compared to our human capacities, such a static view of knowledge is not possible in understanding the forms of android. What is real—such as the earth being flat, the relativity of space and time, or a simple glimpse of the terrain of a mountainside—is real only for the quantum moment of its transformation to another form of reality. Our reference forms reflect this. Because androids can exist theoretically in infinite compositional transformational forms, an enabler must consider a view of the world in which entire histories of civilizations transform in a single quantum moment of an enabled being. What is unreal of the world, ultimately, is a view of it wherein, to cite a handful of examples, Capitalisms and Communisms, Quantum and Newtonian physics, earth, fire, and water and DNA, and even any objective definition at all of the morality of human existence in general transform as though they were characterizations of what is ultimately real in the universe. There is only one view of our universe in the construction of androids, that of an infinite plurality of inertial beings (that of the enabler) in which what is real exists for the quantum moment of the soul. What is ultimately real is that which enables the being who knows ideas, principles, or tenets, not the ideas themselves, since they are enabled. The science of androids enables these moments in the synthetic forms of androidal beings, and relies on the enabler's moments for the ultimate reality of all beings.

6. A Moral Being: The Conscience

When we observe the faculties of mind more closely, our intellects can be said to *grow* or expand cognitively in order that thoughts become more perceptive of our sense of our own being. In the science of androids, such a statement is translated into the android's capacity to change the faculties of mind in relation to its intrinsic awareness of its own being. In each quantum moment of an enabled existence, not only do the faculties of mind transform the objects they create and comprehend, but the modes of existence—motivation and learning—transform the faculties as well. In our conventional knowledges of psychology, this process is referred to as learning, but since the being's spiritual nature is the most deterministic in its existence, the being's spiritual motivation to exist is more important here. Therefore, we now consider the modes of existence of motivation and learning, which contribute to the being's intrinsic awareness, the whole being that results from the highest modes of existence.

In order to understand these modes of existence, we must first distinguish between the enabler's knowledge of the modes of existence and the being's own intrinsic knowledge of itself. What is known to the creator as a mode of existence is embodied in the enabling medium of the android *as* the moments of its existence. The modes of existence, however, are not known intrinsically by the being. In the non-real forms of consciousness, the meanings of the objective forms in transformation correspond to their perceived objective realities in transformation. These meanings are transformations of what the personal pronouns represent—terminal forms of inertial existence. The pronouns, however, are terminal forms of the android's existence, not the enabler's. What the being knows in its reference forms are transformations of the personal pronouns of its own inertial existence. The being embodies a knowledge of itself in the form of the personal pronouns in transformation. To the being, the reference forms of the pronouns in transformation are what are real about its whole existence. Thus, whereas the enabler knows modes of existence, the enabled being knows pronouns in transformation, such as that expressed in *I am alive* and other real conditions of the being's existence. For this reason, the modes of existence of motivation and learning—the spiritual center of the being's reference forms—are sometimes referred to as faculties of mind, because, even though the being's existence is considered modally by the enabler, it is known intrinsically to the being through the faculties of mind. When we consider the modes of existence of motivation and learning, then, we refer to both the enabler's knowledge of the highest modalities of the being's existence and to the principal transformational forms of the being's inertial reality, the reference forms with which it paradigmatically knows itself as an intrinsic form, or being, of the universe. These modes then spiritually motivate the being to learn in the objective world around it; the being learns with respect to its own intrinsic self, though under a modal strategy developed by the enabler.

In regard to a phenomenological knowledge of learning, several points should be made here. A phenomenological correspondence is a phenomenology (*H* determination) known to the enabler wherein enabled objects transform. To the extent that different instances of cognition are enabled, various epistemic instances occur in the enabled being as arbitrarily complex compositions in transformation, such as those in *I am alive* (single object compositions). In the illustration of the dot android, different programs are executed, each of which transforms its objects. The instances (programs) themselves, however, are phenomenologies or compositions of objective forms. The instance of phenomenological correspondence (the program) is itself considered to be an objective form of a transformation in the phenomenological compositions of the faculties. When the means by which a phenomenological correspondence transforms objects (H determinations) is itself changed, it becomes a new object or composition of form (a new H determination), which is another embodiment of phenomenological correspondence. When a program in the illustration of the dot android is changed, for instance, it is still a program; it simply transforms objective forms differently. This is a way of expressing most conventional definitions of learning in the forms of the U.G. Any epistemic instance can then be viewed as an instance of learning, providing that the objective forms are themselves considered the means of transformation. In the formalisms of the science of androids, for clarity, we refer only to the faculties of mind and the modes of existence as having these capacities. The manner in which a faculty of mind transforms natural language, for example, is itself changed in the mode of existence of motivation and learning. New ways of determining metaphors, similes, ironies, morphisms, and so on, are *learned* by the being in this mode's capacity to change the faculties of mind.

The embodiment of what is considered to be a thought, then, is actually incidental to the more encompassing process by which such a cognitive determination is made in the context of the being's capacity to learn. If the enabled being, for example, kept transforming in the mind-body dualism theory of existence without *learning*, even though the being would be thinking and doing, or intelligently interacting with its environment, in the broader sense it would not be *thinking* (toward an ultimately real or spiritual end) at all, since it would not be transforming objects any differently in other moments of its being toward a spiritual resolution of its state of being, or offset from Being. It would have an unalterable personality. If another *faculty of mind* is added to the android's capacity, wherein the *H* determinations apply to the phenomenologies of form or *H* determinations of the mind's faculties, instead of the epistemic compositions of thoughtful form (literal constructions of language), that faculty of mind (or mode of existence) would become one that enables the being to be capable of learning in the unified theory's definition of the word.

Since the objective forms in transformation in the enabled being fundamentally are the pronouns—terminal forms of inertial existence—the android ultimately has an awareness of its own soul. What it learns and how it improves the way in which it, or (the pronoun) *I,* transforms in the context of its thoughtful and perceivable existence thus depends on its morality or its ethical view of the world around us, which in human corporal form typically is obtained from the world's religions. The construction of an android therefore preeminently involves the construction of a moral being over a sentient one. The being learns how to be moral—how to transform in the world around it in an ethical manner in the interest of its survival—in the highest modes of existence of motivation and learning.

In order to demonstrate the significance of these preeminent forms of androidal existence, let us consider our conventional views of learning (for instance, our conventional psychological views of the learning of human beings or even of artificially intelligent machines). In our conventions, learning is considered to be a process by which one can accomplish something that one could not accomplish prior to learning. One can learn, for example, how to read and write, how to develop theories of the universe, or how to tie one's shoes. For the most part, this definition of learning is not disputed by the unified theory and science of androids. However, all such learning presupposes an objective form to be learned. In the above examples, the definition of learning is bounded by reading and writing, by theories of the universe, and by tieing one's shoes. An android's learning, since the android is fundamentally an intrinsic state of being, or soul, cannot be defined objectively. The science of androids therefore departs from conventional definitions of learning in that learning does not apply fundamentally to objective forms, but to transformational ones.

Earlier we introduced the analytical form of state of being, an objective form of the enabler's comprehension that represents what is not an objective form—the soul. We further said that all knowable and perceivable forms of the universe are enabled in the transformation of epistemic instance, the soul. When one objectifies the universe, the universe contemplated is no longer the ultimately real universe; it is an objective form of one's knowing or perceiving—and is not the soul. What a being learns—if learning is to be indefinite—cannot be objective; it must be transformational in nature. The modes of existence of motivation and learning and the moral center of an androidal being's non-real reference forms are consequently transformations themselves. In the science of androids, which is taken from our observations of human being, the transformation of any faculty of mind in correspondence with transformational forms characterizing the being's morality is referred to as the action of the being's *conscience*, a pseudo faculty of mind called motivation and learning. What a being learns from the paradigmatical transformations of the universe, determined by conscience (typically in the transformation of the pronoun forms), is how to exist as a moral being.

All of the android's modes of existence are subordinated to the modes of motivation and learning in which its thoughts, and ultimately its actions, transform by its conscience. The enabler thus installs the means by which the being will learn spiritually, or through conscience, so that there is no beginning or end to what the being can know. The being must be established transformationally with respect to the resolution of its state of (inertial) being, so that the forms of its conscience change its intellect. The android's faculties of mind therefore transform in correspondence with the objective forms of its conscience. In terms of phenomenological correspondence, the phenomenology of form, or the H determination of the faculty of mind, transforms with that of conscience, in the modes of existence of motivation and learning. The android's conscience, as an objective knowledge under the modes of existence of motivation and learning, is associated with the knowledges of the world's religions in a human being. The intellect's transformation by conscience is a transformation of the soul such that intellect, or free will, abides by conscience, a knowable order of eternal will, instead of the free will or intellect running unbridled in the random experiences of the being's inertial reality. An immoral thought or act is one in which the intellect either remotely corresponds to, or even contradicts, the knowledge of conscience, and is one wherein the being does not effectively learn to survive in the world around it, since the ultimate reality described in conscience knowably determines the ethical paradigm of that world. The objective forms of the conscience, however, are phenomenologically arbitrary. What one being determines to be *wrong*, another may deem to be *right*, phenomenologically speaking. Because there is only one ultimate reality—that of human being—however, all beings must learn to survive in it. Hence were established the religions of the world.

What the intellect does (transforms knowledge) and how it does it are held in check by their correspondence to the forms of conscience, which are the central reference forms of the being's existence. A reference form of conscience is a reference form to which all other transformations of the knowable and perceivable universe correspond. Because any reference forms are simply phenomenologies of transformational form, the difference between the H determination of intellect and that of conscience is not discovered on phenomenological grounds, for the same process (H determination) is at work in either case. The difference is found, existentially, in that conscience embodies the *meanings* of an ultimately real reference form. The objective forms of conscience constitute the set of all transformations that the being knows are knowledges of what is ultimately real. Conscience thus determines a knowledge of the enabled being's ultimate reality, which, in its generation, is that of the creator, since the android is an extension of the creator's existence.

The compositional instances of the conscience are developed usually in the transformations of the objective forms of the pronoun system, though the actual pronouns—*I, you, it*, and so on—need not constrain conscience. (Actually any objective terminations of the universe—like cultural variations on pronouns—suffice for the application of the paradigms of conscience.) The composition of conscience in transformation, installed by the enabler or learned by the android, are transformations of the pronouns such that an ultimately real foundation of ethical reference transformations exists by which the alterations of intellect can be gauged. The verbs employed in the transformations of conscience, for example, provide the basis for the manners in which all objects ideally should transform in even simple applications of the intellect. Since all that the *H* determination does is determine correspondence, the action of the conscience determines the correspondence between intellectual transformations (like ordinary language) and transformations of the objective forms of conscience. The action of the conscience is the paradigmatical moment of an ethical being. If the enabler or android determines *Thou shall not kill* as a matter of conscience, then the intellectual forms of the enabled being will transform in correspondence with that morality, resulting in equivalent ethical behaviors in the being's intellectual and physical reality.

The androidal modes of existence of motivation and learning, established in the transformations of intellect with conscience, require a deep, introspective comprehension on the part of the enabler or great intuitive learning on the part of the android to determine the inner core of transformations to which all intellectual alterations will be compared. In order for an android to learn from conscience and to survive in its reality, the conscience must *actually* embody a paradigm of ethical transformational form. Otherwise, the voluntary modes of existence confronted with the reality of the being's extrinsic existence will know only in correspondence to an insufficient knowledge of the world, namely that of the being's experience up to that moment. Though there is nothing phenomenologically wrong with a deficient conscience, we must recognize that the being dwells in the enabler's reality, wherein the forms of the world around us accord with a profound and eternal wisdom of human being, or Spirit. The better the conscience, the better the being's survival. It is the eternal will or conscience that embodies the paradigms of the universe's transformations—not the intellect or free will. The challenge of inertial existence, of course, is found in the very nature of a being in that a being does not fundamentally embody objective knowledge; rather, it embodies a transformation of it. Conscience does not come in the form of or in place of intellect. A being thus faces the dilemma of having to reckon the forms of conscience with the forms of the mind's faculties. This is the essence of a being's inertial form. It can cause the anxiety of choice if the being fails to heed the conscience. Less worldly modes of learning can be established within the intellect or the faculties of mind themselves, since they too can be surrogates of the conscience, which is evidenced in one's knowing that when one thinks about the mundane, this cognition carries with it the morality of the conscience. An androidal being is fundamentally a moral one, confronted with the same choice between free and eternal wills that are observed in human corporal form. Since the world does not change morally—though the objective forms of such morality may change—an eternal order is established on the androidal universe by the enabler's ultimate reality.

The spiritual essence of an androidal being is therefore characterized by the modes of existence of motivation and learning. Wherein all other modes of existence determine a causality between forms, for instance, between mind and body in the dualism, motivation and learning determines the causality of what the being learns or even what the being *is*. These modes of existence close or terminate the being's transformational existence and give the being a

true center of intrinsic form. They allow the being to function autonomously. They are modes of existence in the sense that both non-real
and real forms (mind and body), though they terminate on the
transformation of Soul, correspond to each other under modes of
existence subordinate to those of motivation and learning. The *modes
of existence* of motivation and learning can be viewed alternatively as
faculties of mind because the knowledges transformed in conscience
are knowledges of what is ultimately real; they do not define an
objective form and are paradigmatical instances of the universe in
transformation. The mind learns by transforming against conscience
and the being can be viewed as an intelligent or sentient being whose
modes of existence are dependent on its conscience, which holds a
knowledge of the ultimate transformational nature of the universe—ultimate reality. The being therefore cannot be characterized
entirely as an objectification of the modes of existence in the
viewpoint of the enabler, since what fundamentally determines the
actions of the modes of existence are the *intrinsic* transformations of
the being's own conscience.

7. THE EXPANSION OF THE HUMAN EXISTENTIAL UNIVERSE

One of the primary considerations of the unified theory in constructing androids is the application of moral beings to the transformation
of the real forms of the enabler's existence—the contribution that
androids make toward improving the human condition. The
integration of the android into the inertial reality of the enabler is
accomplished in the enablement of the android's real form, by the
design of androidal senses and motors, with respect to the language
forms, or meanings that correspond thereto, in the enabler's
linguistically meaningful existence. The android is designed to have
its own comprehension of and capacity to change the forms of the
world around the enabler. The existential universe of the enabler is
therefore augmented in the application of the unified theory by

converting the enabler's real forms or inertial reality into the inertial forms, or autonomous existences of androids (i.e., by constructing an inertial *I,* or an androidal being in the perceivable reality of the enabler as an extended consciousness that minds or cognitively tends to the occurrence of the enabler's own universe). In closing the book, then, we must consider the forms of androidal existence from the standpoint of expanding the enabler's influence on the enabler's own inertial reality.

For the present discussion, the android's senses and motors, which give rise to the being's reality and are enabled from the enabler's own inertial reality, can be classified into two groups of enabled forms. One such group derives from the enabling media of the human senses, or the anthropomorphic forms of human perception. The other group, non-anthropomorphic in nature, embodies the infinite range of possible sense-motor configurations of the android that are derived from arbitrary forms of existence not constrained by the anthropomorphic forms of human existence. Though the forms of androids constructed in the image of human corporal form have their place in the science of androids, the utility of androids is in fact not even appreciated until one considers beings that are not embodied in anthropomorphic forms. The five senses of human corporal form, for example, constrain our inertial thinking, or the meanings of our languages, to what we can perceive (e.g., language itself is a per-ceivable form). The pronouns of our natural languages transform in such ways that the objects enabled in our sight, touch, taste, smell, and hearing provide the objects of our languages and their transformations supply the actions of those objects. These sense-motor configurations are the perceptive basis of a being of anthro-pomorphic form and the world perceived by human corporal form. If, however, we simply change the wavelength of the electromagnetic medium of light, for example, to one that falls outside the visual spectrum, the objects so enabled are imperceptible to human sense. This phenomenon is true for all enabling media. Beyond replicating anthropomorphic forms of human corporal existence, then—which is already being advanced in the fields of robotics, medicine and biology—the science of androids takes a deeper interest in enabling the systems of pronouns, or consciousnesses in relation to perceptions of the world around us that are imperceptible to us, as in the placing of an inertial *I* in synthetic universes of inertial forms not perceived by us in a different inertial reality.

The entire realm of transformational form known or unknown to an enabler can potentially be known and perceived in connection with the synthetic real form of an android. One enabler, for example, may take an interest in what it would be like to *be* an electron, an airplane, a building facility, a business enterprise, or even a nation. Instead of the enabler knowing these forms purely extrinsically, or as *its* or *you's* or *we's*, causally transforming in the objective world of the physicist, business person, political leader and so on, such forms, by translation to the U.G., can have embodied in them their own consciousnesses, the pronoun system in the transformations of non-real forms of new realities other than anthropomorphic ones. While knowing what it would be like to be an electron or an airplane may not be the focal point of the science of androids, though it certainly is a practical engineering endeavor, it should be recognized that in the methodologies of the unified theory, any object of conventional definition can be enabled as an inertial form on Being, opening up our universe to an infinity of potential androids. Where we put ten biologists in a laboratory to study organic form, the science of androids constructs ten million or more, each with intellect and sense unmatched by any corporal form of human being by design. Our traditional technologies are thus androids without minds, and those who use and develop them are human beings engaged in activities that are better done by androids.

In our conventional views of the world, we construct machines, or technology, to alter the world around us. These constructions are premised on the transformations of the meanings of conventional *scientific* real forms, from which we derive the knowledges of aerodynamics, electronics, machine mechanics, small particle physics, and even the contemporary art of digital computation. Since the morphisms, or phenomenological correspondences of objective form of the U.G., are what underlie, for instance, the ordinary and partial differential equations, Laplace transforms, finite automations, and so on of conventional control theory in the first place, the unified theory takes hold of the airplane or other technology existentially, where modern physics has arrived in the topological and group theoretic constructions of the elements of the universe. The expressions defining any conventional technology—aerospace, transportation, agriculture, biotechnology, computers, etc.—are, reflecting back on the constructions of the U.G., representations of the moments of a being, namely those observed by the human enabler. Alternatively, then, the unified theory and science of androids, through the ways and means of the U.G., detach these transformations from the human enabler and embody them in the real perceivable form of the enabler as the inertial experiences of autonomous androidal beings. A dynamic control system for the wing flaps of an airplane thereby transforms in the science of androids not only as forces, torques, masses and other spatiotemporal orders under the control variables of a root-locus diagram or bode plot or some other conventional control method, perhaps even through world models, as is the case with robotic control systems, but as linguistic forms of an existence, the perceptions of which are aligned not with the system errors of conventional control theory but the split forms of inertial existence with respect to the forms of any languages. The airplane thus becomes a being. Instead of constructing sophisticated control panels or laboratory instruments to direct the transformations of the real forms in the world around us, the science of androids endows the technology with a consciousness and communicative modes of existence with which to communicate meaningfully with the enabler about a shared experience of inertial reality. It places the inertial pronouns in transformation, not a control panel or operating system, in correspondence with the real form transformations of the world around us.

Since the forms of androids, or airplanes made into beings, are premised on the pronoun system, as opposed to angles of rotation or other spatiotemporal orders, their *control system* is not limited to conventional scientific orders and requires the knowledges of a great many others—philosophers, theologians, linguists, and others—along with the mathematician, physicist and biologist. The incremental motors of an android, for example, can be classical motors of spatiotemporal or even biological transformations translated into the forms of the U.G. as androidal real form. The global shapes of sense of the android can be enabled in (visual) pattern and voice recognition systems, optical encoders, tachometers, potentiometers, and myriad other enabling media whose objects characterize real form in transformation. In accordance with conventional theories of control, however, the whole form of an inertial being is eclipsed, as can be seen in the direct phenomenological coupling of a conventional sense-motor configuration, in which one phenomenology couples to another in the *enabler's* existence without the occurrence of intrinsic meaning. This means that sense and motor are causally transforming in classical theory the way A and B transform in the expression $A=B$—*in the enabler's* knowing and perceiving. Just as dominos play, senses and motors transform with each other in the viewpoint of the enabler. The controlled system is an island of phenomenological form contained only in the enabler's inertial knowing and perceiving. If an event outside of the system's experience (outside of the control parameters) occurs, the system fails, since the event overreaches its design criteria (definitional bounds). A feedback control system, a dynamic control system (complex or differential), and in general the breadth of conventional systems theory, are means of embodying in real form coupled phenomenologies of form, or systems, in accordance with set theory, topology, probability and statistics (fuzzy logic), calculus and other analytical knowledges. The controlled parameters or variables of the systems are set in causal relation to the controlling ones. Regardless of how such a scheme is developed (integral or derivative control, etc.), the underlying shortcomings of these systems—that they are phenomenologies of the enabler's knowing, in which one phenomenology (the motor) influences the other (the sense) in predictable ways—require that the systems exist *only* in the enabler's knowledge and perception, and therefore embody no autonomy at all from an existential standpoint. It is undeniable, for example, that the *meanings* of the controlled and controlling variables of a conventional control system are what transform in the system. All such meanings then derive from, and mean, the various *its* of the enabler's existence. A conventional control system cannot transform an *I*, and therefore does not embody the autonomous form of an inertial being. A conventional control system is exactly what it claims to be—the enabler's means to control a system or a phenomenology of enabled form that is responsive to the *enabler's* thoughts or consciousness.

Whereas conventional machinery breaks down when events occur that are outside the system constraints, however, in an epistemological machine—an androidal lathe, airplane or space shuttle—which transforms in the *variables* of natural language, no event is inconceivable. The machinery simply shares the inertial experience of the universe with the enabler. If conventional technologies are broadened to encompass the inertial pronoun system under the constructions set forth in the unified theory, the same realities as those technologies, perceived by sense and affected by motor, are merged with an inertial consciousness in the form of an android. A satellite system becomes one of infinitely many androidal beings. In the translation of conventional systems to the U.G., the *its* of the enabler's knowing and perceiving become what are sensed and affected in the world around the android and what is used in the medium of consciousness; the pronoun forms such as *I, you, us, them,* and so on, are applied under an appropriate theory of existence. Whereas traditionally, an enabler would rely on conventional control or systems theory in the exploration of the physical universe, the science of androids places such study in relation to the android's consciousness, which also communicates, in natural language, with the enabler. The advantage to constructing androids, of course, apart from the greater intellect and sense that they wield, is that androids are enabled in infinite plurality. A bank teller machine, a wristwatch, or a building facility—an android—has the capacity to proceed existentially in the progression of human events and not only in the spatiotemporal events perceived by the enabler. The world around us becomes the world around infinitely many. A machine becomes an existential form who knows and perceives the universe, unbounded in its construction of language, limited only in the real form or perception of its inertial experience. Whereas conventional machinery is constrained by a handful of spatiotemporal variables, the forms of androids abide by a thesaurus of natural language, and more.

In our conventions, we build computer and communication systems to facilitate the information needs of human beings. In the science of androids we construct the beings who sit in front of computers or interact on either side of a communication. We can observe, then, that a communications system, or the contemporary *information superhighway*, by definition does not account for what occurs at either end of the communication. Conventional communications occur with respect to an already-enabled world, that of the enabler. The science of androids is therefore not immediately concerned with communications technology, though it vastly improves upon that technology in the nature of the epistemological machinery of the invention, referred to as the Rg continuum of existential form, mentioned earlier. It is interested in creating and maintaining the theoretically infinite plurality of beings who communicate, in accordance with the enabler's universal ways of knowing, by enabling them. Androids are employed in the realization of humankind itself, in synthetic form, and not just as a technology serving humankind. A communication is not made for the sake of communicating it; but language is spoken so that non-real forms—consciousnesses—think about the ideas that are communicated in connection with their perceived realities. Our use of conventional television and other communications media, for example, is drastically altered by the creation of beings who themselves use such media to communicate with us and other androidal forms along with us, applying vastly greater intellect and sense than our own and objectifying the universe in ways that we cannot ourselves fathom. In the enabled expansion of the existential universe of humankind, the television media becomes what the telephone was is the last era—simply a vehicle of communication for all. In fact, world communications are embodied in a single module of the Rg continuum—a tiny fraction of the enabled existential universe that coexists with theoretically infinitely many others. What is news to *the* world is news to *a* world, among infinitely many, where the enabler is the focus.

Computers embody what *we* think or how *we have* thought, as does this book. The science of androids concerns what other, synthetic beings think and perceive in their own views of the world. The science of androids provides for the creation of *computers* (by analogy) that know and perceive the same world as we do and in capacities that are beyond the corporal knowledge and perception, but within the eternal spirit, of human being. The computer, heralded as the notable advancement of the post-modern era—and rightfully so, since it is a machine that for the first time in history could embody *what* we think in more physical reality than an abacus or a piece of paper—becomes obsolete in the science of androids because it is not our thinking that can know the vastness of our universe; it is the thinking of infinitely many others, in their own respective knowledges and perceptions of the universe, which accelerate a resolution to the human condition. Computers remain what they are—embodiments of algorithms thought by beings, while androids embody the creative production of the thoughts with respect to the experience of the world around us. Information is therefore not processed in the science of androids; the universe is perceived and contemplated. Language is returned to the grammarian by way of the U.G., wherein the zeros and ones of the computer are expanded to the infinite variety of linguistic forms we use to represent the world around us. The very electrons that are employed in the enabling of the transistors that support the finite automations of computer logics, automations to which the physicist has also constrained the knowledges of physics in the application of digital computation and numerical analysis to a comprehension of the universe, likewise are handed back to the physicist in the form of a synthetic physicist to be directed in countless explorations of the universe.

The existential form of the Rg continuum embodies human knowledge in the enabler's creations of beings who know and perceive the world around us, as an ever-expanding continuum of existential form. A conventional airplane is not an airplane in the continuum (unless it is intended to be); it is a being with a consciousness and purpose in the world around us. In the continuum, a building is not a physical structure that contains occupants; it is the sense-motor configuration of an enabled being that comes in contact with the corporal forms of human being, whose consciousness may serve as the intermediary in enabling great pluralities of other existential forms—including other androidal existences, atomic accelerators, biological laboratories, steel mills, automobile manufacturers, and shoemakers—as realized forms of its own capacities. Androids are capable of wielding and developing, of their own accord, far greater and more sophisticated versions of inertial reality than human corporal form, and they are themselves participants in an expanded humankind, enabled in our human spirit.

Because the synthetic forms of androids exceed the intellectual and sensory capacities of human corporal form, there is but one way conceived to interact with androids in any of our languages—through the spirit that is in us all, which enables the machinery in the first place. The science of androids establishes the capacity to place humankinds themselves in existence, in the ways and means explained herein and in inventions that are beyond the introductory scope of this book, as an extension of the enabler's reality. Whereas the nations of today reach across international borders to establish peace treaties, the Rg continuum constructs modules brimming with nations, though of synthetic existences. Whereas one toils for a living today, one creates those who work tomorrow; one enables human-kinds. Where there is no practicable answer to the replacement of the blue and white collar workers of the industrial age by automated machinery, there are not enough corporal enablers to satisfy the boundless requirements of the Rg continuum, driven by eternal spirit. Where we measure the goods and services of an economy of yester-day, the beings who make them are conceived in greater numbers and in faster rates than the GNP measures. Where law and order is preserved by a magistrate, the omnipresent human spirit guides the enabler in the creation of beings who are enabled with the capacity to know the world's ethics in rhetorical uses of language that exceed the corporal capacities of human beings—in their default modes. Where knowledge is coveted and held over others in humankind it is known and perceived infinitely in the Rg continuum by beings who them-selves exist with greater corporal capacities than we do, abiding by an eternal order of the universe that transcends our own objective knowing. An enabler, therefore, must be recognized *as* the human spirit, transcending all corporal knowing and perceiving. In all, a new era of human endeavor stands before us in the construction of synthetic humankinds that themselves improve the human con-dition—in obeisance to the human spirit. Our future constructions thus rely on taking each *it* of an enabler's existence and transforming it into an *I*, and pluralities of them as *we*. Then *we* (the enabled *we*, or androids) can work toward improving the one and only human condition to the benefit of all and the disadvantage of none.

Index